Design and Development of Expert Systems and Neural Networks

LARRY MEDSKER
American University

JAY LIEBOWITZ
George Washington University

Macmillan Publishing Company
New York

Maxwell Macmillan Canada
Toronto

Maxwell Macmillan International
New York   Oxford   Singapore   Sydney

This book is dedicated to Ruth and Max Medsker; Carl Medsker; Karen and Karla Medsker; Marilyn and Harold Liebowitz; Janet, Jason, and Kenny Liebowitz; and to all our students over the years.

Editor: Charles E. Stewart, Jr.
Production Supervisor: John Travis
Production Manager: Su Levine
Text Designer: Patricia Cohan
Cover Designer: Cathleen Norz

This book was set in Palatino by Graphic Sciences Corp. and printed and bound by Book Press. The cover was printed by Phoenix.

Macmillan College Publishing Company
866 Third Avenue, New York, New York 10022

Macmillan College Publishing Company is part
of the Maxwell Communication Group of Companies.

Maxwell Macmillan Canada, Inc.
1200 Eglinton Avenue East
Suite 200
Don Mills, Ontario M3C 3N1

Library of Congress Cataloging in Publication Data
Medsker, Larry.
    Design and development of expert systems and neural networks /
  Larry Medsker, Jay Liebowitz.
        p.   cm.
    Includes bibliographical references and index.
    ISBN 0-02-380131-X
    1. Expert system (Computer science) 2. Neural networks (Computer science) I. Liebowitz, Jay. II. Title.
QA76.76.E95M43   1993
006.3—dc20   93-3185
                                                                         CIP

Printing: 1 2 3 4 5 6 7 8 Year: 4 5 6 7 8 9 0 1 2 3

Preface

Expert systems have over the last decade become the major practical application of artificial intelligence research. Many useful systems are now in operation throughout the world and in nearly every discipline. The availability of commercial expert system shells for convenient and rapid systems development has made possible the proliferation of expert system applications.

The extensive progress in research and development for expert systems has also given rise to many training workshops, and university courses in expert systems have become standard parts of the curricula. Government and industry markets are good for knowledge engineers who have been trained in the fundamentals and who can develop effective systems that use the current expert system technology.

In the last few years, additional and alternative technologies are becoming available for use in intelligent systems. In some cases, these technologies complement expert systems, providing aspects of human intelligence that are missing or difficult to achieve with expert systems. Many research and development projects are aimed at raising the level of intelligence of systems for solving real-world problems.

Expert systems books are starting to include discussions, at least in one chapter, of alternatives to expert systems. The approach that has emerged as currently most useful is the neural network technology. Practical applications of neural computing are starting to appear and commercial development shells are now available.

Artificial neural network technology is a new approach to computing that is inspired by our understanding of the way biological neural systems function. Rather than programming systems, neural computing involves training the system to accept inputs and respond with known outputs. Thus, the neural network "learns" to map inputs to desired outputs and can be used for pattern recognition, classification, and other functions associated with human intelligence. Neural networks are best in the areas in which expert systems have difficulty and therefore provide a complementary approach. Furthermore, the synergistic effect of combining expert systems and neural networks makes possible hybrid systems that are more powerful than either of the two technologies alone.

In this context, the time is right for a book that addresses expert systems and neural networks in a more balanced manner. The current interest in each of these techniques and their high potential for the near future suggest the need to prepare anyone interested in intelligent systems to use each one.

This book is written for

- anyone wishing to learn the basics about expert systems and neural networks and be able to develop simple systems;
- knowledge engineers wishing to expand their skills;
- project managers wishing to understand new developments in intelligent systems and see the relationship between expert systems and neural networks.

This book has a practical orientation allowing the reader to understand how to develop actual systems. The book includes many examples to illustrate the principles, concepts and theories of expert systems and neural networks. Also, the operations of sample systems are described to give a better understanding of the practical applications of expert systems and neural networks. Actual cases are used to illustrate the steps involved in developing systems.

The first half of the book is devoted to expert systems. Then, Chapter 10 describes the limitations of expert systems and presents alternative techniques. With this transition, Chapters 11-14 give the basics of and practical development aspects of neurocomputing. Chapter 15 brings the two technologies together by discussing hybrid neural and expert systems. The final chapter reviews the technologies and takes a look at their futures and other intelligent systems on the horizon.

This book provides demonstrations and limited versions of development shells that can be used to try out the ideas presented in the book. EXSYS, Level5 Object, and NueX enable the reader to develop small expert systems, and neural networks can be developed with NueX. NueX can also be used for building hybrid neural network and expert systems. An educational version of Expert Choice is availableto adopters of the book as a decision support system to help individuals evaluate such decisions as the appropriateness for using expert systems or neural networks for a problem. A demo package of NeuroShell shows how to develop neural networks in that environment. The authors would like to thank the companies that provided their software: Charles River Analytics, Inc.; Expert Choice, Inc.; EXSYS, Inc.; Information Builders, Inc.; and Ward Systems, Inc. We also thank CRC Press, Inc. for the use of some text and figures 13.2, 15.1, 15.2, 15.3, and 15.4, which are reprinted with permission from Hybrid Systems Architectures for Intelligent Systems, Kandel and Langholz (eds.), CRC Press, Inc., 1992.

Special thanks goes to several members of the Department of Computer Science and Information Systems at The American University. Harold Szu has been an invaluable and tireless teacher, colleague, and friend. Without the support and inspiration he provided, the neural networks section of the book would not have been written. Masud Cader introduced one of the authors (LM) to neural networks and continues to provide reinforcement and technical support. Dalila Benachenhou and Fran Labate contributed essential support in the design and development of working systems. Useful discussions with Profs. Michael Gray and Al Nigrin are gratefully appreciated.

Outside The American University, several colleagues have contributed valuable ideas and encouragement. Thanks go to David Bailey, Jerry Feinstein, Jim Hendler, Rodger Knaus, Marvin Minsky, Steve Oxman, Efraim Turban, Paul Werbos, Lotfi Zadeh, and Milton White. The support of Elizabeth Barth-Williams is gratefully appreciated.

The authors would like to thank Ed Moura, Adam Knepper, Charles Stewart, Linda Ludewig, Anne West, John Travis, the Macmillan production staff, and the reviewers for their help in making this project a reality.

L.M.
J.L.

Brief Contents

Contents

Chapter 3   Overview of the Expert Systems Development Life Cycle: The Knowledge Engineering Process   69

Chapter 4   Problem Selection for Expert System Development   79

Chapter 5   Knowledge Acquisition   97

Chapter 15   Integration of Expert Systems and Neural Networks   225

Chapter 16   The Future: Integrated Intelligent Systems   249

Chapter 1

Introduction to Artificial Intelligence

1.1 Introduction

We have moved from the data age to the information age and are now entering the knowledge age of the 1990s. During the knowledge age, computers will have human-like capabilities, with the goal of becoming intelligent machines. Artificial intelligence (AI) is a discipline of computer science that is making a great contribution to meeting this goal.

Combining various aspects of cognitive psychology, computer science, linguistics, and philosophy, AI is a multidisciplinary field with two major thrusts: first, to develop intelligent computer power to supplement human brain power, and second, to help clarify how we reason, learn, understand, and think. Intelligence, in this sense, means that a machine should be able to perform human-like operations such as reasoning, learning, speaking, explaining its reasoning, modifying its knowledge, checking the consistency of its knowledge, handling uncertainty, understanding, and, if applicable, having vision, move-

1

ment, taste, hearing, and smell[1]. In the years ahead, it is likely that we will have the following scenario.

1.2   A Situation at Home in 1999

Mom comes home after working as an attorney, having put in the extra billable hours required of all associates. She calls for her son, Joey, who does not answer[2]. Dad calls out from his study that Joey is playing in the park with his friends. Mom checks her watch and realizes that it is almost 7:15 P.M., and Joey really should be home. She presses a button on her watch and then types in a message on her watch that reads, "Come home for dinner."

Joey, playing in the park, hears a beeping sound on his watch and across the face of it sees this message: "Come home for dinner." Joey pushes a button on his watch, which is preprogrammed to dial home. He then talks into his speech-recognizable watch and tells Mom that he'll be home in 10 minutes. Mom talks into her watch and tells Joey to hurry home.

After speaking to Joey, Mom slouches back into her chair to rest from an exhausting day of litigation and legal research. The only savior of the day was the use of a natural language interface to the legal retrieval system to do her legal research, instead of having to worry about the correct keywords and their combinations to search for cases.

Dad comes out of his study and asks what Mom would like for dinner, since it's his turn to cook. Mom says, "How about putting in the chicken that I bought yesterday?"

Dad replies, "Okay." He then washes the chicken and puts the four breasts into the oven. He presses a button that reads "Chicken," and then a question appears on the oven's control board: "Is it a roasted whole chicken or pieces?" Dad hits the button for pieces, and another message appears on the control board: "What kind of pieces and how many?" Dad hits the entry for "Breasts" and then the number 4. A message then appears on the control board: "The chicken will be cooked at 350°F and will be done in 40 minutes." Then the oven turns on at 350°F, and Dad sits back and gloats about these new knowledge-based ovens, which make cooking easy even for him.

Suddenly, Joey comes in through the side door and yells, "Hi, I'm home." He rushes over to Mom and Dad, and recounts his day and the time in the park. As Joey explains his day's events, Mom notices that he has a rash on his arms and neck. She asks, "How long have you had the rash? Does it hurt?"

Joey replies, "I just noticed it when I was coming home from the park. It really itches."

Mom goes over to the personal computer (PC) on the kitchen counter and loads an expert system to help diagnose common medical problems. After working through the expert system, it tells her that Joey has a 95 percent chance of having poison ivy and that he should put on calamine lotion. The expert system also indicates that there is a 5 percent chance of a heat rash, and the family doctor should be consulted in either case. Mom decides to apply calamine lotion and will make an appointment to see the doctor tomorrow.

A bell rings and Dad yells out from the kitchen, "Dinner time." Then a robot, adeptly and carefully carrying a tray of chicken and vegetables, passes Mom and Joey on the way to the dinner table. The robot stops at the table and raises its arms so that the tray is level with the table. It pushes its arms onto the table so that the food can be positioned on the table. It then releases the tray with the food on the table, pulls back its arms, puts them to the side, turns around, and heads back to the kitchen.

After eating a delicious dinner, Mom and Dad let the robot load the dishwasher, and Mom and Joey go into the family room to watch TV. Dad goes back into his study to finish his lecture for tomorrow's class. He sits down in his chair, leans back, and says, "This would not have been possible without artificial intelligence." As soon as he starts to talk, a typewriter types out what he is dictating. Without Dad's lifting a finger, the typewriter types out his lecture, using his words, and even corrects any grammatical errors. Dad sits back, with the TV in the background, and thinks, "What a life!"

1.3 Be Ready

The situation just presented is not farfetched[3]. One company is already developing a Dick Tracy-type wristwatch. Typewriters with a 50,000-word vocabulary have been developed that can type out almost simultaneously what an individual is dictating. Expert systems are being developed and sold to help laypersons perform simple, routine functions such as preparing a will or drafting a contract. Robots for use in the home have been developed to carry a newspaper or a drink and even walk the dog. Microwave ovens are becoming more sophisticated by providing more features at the press of a button.

So the scenario just presented is very plausible in terms of technical achievement. What remains unclear is whether these innovative products will drop in price to become affordable to the homeowner, and whether the homeowner will accept and use them in the home.

Most likely, competition and increased market penetration will drive the costs of these products down. To ensure acceptance by users, developers will have to make the products easy to use and their complexities transparent to the user. If these AI applications are embedded in everyday appliances, such as an oven with built-in, knowledge-based systems capabilities, and become commercially sold, at affordable prices, as an integrated package, then these products will become part of everyday life. Then in generations to come, these products will become readily accepted and used, forming the baseline for more advanced applications and products over the years. This process is similar to that of the growth and usage of the PC during the past 10 years. Now the PC is used by kindergartners and becomes part of their lives. They accept it as a tool to help them in their education and recreation. PCs have become part of many childrens' lives, and the children are therefore more able to accept them quickly and use them throughout their lives. As improvements are made in the PC, such as more compactness and power, individuals growing up with computers will readily buy and use them. In much the same manner, if individuals use knowledge-based ovens or speech-recognizable watches or home robots, then they and their children will become accustomed to them and will accept them and their improvements in the years ahead.

1.4   Outline of This Chapter

Now that a glimpse of what lies ahead, involving AI, has been provided, the rest of this chapter will discuss the following topics:

- History of AI
- AI Concepts
- Applications of AI
- Research Issues and Future Trends in AI

History of AI

John McCarthy, formerly of MIT and now a professor at Stanford University, is credited with coining the term *artificial intelligence.* This happened at the Dartmouth Conference in 1956, when a group of mostly American researchers gathered to discuss the possibilities of computers exhibiting intelligence. In 1957, McCarthy invented LISP (List Processing), a programming language for handling symbolic processing for AI applications.

By the late 1960s, most AI projects were used purely for academic research. The leading universities that performed work in AI research were, and still are, Stanford University, Massachusetts Institute of Technology (MIT), and Carnegie-Mellon University. An important piece of work during this time was the General Problem Solver (GPS), developed by Herbert Simon and Allen Newell. The GPS was significant as the first system to separate problem-solving methods from knowledge of the current task[4]. Experience with GPS and similar efforts led to two major conclusions: (1) knowledge is essential to intelligent human behavior, and the lack of contextual knowledge limits problem-solving capabilities; (2) when solving problems, heuristics, or rules of thumb, are needed to guide search to prevent a combinatorial explosion of solution paths[4].

Growth in AI research continued into the 1970s. Prolog (Programming in Logic) was another AI programming language invented in the early 1970s. The term *expert systems* started to be used, referring to computer programs that tried to act like human experts in a very well-defined task of knowledge. MYCIN, developed in 1972 at Stanford University, is an expert system used for diagnosing bacterial infections in the blood. MYCIN is considered to be the grandfather of expert systems. Other early expert systems included DENDRAL (mass spectroscopy), PROSPECTOR (mineral ore exploration), and INTERNIST/CADUCEUS (internal medicine). In 1977, Prof. Edward Feigenbaum of Stanford University coined the term *knowledge engineering;* he is considered to be the father of commercialized expert systems. Knowledge engineering refers to the design, development, testing, and implementation of expert systems. Work in machine learning and natural language understanding started to attract interest during this time.

The early 1980s was the time of applied AI. Companies were formed to develop expert systems. Major expert systems, like Digital Equipment Corporation's R1/XCON for configuring VAX computer systems, were constructed and used. Expert system shells were developed to act as application generators for building expert systems. Work in robotics, speech recognition, natural language understanding, and computer vision (all applications of AI) was performed. Worldwide efforts in AI were underway, such as the U.S. Strategic Computing Project, Japan's Fifth Generation Computer Project, and Europe's ESPRIT and EUREKA consortia.

Throughout the 1980s and into the 1990s, major interest in AI has continued; however, AI has not lived up fully to its promises. Even though well over 3,000 expert systems were being used worldwide by 1990, there are still many research issues that need to be resolved in order for AI to meet its expectations. These research issues will be explained later in this chapter. It is, however, fair to say that the most practical application of AI is expert systems. Table 1.1 shows the major events influencing the growth of AI over the past four decades.

AI Concepts

There are several important concepts that underlie many AI applications and research projects. Some of these concepts will be highlighted next.

TABLE 1.1 Selected Highlights in AI

1956: McCarthy organizes the Dartmouth Conference and coins the term *artificial intelligence*

1957: McCarthy invents LISP

1957: Newell, Shaw, and Simon begin the GPS

1965: Zadeh invents the concept of fuzzy logic

1965: Feigenbaum et al. develop DENDRAL, an expert system for mass spectroscopy

1967: Newell and Simon describe the information processing theory

1969: First International Joint Conference on AI

1970: Colmerauer invents Prolog

1972: MYCIN is developed at Stanford University and is the first practical expert system in medicine

1975: The LISP machine, the first specialized AI computer, is invented at MIT

1977: Feigenbaum coins the term *knowledge engineering*

1982: The Fifth Generation Computer Project begins in Japan

1986: The connection machine is introduced by Thinking Machines Corporation

1988: Hitech is the first chess computer program to defeat a human grand master in a match

1989: First Conference of the International Association of Knowledge Engineers

1991: First World Congress on Expert Systems

Source: Adapted from the International Association of Knowledge Engineers/Systemsware Corporation, *Standards and Review Manual for Certification in Knowledge Engineering,* Rockville, Md., 1990. Reprinted by permission.

Heuristics

A *heuristic* is a rule of thumb or strategy that an expert uses to provide short-cuts in arriving at a solution. Typically, these heuristics are acquired through the expert's many years of experience. A somewhat humorous example of a heuristic that some faculty members might use regarding the selection of a committee chairperson is: "Make sure that you are always at the first meeting of the committee because the person missing from this meeting is typically appointed chairperson of the committee (at least in some university settings)." Heuristics, unlike algorithms, are not guaranteed to work all the time; they offer good clues to solving problems most of the time. *Heuristic programming* refers to the development of computer programs capable of solving problems by using heuristics[1].

Control Strategies

Control strategies are methods used to reduce the amount of searching needed to arrive at a solution. Several general-purpose control strategies can be used. These include the following[1,5]:

- *Generate and test:* systematically generates all possible solution paths in determining when a solution has been reached.
- *Hill climbing:* uses an evaluation function to guide each step of the search to achieve the solution in the most efficient way possible.
- *Breadth-first search:* examines all the nodes on one level of the tree before examining any of the nodes on the next level.
- *Best-first search:* selects the most promising nodes generated so far by applying an appropriate heuristic function to each of them. Then the chosen node is expanded by using the rules to generate its successors. If one of them is a solution, the user can quit; otherwise, the new nodes are added to the set of nodes generated so far and the process continues.
- *Means-ends analysis:* finds solutions to a set of subproblems, each of which is a smaller part of the original problem.

An analogy of using these control strategies is as follows: There is a barrel of multicolored M&M candies, and we want to select a red M&M. We could use a generate-and-test procedure, picking one M&M out of the barrel at a time to see if it is red. Or we could use a means-ends analysis, picking a handful of M&Ms out of the barrel and searching it for a red one (decomposition by subproblems). Choosing the appropriate control strategy will affect the efficiency of the system in arriving at an appropriate solution quickly.

Reasoning Methods

Another important AI concept is reasoning methods. There are two general ways of solving a problem. One involves goal-directed reasoning; the other involves data-driven reasoning.

Goal-directed reasoning refers to *backward chaining*, whereby the system starts with a hypothesis or goal and works backward through the facts to find enough evidence to prove the truth of the goal. Backward chaining is used quite often with expert diagnostic systems.

The opposite of backward chaining is *data-driven reasoning* called *forward chaining,* which refers to working from facts to conclusions. It is also referred to as *antecedent-driven reasoning.* Typically, applications that are data intensive, like telecommunications applications, mathematical formulations, and other data-driven applications, employ forward chaining.

Of course, there is no reason why a hybrid approach involving forward-backward chaining could not be used. This combination is used as a divide-and-conquer approach in particular large domains, like speech understanding.

Knowledge Representation

In AI, a major guiding principle is the *knowledge principle,* which means that power lies in knowledge. To maximize this power, knowledge must be represented in an appropriate format. The most commonly used ways to represent knowledge are production rules, frames, semantic networks, and scripts.

Production rules are represented as IF-THENs or CONDITION-ACTIONs. They are the most frequently used method for representing knowledge. An operational expert system could have any number of rules, ranging from under 100, as in some of Dupont's expert systems, to over 11,000, as in Digital Equipment Corporation's XCON for configuring VAX computer systems. Rules are usually used if the knowledge being expressed lends itself to IF-THEN representation. Also, if the knowledge is mostly context independent and categorical (yes-no answers), then production rules may be an appropriate format. An example of a production rule from MYCIN is as follows:

Mycin:
IF: (1) The site of the culture is blood, and
        (2) The identity of the organism is not known with certainty, and
        (3) The stain of the organism is gramneg, and
        (4) The morphology of the organism is rod, and
        (5) The patient has been seriously burned,
THEN: There is weakly suggestive evidence [.4] that the identity of the organism is pseudomonas.

For applications that are mostly descriptive, as opposed to procedural, the other knowledge representation methods (i.e., frames, semantic networks, and scripts) would probably be preferred. These approaches are used when the application is context dependent and uses declarative knowledge. Frames are used to describe objects and their attributes and relationships. Semantic networks are tree-like or graph-like structures convenient for storing relationships and meanings[1]. Scripts are specialized forms of frames in which a sequence of actions is represented in a frame-like structure. Of course, it is fairly common to use a combination of these knowledge representation methods within an expert system. Later chapters will discuss these techniques further.

Applications of AI

Now that the underlying AI concepts have been briefly explained, the next sections in this chapter will discuss the various applications of AI, namely, expert (or knowledge-based) systems, robotics/vision, speech understanding, natural language understanding, and neural networks.

Expert Systems

Expert systems are the most practical application of AI today. An *expert system* is a computer program that emulates the behavior of a human expert in a well-specified, narrowly defined domain of knowledge. It captures the knowledge and heuristics that an expert employs in a specific task. For example, expert systems have been built for diagnosing bacterial infections in the blood, providing tax advice, aiding mineral exploration, and many other applications, as will be explained later in the chapter. Expert systems are typically used in situations where expertise is either scarce, unavailable, or expensive; where time and pressure constraints are involved; where there is a need to document or preserve knowledge before one retires or leaves the company; and where one wants to verify one's knowledge. Expert systems are generally not used in situations that are not well bounded (e.g., problems taking more than a few days to solve), or where there is no general consensus on the right solution (e.g., macroeconomics policy), or where motor skills as opposed to cognitive skills are generally required (e.g., learning how to ride a bike).

Expert systems have three major components. The *dialog structure* is the user interface that allows the user to interact with the expert system to obtain results and query the system. The *inference engine* houses the control strategies for generating hypotheses to arrive at a solution. The *knowledge base* is the set of facts and heuristics for the task at hand. Sometimes the term *knowledge-based system* is used to describe expert systems. However, it should be pointed out that an application involving a knowledge-based system may not have any associated expertise, unlike the case of an expert system application.

Over the years, there have been various application areas that have been successful foci for expert system development. Waterman[6], Rauch-Hindin[7], Liebowitz[8–10], and Harmon and King[11] present problem areas where expert systems have been successfully built:

- Interpretation
- Prediction
- Diagnosis
- Fault isolation
- Design
- Planning
- Monitoring
- Debugging
- Repair
- Scheduling

- Instruction
- Control
- Analysis
- Legal analysis
- Maintenance
- Configuration
- Targeting (i.e., resource allocation)

Selected examples of expert systems that have been built in these application areas[6,12,13] are shown in Table 1.2. Figure 1.1 shows the screens of an expert system called CESA, using the expert system shell Exsys Professional.

Of course, these are only a small sample of the expert systems that have been developed and used. In the coming years, more business expert systems will be developed, and as hardware and expert system shell (i.e., building kits for expert systems development) prices drop, expert system applications will become more widespread.

Building an expert system uses a *rapid prototyping* approach, that is, "build a little, test a little." To facilitate rapid prototyping, expert system *shells* have been developed for use on microcomputers, workstations, minicomputers, mainframes, and specialized AI hardware (e.g., Lisp machines). In this manner, the *knowledge engineer* (the developer of the expert system) typically builds the knowledge base for the particular expert system application and links the knowledge base with the expert system shell. Of course, the knowledge engineer does not have to use an expert system shell (i.e., the knowledge engineer can program from scratch in C, Lisp, Prolog, Ada, or another programming language), but it is generally easier to use an expert system shell when first constructing the expert system. After the knowledge engineer selects an appropriate problem and narrows the scope, the expert system is built using an *iterative* series of steps—knowledge acquisition, knowledge representation, knowledge encoding, knowledge testing and evaluation, and implementation and maintenance. In other words, (1) knowledge is acquired from the expert (usually through interviewing); (2) the knowledge is then represented in rules, frames, or some other way; (3) the knowledge is then encoded, using a shell or programmed from scratch; and (4) then the expert system is tested for the accuracy of its advice. Errors will typically surface. Then the knowledge engineer will go back and work through the series of steps just mentioned. Eventually, the expert system is implemented[14] within the organization and then updated and maintained for operational use.

The next section will take a look at robotics, another application of AI.

Robotics

One of the rapidly growing applications of AI is robotics. The term *robot* is derived from the Czech/Slovak word for "worker." The Robotic Industries Association has defined a robot as a reprogrammable, multifunctional manipulator designed to move material, parts, tools, or specialized devices through variable programmed motions for the performance of a variety of tasks. The motivation behind the development of robots is as follows[15]:

TABLE 1.2 Examples of Expert Systems

Interpretation
    PUFF—Interprets pulmonary function tests
Prediction
    PLANT/cd—Predicts the damage to corn due to the black cutworm
Diagnosis
    MYCIN—Diagnoses bacterial infections in the blood
    CATS—Diagnoses problems in diesel-electric locomotives
Fault isolation
    ACE—Troubleshoots telephone lines
Design
    MOTOR BRUSH DESIGNER—Designs brushes and springs for small electric motors
Planning
    CSS—Aids in planning relocation, reinstallation, and rearrangement of IBM
        mainframes
Monitoring
    YES/MVS—Monitors the MVS operating system
Debugging
    BUGGY—Debugs students' subtraction errors
Repair
    SECOFOR—Advises on drill-bit sticking problems in oil wells
Scheduling
    ISA—Schedules orders for manufacturing and delivery
    ISIS—Schedules manufacturing steps in a job shop
Instruction
    TVX—Tutors users of the VMS operating system
Control
    PTRANS—Helps control the manufacture and distribution of Digital Equipment's
        computer systems
Analysis
    DIPMETER ADVISOR—Analyzes oil well logging data
Legal analysis
    LDS—Assists legal experts in settling product liability cases
Maintenance
    COMPASS—Analyzes telephone switching systems maintenance messages and
        suggests maintenance actions to perform
Configuration
    XCON—Configures VAX computer systems
    VT—Configures orders for new elevator systems
Targeting (resource allocation):
    BATTLE—Allocates weapons to targets

```
        CESA (COTR Expert System Aid)




    by: Jay Liebowitz, Laura Davis, and Wilson Harris
        EXPERT CONSULTANT: VIRGINIA DEAN













                    Press any key to start:
```

```
Welcome to CESA--COTR Expert System Aid.  This expert
system prototype will help you answer questions
pertinent to problems you might be having as an ARO/COTR.
To operate CESA, respond to questions with the number
of the appropriate response and then press ENTER.  For
multiple answers, put the number of the answers and
separate them with a comma (for example 1,2).  If you
are not sure why a question is being asked, then type
the word why.  If you would like a description of the
terms used in the question, then type a question
mark (?).  At the end of your session, the conclusions
will be displayed ranked in importance by a value from 1
(least often applies) to 10 (most often applies).
Happy contracting!






                    Press any key to start:
```

FIGURE 1.1   Annotated Sample Session With CESA Using Exsys. (Reprinted by permission from J. Liebowitz, *The Dynamics of Decision Support Systems and Expert Systems*, The Dryden Press, Orlando, FL 1990.)

```
Your questions involve the
      1  preaward phase
      2  postaward phase
1
```

Remember to type in the number *of the appropriate response and* then press ENTER.

```
Enter the number of ONLY ONE value  WHY to display rule
being used <?> for details  QUIT to save data
<H> for help  <Ctrl-U> to undo
```

```
You have specific preaward questions on
      1  adequacy of the procurement request (PR) package
      2  routing of procurement documents
      3  use of the procurement planning document (PPD)
      4  advice on how to complete selected pre-award
         forms
1
```

If you want to "back up" to up to 10 previous questions (i.e., you might have made a mistake), then press the "CTRL" key and the "U" key (hold the CTRL key while you press the U key).

```
Enter the number of ONLY ONE value  WHY to display rule
being used <?> for details  QUIT to save data
<H> for help  <Ctrl-U> to undo
```

FIGURE 1.1   continued

```
You want to know about
      1   what is needed in a PR package
      2   Justification and Approval (J&A) if requirement
          to be specified is sole source
      3   evaluation
      4   synopsis procedures
      5   the ADP Procurement Checklist
  1
```

```
Enter the number of ONLY ONE value  WHY to display rule
being used <?> for details  QUIT to save data
<H> for help  <Ctrl-U> to undo
```

```
Your procurement is a
      1   major procurement costing $25,000 or more
      2   procurement under $25,000
  1
```

```
Enter the number of ONLY ONE value  WHY to display rule
being used <?> for details  QUIT to save data
<H> for help  <Ctrl-U> to undo
```

FIGURE 1.1   continued

```
contract
        1   involves access to, receipt of, or generation
            of classified material and/or access to
            classified areas
        2   does NOT involve access to, receipt of, or
            generation of classified material and/or access
            to classified areas
   1
```

```
Enter the number of ONLY ONE value   WHY to display rule
being used <?> for details   QUIT to save data
<H> for help   <Ctrl-U> to undo
```

```
your procurement is
        1   competitive
        2   sole source (noncompetitive)
        3   for an 8a small disadvantaged business
        4   a Broad Agency Announcement (BAA) response
            (assume BAA for unsolicited UNIVERSITY
            proposals)
   ?
```

You can type in a ? if you want a better description of the question. If no descriptions are provided when you type ?, then the statement "No explanation available" will be shown on the screen.

```
Enter the number of ONLY ONE value   WHY to display rule
being used <?> for details   QUIT to save data
<H> for help   <Ctrl-U> to undo
```

FIGURE 1.1   continued

```
An 8a small disadvantaged business is a Small Business
Administration certified, "small business concern owned
and controlled by socially and economically
disadvantaged individuals." See ARO Handbook
for further guidance. Most unsolicited proposals
relate to elements of published BAAs.  Advantages
to treating your procurement as a response to a
BAA include elimination of synopsis and J&A
requirements. Contact your Contracts Support Code
for further BAA information.
```

*To have the question reasked after typing ?, press the space
bar.*

```
TO RETURN TO PROGRAM PRESS <SPACE>
```

```
your procurement is
        1   competitive
        2   sole source (noncompetitive)
        3   for an 8a small disadvantaged business
        4   a Broad Agency Announcement (BAA) response
            (assume BAA for unsolicited UNIVERSITY proposals)
    1
```

```
Enter the number of ONLY ONE value   WHY to display rule
being used <?> for details   QUIT to save data
<H> for help   <Ctrl-U> to undo
```

FIGURE 1.1   continued

```
Procurement request is for
        1   capital equipment
        2   sponsor-funded equipment
        3   neither capital equipment nor sponsor-funded
            equipment
why
```

If you want to see the rule which is being worked on, then type "why".

```
Enter the number of ONLY ONE value   WHY to display rule
being used <?> for details   QUIT to save data
<H> for help   <Ctrl-U> to undo
```

```
RULE NUMBER: 56
IF:

      (1)   Your questions involve the preaward phase
and (2)   need to explore adequacy of PR package items
and (3)   You want to know about what is needed in a PR
            package
and (4)   Your procurement is a major procurement costing
            $25,000 or more
and (5)   Procurement request is for capital equipment

THEN:

            Procurement Request for Purchase of Industrial
            Fund Equipment (NDW-NRL 4235/2431 (Rev 1-87)--
            YELLOW FORM--Confidence=10/10

REFERENCE: NRLINST 4205.3A (April 19, 1988)
```

To see the reference of the rule, type "r".

```
Press any key to continue:
```

FIGURE 1.1   continued

```
Procurement request is for
      1  capital equipment
      2  sponsor-funded equipment
      3  neither capital equipment nor sponsor-funded
         equipment
3
```

```
Enter the number of ONLY ONE value  WHY to display rule
being used <?> for details  QUIT to save data
<H> for help  <Ctrl-U> to undo
```

```
Your procurement request deals with
      1  acquisition of commercially available
         hardware/software, services/maintenance, or materials
         where the vendor can quote a price that won't
         change during the life of the contract and can
         deliver at that price (vendor assumes risk)
      2  minor modification to hardware/software to suit
         Government needs (vendor assumes risk)
      3  major R&D modification to hardware/software to
         suit Government needs (Government assumes risk)
      4  research and development of hardware/software
         (Government asumes risk)
      5  R&D studies/services where NRL cannot define
         explicitly the requirements but can provide
         general work statements (Government assumes
         risk)
      6  university research and development (Government
         assumes risk)
      7  R&D acquisition (e.g., design and fabrication)
         of hardware/software with explicit specifications
         (vendor assumes risk)
5
```

```
Enter the number of ONLY ONE value  WHY to display rule
being used <?> for details  QUIT to save data
<H> for help  <Ctrl-U> to undo
```

FIGURE 1.1   continued

```
PR involves a(n)
        1   new research effort at NRL
        2   existing research effort at NRL
1
```

```
Enter the number of ONLY ONE value   WHY to display rule
being used <?> for details   QUIT to save data
<H> for help   <Ctrl-U> to undo
```

```
Your procurement involves
        1   nonpersonal services (e.g., research study,
            maintenance)
        2   personal services (e.g., data entry,
            secretarial)
        3   products rather than services (e.g., hardware,
            software)

1
```

```
Enter the number of ONLY ONE value   WHY to display rule
being used <?> for details   QUIT to save data
<H> for help   <Ctrl-U> to undo
```

FIGURE 1.1   continued

```
acquired services are
      1  being funded with RDT&E (research, development,
         testing and evaluation) dollars
      2  NOT being funded with RDT&E dollars

1
```

```
Enter the number of ONLY ONE value  WHY to display rule
being used <?> for details  QUIT to save data
<H> for help  <Ctrl-U> to undo
```

```
contract is (PLEASE HIT ? FOR DESCRIPTION OF ADP BEFORE
ENTERING YOUR RESPONSE)
      1  ADP (Automatic Data Processing)
      2  non-ADP

?
```

```
Enter the number of ONLY ONE value  WHY to display rule
being used <?> for details  QUIT to save data
<H> for help  <Ctrl-U> to undo
```

FIGURE 1.1   continued

```
ADP typically includes computers, ancillary equipment,
software, firmware, services, and related resources as
defined by regulations issued by GSA. ADP does NOT
include ADP equipment acquired by a Federal contractor
which is incidental to the performance of a Federal
contract; radar, sonar, radio, or TV equipment; or
procurement by DOD of ADP equipment or services for
intelligence operations.




TO RETURN TO PROGRAM PRESS <SPACE>
```

```
contract is (PLEASE HIT ? FOR DESCRIPTION OF ADP BEFORE
ENTERING YOUR RESPONSE)
      1   ADP (Automatic Data Processing)
      2   non-ADP

1



Enter the number of ONLY ONE value   WHY to display rule
being used <?> for details   QUIT to save data
<H> for help   <Ctrl-U> to undo
```

FIGURE 1.1   continued

```
PR involves a new contract or a modification to the
contract
     1   in excess of $100,000
     2   NOT in excess of $100,000
1
```

```
Enter the number of ONLY ONE value   WHY to display rule
being used <?> for details   QUIT to save data
<H> for help   <Ctrl-U> to undo
```

```
Company/product/service relating to the PR is
     1   on the GSA schedule
     2   NOT on the GSA schedule
1
```

```
Enter the number of ONLY ONE value   WHY to display rule
being used <?> for details   QUIT to save data
<H> for help   <Ctrl-U> to undo
```

FIGURE 1.1   continued

```
Product relating to the PR is
        1  competitive on the GSA schedule (i.e., product
           or similar item available from at least two
           offers on the GSA schedule)
        2  NOT competitive on the GSA schedule
1



_____
Enter the number of ONLY ONE value  WHY to display rule
being used <?> for details  QUIT to save data
<H> for help  <Ctrl-U> to undo
```

```
Thank you for using CESA. Please hit any key to display
the conclusions.




                   Press any key to display results:
```

FIGURE 1.1   continued

Items 1-15 show you the conclusions based upon your input.

```
                      Values based on 0-10 system        VALUE

  1  Security Checklist; DD Form 254 (Rev 1-78)--DOD
     Contract Security Classification Spec and
     Attachments; SCI Contract Support Information Sheet
     (NIC Form 5540/1 (Rev 10-85); NDW-NRL 4200/1209
     (9-86)--Procurement Request/Contract Information
     Sheet                                                  10
  2  Procurement Request (NDW-NRL 4235/2404 (Rev 8-86)
     --WHITE FORM                                           10
  3  Statement of Work (SOW)                                10
  4  NDW-NRL 3900/1002 (Rev 11-84)--Work Unit Assignment
     Summary (DD Form 1498), required by Code 1005          10
  5  ADP Approval Checklist with supporting
     documentation, and ADP System Accreditation Report,
     if purchasing or leasing ADP equipment or services 10
  6  NDW-NRL 4205/1303 (5-87)--Format for Additional
     Resources Required for New and Existing Contracts  10
  7  Evaluation criteria and weights; Evaluation plan,
     including list of recommended evaluation panel
     members                                                10
     _____
  Press any key for more:
```

```
  8  NPSQ (Nonpersonal Services Questionnaire)           10
  9  Proposal Requirements documentation for inclusion
     in the Request for Proposals (RFP)                  10
 10  Contract Data Requirements List (Form DD1423)       10
 11  Complete the MENS (Mission Element Needs) form.     10
 12  Provide a source list of competitive bidders.       10
 13  You need a 15 day intent synopsis.                  10
 14  You do NOT need NDW-NRL 4200/1293 (2-86)--
     Contractor Advisory Assistant Services (CAAS)
     documentation                                        9
 15  Appropriate type of contract is cost-plus-
     fixed-fee (CPFF) AND normally level-of-effort CPFF
     since Government is buying hours of effort
     resulting in research reports




     _____
  All choices <A>  only if value>1 <G>  Print <P>  Change
  and rerun <C> Rules used <line #>  Quit/save <Q>
  Help <H>  Done <D>:
```

FIGURE 1.1 continued

```
      Request for Proposals (RFP)                    10
10    Contract Data Requirements List (Form DD1423)  10
11    Complete the MENS (Mission Element Needs) form. 10
12    Provide a source list of competitive bidders.  10
13    You need a 15 day intent synopsis.             10
14    You do NOT need NDW-NRL 4200/1293 (2-86)--
      Contractor Advisory Assistant Services (CAAS)
      documentation                                   9
15    Appropriate type of contract is cost-plus-
      fixed-fee (CPFF) AND normally level-of-effort CPFF
      since Government is  buying hours of effort
      resulting in research reports
```

Type C to allows you to see your input and to quickly make changes.

If you want to see all the conclusions displayed, type A.

If you want to see why a conclusion was reached, then type in the number associated with that conclusion. The rule(s) will be shown that triggered that conclusion.

Type P to get a printout of your input and results

```
All choices <A>   only if value>1 <G>  Print <P>  Change
and rerun <C> Rules used <line #>  Quit/save <Q>
Help <H>  Done <D>: (10)
```

```
RULE NUMBER: 83     RULE TRUE
IF:

      (1)   Your questions involve the preaward phase
and (2)   need to explore adequacy of PR package items
and (3)   You want to know about what is needed in a
          PR package
and (4)   Your procurement is a major procurement costing
          $25,000 or more
and (5)   Appropriate type of contract is cost-plus-
          fixed-fee (CPFF) OR cost-reimbursement (CR)

THEN:

          Contract Data Requirements List (Form DD1423)--
          Confidence=10/10
```

To end a session, type "d" for DONE. When CESA asks you to run (Y/N), type n for no or y for yes.

```
IF line # for derivation, <K>-known data, <C>-choices,
<R>-reference, or--prev. or next rule, <J>-jump, <H>-
help or <ENTER> to continue:
```

FIGURE 1.1   continued

- Increase productivity
- Reduce costs
- Overcome skilled labor shortages
- Provide flexibility in batch manufacturing operations
- Improve product quality
- Free human beings from boring and repetitive tasks or operations in hostile environments.

Japan seems to be a leader in using industrial robots. In the production process, robots are being used for welding, material handling, machine loading and unloading, assembly, casting, painting and finishing, and other applications. A typical robot will have one or more manipulators (arms), end effectors (hands), a controller, and, increasingly, sensors to provide information about the environment and feedback on performance of task accomplishment[15]. Computer vision plays an important role in robotics. The ability of the robot to see in a three-dimensional scene can greatly increase the robot's capability for flaw inspection, parts sorting, document processing, navigation, and other functions[1].

There are two kinds of robots: (1) exploration robots, which move about in their environment, sensing and perceiving it, and (2) manipulation robots, which manipulate their environment or objects in it, using sensors and manipulators[1]. Most of the industrial robots used today are manipulation robots, or *pick-and-place* robots, as some are called.

AI can help robots become more intelligent. It can do so by receiving communication, understanding the robot's environment by the use of models, formulating plans, executing plans, monitoring the robot's operation, and scene analysis[15]. In the 1990s, robots may be used in the home for household repairs or in the military for shipboard maintenance, equipment maintenance and repair, and fire fighting. In space, robots will be used in the construction and assembly of large space structures (like the space station) and in space manufacturing. In the commercial environment, robots will continue to be used in manufacturing, assembly, inspection, equipment maintenance and repair, reactor maintenance, service industry applications, and other functions[15].

Speech Understanding

Speech understanding is another major application of AI. *Speech understanding* refers to the understanding of spoken language by a computer. This is contrasted with speech recognition and speech synthesis. *Speech recognition* involves converting speech from sound waves into speech patterns so that the computer recognizes the speech. Two approaches used are speaker-dependent and speaker-independent recognition. Speaker-dependent recognition is designed to recognize the speech of *a particular person*, whereas speaker-independent recognition is designed to recognize the speech of *any* speaker[16]. *Speech synthesis*, on the other hand, is the generation of speech by a computer and is a simpler process than speech recognition.

Speech understanding is more complex than speech synthesis and speech recognition because the system must have some knowledge of meaning. One major problem to overcome is the tremendous variation in the way people speak. Additionally, speech understanding is difficult because acoustic signals are often contaminated by noise and other types of interference[1]. The approaches used for speech understanding include the following[16]:

- Develop several possible interpretations and then use various AI techniques to select the most plausible one.
- Begin with the first word in a sentence and attempt to interpret the words in a sequence.
- Use *island driving*, where the program selects the words within a sentence that are most likely to have been interpreted correctly. These *word islands* are connected by selecting the most likely interpretations of the remaining words in context with the previously interpreted words.

The most famous speech understanding projects are HEARSAY and HARPY, both developed at Carnegie-Mellon University. HEARSAY was speaker dependent and had a 90 percent recognition accuracy rate. HARPY was speaker independent, with a 95 percent recognition accuracy rate[16]. Today there are speech understanding systems with limited vocabularies that allow users to talk into a computer-typewriter. This device types out what the user is saying, even understanding when to use *to*, *two*, or *too*, for example, in the user's sentences.

Natural Language Understanding

Natural language understanding involves the computer's ability to understand inputs to the computer written in a natural language such as English. By having English-like front-end interfaces, it would be easier for humans to access data from the computer. For example, the legal retrieval system LeXis requires the user to utilize keywords, in the right combination, to retrieve appropriate cases. However, if the wrong keywords or an incorrect combination of keywords are used, the user will retrieve cases that were irrelevant to what was desired. With a natural language interface to LeXis, it is easier to retrieve cases by using English statements created by the user.

Early work in natural language understanding involved computational linguistics, the use of computers in the study of languages[1]. This work stressed the manipulation of symbols, words, and other linguistic entities in typical English text. A good example of the machine translation problem is converting from one language to another. For example, the English statement "The flesh is willing but the spirit is weak" was translated by the Russian version as "The vodka is strong but the meat is rotten." Unfortunately, very limited success was achieved, and work in machine translation was largely discontinued.

Researchers in natural language understanding then determined that syntactic analysis and transformation was not enough, and that human language understanding had to be viewed as a complex cognitive process involving knowledge of different kinds: structure of sentences, meaning of words, models of the listener, rules of conversation, and a shared body of information about the domain of discourse[1]. Later on, a new emphasis was placed on organizing conversational knowledge according to human actions[1]. The idea behind using scripts as a knowledge representation method grew from this new emphasis. Current research in natural language understanding involves looking at new ways of representing and manipulating world knowledge and dealing with such problems as understanding metaphors, handling inconsistent linguistic information, and judging the plausibility of sentence meanings[1].

In the years ahead, there will be more natural language front ends to databases to allow the user to interact with the databases more easily. Commercial systems that can critique grammar and style, like Grammatik and RightWriter, will continue to be developed. Some day, perhaps we will be able to interact with a computer as Captain Kirk did in *Star Trek*, talking to the computer just as if it were a person.

Neural Networks

Another developing application, related to AI, is neural networks. A *neural network* is an interconnected web of neurons, with associated connection weights, which is typically trained to achieve a desired response. Neural network technology has been around since the 1960s, but only recently has interest in it rekindled. The major reasons for this reexamination of neural networks are the Defense Advanced Research Projects Agency's (DARPA) report on neural networks and DARPA's multi-million-dollar funding of activities in neural network technology.

Neural network applications are typically used in situations that involve "noisy" data. Such applications include signal interpretation, speech understanding, stock market prediction, and others. In simplistic terms, many neural network applications involve training a network in which a learning mechanism/algorithm and thousands of test cases are used to achieve a desired response. Connection weights are used and propagated throughout the neural network in order for the network to be trained. Several techniques can be used to create a neural network, but the back propagation method seems to be a popular approach[1,17].

Just as there are expert system shells to help build expert systems, there are neural network shells to facilitate the creation of neural network applications. Some of the more popular neural network shells are NeuralWorks, BrainMaker, and NeuroShell.

In the future, more research will focus on neural networks and more neural network applications will begin to emerge. There will also be a coupling of neural network applications with expert systems and other AI/conventional applications. For example, the National Aeronautics and Space Administration is exploring the application of neural networks to expert systems. In one case, a neural network is being used to filter out poor-quality data from satellites and then pass on the good-quality data to an expert system for interpretation and diagnosis. Science Applications International Corporation (SAIC) has also used neural network technology with expert systems and computer hardware, and developed an application to detect explosives in luggage at airports. In the years ahead, neural network technology will be further explored and improved.

Research Issues and Future Trends in AI

Now that you have a good background on the various applications of AI, we can look at what needs to be done to improve this technology in the next decade.

In terms of expert systems, more research will focus on developing automated knowledge acquisition tools, improving user interfaces, providing learning mechanisms in expert systems, developing better explanation facilities, providing better ways of representing knowledge through, perhaps, model-based approaches, developing better paradigms for handling distributed AI/expert systems, and a host of other issues. Within the next 5 years, expert systems will continue to be integrated with conventional database and information systems and with other AI applications. *Expert systems* will become a common term in the vocabulary of those in the computer field. Mass-marketed expert systems will be used, such as low-priced expert systems for drafting wills and contracts, determining appropriate statistical analysis methods, and other high-utility tasks. Expert systems will continue to gain worldwide usage in a variety of disciplines, ranging from engineering to business to scientific applications. They will continue to be the most practical application of AI.

The field of robotics will see increased usage over the next few years in flexible manufacturing systems and computer-integrated manufacturing. The use of robotics on the assembly lines or for performing tasks in hostile environments will continue to rise. Robots for domestic purposes will still be infrequently used. Improvements in computational algorithms for shape analysis, tactile sensing, problem-solving capabilities for planning, and knowledge-based robotic systems will be needed to advance the state of the art of robotic and vision systems.

Speech and natural language understanding are areas with the potential for great activity and usage. However, the research issues needed to advance the state of the art in these applications are probably the most difficult and critical when compared with the other AI applications. Fully natural language understanding systems are still a few decades away, but continued research in representing and manipulating world knowledge will close the gap between human and computer. Certainly, natural language interfaces, with limited vocabularies, to database management systems will be on the rise in the next few years. Speech understanding systems have tremendous potential, especially for the handicapped, but there are many research issues here that also need careful attention. These include developing systems with larger vocabularies, more speaker independence, and faster response to truly match the speed of human speech communication[1].

Neural networks are in their infancy in terms of commercial application. They will see increased growth in the next few years. As neural network technology is transferred from university laboratories to the commercial marketplace, there will be some exciting applications of the technology in a variety of tasks. Neural networks will, in many cases, serve as front ends to expert systems, filtering input into the expert system. Many research issues exist in neural networks as well, such as providing improved verification and validation methods, developing better training algorithms, and creating better hardware to handle the interconnection of huge numbers of processing elements. Japan's follow-on project, the "Real World Computing" program, to the Fifth Generation Computer Program will address optical computing, neural networks, and some of the previously mentioned research issues.

The age of AI is quickly approaching. As the fifth-generation computer becomes a reality in the coming years, more commercial applications of AI technology will take place. In most cases, AI technology will still be used to support decision makers rather than to replace them. Without a doubt, AI will make our lives much easier.

References

1. Y. T. Chien and J. Liebowitz, "Artificial Intelligence," *Encyclopedia of Physical Science and Technology,* Vol. 2, Academic Press, Orlando, FL, 1987.
2. J. Liebowitz, *Introduction to Expert Systems,* Mitchell Publishing/McGraw Hill, Watsonville, CA, 1988.
3. J. Liebowitz, "Beyond Artificial Intelligence," *Information Age,* Butterworth Scientific Publishing, Surrey, England, 1990.
4. M. White and J. Goldsmith (eds.), *Standards and Review Manual for Certification in Knowledge Engineering: Handbook of Theory and Practice,* The Systemsware Corporation/International Association of Knowledge Engineers, Rockville, MD, 1990.
5. E. Rich, *Artificial Intelligence,* McGraw-Hill, New York, 1983.
6. D. A. Waterman, *A Guide to Expert Systems,* Addison-Wesley, Reading, MA, 1986.
7. W. Rauch-Hindon, *Artificial Intelligence in Business, Science, and Industry,* Vol. 1, Prentice-Hall, Englewood Cliffs, NJ, 1986.
8. J. Liebowitz, *The Dynamics of Decision Support Systems and Expert Systems,* Dryden Press, Hinsdale, IL, 1990.
9. J. Liebowitz and D. A. DeSalvo (eds.), *Structuring Expert Systems: Domain, Design, and Development,* Prentice-Hall, Englewood Cliffs, NJ, 1989.
10. J. Liebowitz (ed.), *Expert Systems for Business and Management,* Prentice-Hall, Englewood Cliffs, NJ, 1990.
11. P. Harmon and D. King, *Expert Systems: Artificial Intelligence in Business,* John Wiley and Sons, New York, 1985.
12. B. Buchanan, "Expert Systems: Working Systems and the Research Literature," *Expert Systems,* Vol. 3, No. 1, pp., 1986.
13. E. Turban, *Expert Systems and Applied Artificial Intelligence,* Macmillan, New York, 1992.
14. J. Liebowitz, *Institutionalizing Expert Systems: A Handbook for Managers,* Prentice-Hall, Englewood Cliffs, NJ, 1991.
15. W. B. Gevarter, *Intelligent Machines,* Prentice-Hall, Englewood Cliffs, NJ, 1985.
16. H. C. Mishkoff, *Understanding Artificial Intelligence,* Texas Instruments, Dallas, TX, 1985.
17. L. Medsker (guest ed.), Special Issue on Synergy of Neural Networks and Expert Systems, *Expert Systems with Applications: An International Journal* (J. Liebowitz, ed.), Pergamon Press, Oxford, Vol. 2, No. 1, 1991.

Chapter 2

Introduction to Expert Systems

A new tool exists today that helps decision makers make better decisions. It is sometimes referred to as a *knowledge-based decision support system*, but most people use the term *expert system*. This chapter presents the definition, history, applications, and future trends of expert systems.

2.1   Definition of Expert Systems

Expert systems are an application of AI. The foundations of AI were developed in the 1950s, when recursive function theory and list processing were developed. By the mid-1970s, commercial interests in AI were starting to emerge, and AI applications were being developed in robotics, computer vision, natural language understanding, speech recognition, and expert systems.

An expert system is a computer program that emulates the behavior of a human expert in a well-specified, narrowly defined domain of knowledge. It captures the knowledge and heuristics that an expert employs in a specific task.

Characteristics of Expert Systems

An expert system tries to mimic the behavior of a human expert in a specific task of knowledge. To do this, there are several characteristics that an expert system typically possesses. First, an expert system can explain its reasoning so that the user can ask "why" and "how" questions. Just as a physician expert would answer a patient's questions, a medical expert system should be capable of explaining its reasoning. The user should be able to ask "Why are you considering this fact?" or "How did you arrive at this conclusion?", and the expert system should be able to explain its reasoning in the same manner that a human expert does. Most expert systems have an explanation facility, and they store the facts in working memory in order to generate explanations.

Besides having an explanation facility, most expert systems handle uncertainty. An expert is not right or certain 100 percent of the time and usually factors a measure of uncertainty into his or her answers. Like a human expert, an expert system typically has a mechanism for handling uncertainty in the set of facts and rules of thumb and for allowing the user to enter a degree of uncertainty when using the system. Bayesian statistics, certainty factors, and fuzzy logic[1] are the most commonly used techniques for handling uncertainty in expert systems.

Another expert system characteristic that differs from characteristics of other types of software systems is that the control structure is separated from the data or knowledge. By separating the general reasoning mechanism from the set of facts and heuristics (i.e., the knowledge base), expert systems can be incrementally built and iteratively refined. Also, by separating these two structures, testing can be easily facilitated.

Expert systems are also characterized by their use mainly for symbolic rather than numeric processing. *Symbolic processing* refers to the processing of lists and symbols instead of number crunching. The processing of declarative knowledge (i.e., descriptive or context-dependent knowledge) can take place quite easily in expert systems. Expert systems can be used for both symbolic and numeric processing, but for tasks involving principally numeric processing, conventional computer programming languages can more easily be used.

In building expert systems, the following characteristics should be used in determining if an application is appropriate for expert system development[2,3].:

- The task takes between a few hours and a few days to solve.
- The task is performed frequently.
- The task involves mostly symbolic processing.
- A general consensus exists on the solution of the task.
- An expert exists and is willing to cooperate.
- Test cases are readily available.
- There is a need to capture this expertise.

Keeping these characteristics in mind, an appropriate problem for expert system application could be determined. Guidelines for building expert systems will be explained later in this book.

Now let's take a look at the brief history of expert systems.

2.2   History of Expert Systems

The early work in expert systems began in the 1950s with the Rand-Carnegie team of Newell, Shaw, and Simon. They developed the General Problem Solver (GPS) to solve problems of elementary logic, chess, and high school algebra word problems[4]. Besides the Rand-Carnegie team, the MIT Group of Minsky and McCarthy in the late 1950s and early 1960s developed a foundation for expert systems. McCarthy invented the LISP programming language, which is the dominant language used in AI and expert systems. Also in the 1960s, an expert system called DENDRAL was created by Lederberg, Buchanan, and Feigenbaum, which inferred a structure of molecules by mass spectography data. Other work on expert systems in the 1960s included SAINT, by Slagle, for symbolic integration; STUDENT, by Bobrow, for solving high school algebra word problems; and an expert system by Raphael for answering questions using trivial databases.

In the 1970s, industrial interest in developing expert systems increased; this interest has increased up to the present. Expert systems are being developed in application areas such as diagnosis, perception, instruction, learning, game playing, programming, theorem proving, and pattern and speech recognition. PROLOG was also developed during the 1970s and is used for logic programming applications.

Industrial interest has been shown by Digital Equipment, Texas Instruments, Xerox, Schlumberger, Hewlett-Packard, General Motors, IBM, Teknowledge, the Carnegie Group, Inference Corporation, Intellicorp, and others. Universities, such as Stanford, MIT, Carnegie-Mellon, Rutgers, and others continue to pursue expert system technology.

By applying AI ideas to expert systems over the years, two major facts have been learned[5]. The first is that an expert system must be knowledge rich to work successfully, even if it is methods poor. The second fact, derived through work with expert systems, is that a specialist's knowledge is largely heuristic—experiential and uncertain.

2.3   Applications of Expert Systems During the Knowledge Age

As expert systems technology matures and becomes even more affordable, expert systems will penetrate more deeply into the marketplace[3,6–10,12,16,17]. Many expert systems are already being used on a worldwide basis, as shown in a sample of expert systems in Figure 2.1[17]. In some areas, such as medical diagnosis, consulting an expert system may become part of the standard practice of care. This section presents 10 examples of expert systems technology that could become common in the coming years. Figures 2.2 through 2.4 show sample runs of expert system prototypes in different domains.

Example One: The Home Entertainment Market Via the Video Store in 1995

Imagine how expert systems could play a role in the home entertainment industry if they were used in the following manner. Let's picture the video store in 1995. Perhaps, instead of selling today's videotapes, the video store will sell videodiscs of movies to be played on one's home CD player. Expert systems could be used to help the patron determine what movie tape/disc is best for that customer. An expert system could be created that would help the patron narrow down the choices in selecting an appropriate movie. The expert system might first ask what type of movie the patron wants to see, such as a comedy, adventure, science fiction, horror, drama, or documentary. Then questions delving deeper into this subject area would be asked to determine the best movies for the patron's interests. When the recommended movies are finally listed, hypertext might be used to allow the patron to explore the recommended movies in more detail. The expert system would also be linked with videodiscs that would show 30-second segments of actual scenes from the recommended movies. The expert system would be tied into the inventory system in order to check the in-stock status of the recommended movies to see if they had been checked out. This application is not farfetched at all. The technology already exists to make it a reality, but the economics do not now warrant the use of this expert system application.

Example Two: The Expert Tax Form Selector System

With the myriad tax forms available and the fact that many individuals may not have accountants, it might be difficult to determine what tax forms and supporting schedules are needed in order to file your tax form. This is where an expert system might help. Imagine having a microcomputer-based expert system available in libraries and post offices (where tax forms and schedules are usually displayed) for assisting you in determining what tax forms and schedules you need. Taking this one step further, imagine having this expert system linked to software for actually completing your taxes. Thus, the expert system would not only tell you what forms and schedules you need but would also allow you to fill out your forms and schedules. Pushing this concept even further, the expert system might be able to provide some tax advice (like Tax Cut, an integrated expert system package that already exists for providing tax advice) to help you in your tax planning. Again, as in the first example, the technology already exists to provide this application. Now the usefulness of such an application needs to be assessed.

Europe
- The safety-bag expert system in the electronic railway interlocking system ELEKTRA (ALCATEL Austria-ELIN Research Center, Vienna, Austria);
- An expert system to support the treatment of cases concerning the import and export of sugar products (Belgium Institute of Management, Everberg, Belgium)
- An expert system (ERASMUS) for decision making in road maintenance (ILOG, Gentilly, France)
- An expert system (GESPI) for solving the management problem of allocating platforms to arriving trains and then planning a route for their departure that does not conflict with those of other incoming trains (GSI-ERLI, Charenton-Le Pont, France)
- An expert system (XUMA) for assisting environmental protection authorities in the assessment of contaminated sites (Kernforschungszentrum [Nuclear Research Center], Karlsruhe, Germany)
- An expert system for fault diagnosis on computerized numerical control machines (IAO, Stuttgart, Germany)
- A diagnostic expert system (DAX/MED2) for quality assurance of an automatic transmission control unit (Karlsruhe University, Karlsruhe, Germany)
- An expert system (PECUNIA) for personal portfolio management (QUINARY, Milan, Italy)
- An expert system (LAIDA) for the analysis of disturbances in electrical networks (LABEIN, Bilbao, Spain)
- An expert system for controlling experimental sites in high-energy physics (CERN/ECP, Geneva, Switzerland)
- An expert system to help in the options market (University of Geneva, Geneva, Switzerland)
- An expert system (AMETHYST) for the automatic diagnosis of rotating machinery faults (Intelligent Applications, Ltd., West Lothian, Scotland)
- An expert system (PFES) for product formulation (Logica, Cambridge, England)
- An expert system (RAP) for naval resource allocation (SD-Scicon, Surrey, England).

Far East
- An expert system for blast furnace operation (NKK Corporation, Hiroshima, Japan)
- An expert system for large-scale fault diagnosis in steel manufacturing (Nippon Steel Corporation, Japan)
- An expert system for predicting blast pressure in blast furnace operations (RIST, Pohang, Korea)
- An expert system for elevator design (Mitsubishi Electric Corporation, Japan)

FIGURE 2.1 Sample of Operational Expert Systems Worldwide.

- An expert system as an alarm-based operational guidance system (Toshiba Corporation, Tokyo, Japan)
- A diagnostic expert system for a gas turbine air conditioning plant (China Light and Power Company, Hong Kong)
- An expert system for diagnosing steel structures at hydropower stations (CRIEPI, Tokyo, Japan)
- A diagnostic expert system for automobiles with electronic control units (Hyundai Moter Service Company, Seoul, Korea)
- An expert system (UNIK-PCS) as a crude oil delivery scheduling system (Yukong, Ltd., Seoul, Korea)
- An expert scheduling system for paper production (Oji Paper Company, Japan)
- An expert system for cockpit crew scheduling (NEC/Japan Airlines, Tokyo, Japan)
- An expert system for airport staff rostering (Singapore Air Lines, Singapore)
- An expert system for supporting construction planning for shield tunneling works (Hitachi, Osaka, Japan)
- An expert system (BRAINS) as a stock portfolio management system (Lucky Securities, Seoul, Korea).

Mexico
- An expert system (SECAL) for diagnosing problems in boiler operations (ITESM/CRYSEL, Monterrey, Mexico)
- An expert system (SEMPREP) for fault diagnosis in textile machinery (ITESM, Monterrey, Mexico)
- An expert system to help varnish plant operations (Electric Research Institute/CONDUMEX Group, Cuernavaca, Mexico)
- An expert system for problem diagnosis during the synthetic thread dyeing process (ITESM/CRYSEL, Monterrey, Mexico)
- An expert system (SEND) for controlling tone deviations in colorant direct-black-38 (ITESM/PYOSA, Monterrey, Mexico)
- An expert system (SEMAT) for diagnosing problems in toothpaste tube machines (ITESM/CYDSA, Monterrey, Mexico)
- An expert system (CELLOS) for diagnosing quality defects in cellophane film production (ITESM/CYDSA, Monterrey, Mexico)
- An expert system (AFFIN) for the evaluation of industrial investment projects (ITESM/FONEI, Cuernavaca, Mexico)
- An expert system for risk assessment in an individual's life (Seguros America, Mexico City, Mexico)
- An expert system (OPTAR) for optimizing the design of automotive electrical wire harnesses (CONDUMEX, Mexico)
- An expert system for the design of capital goods (Sistemas Inteligentes, Monterrey, Mexico)

FIGURE 2.1   continued

- An expert system (SEHUSI) for describing human behavior in a work environment (ITESM/CYDSA, Monterrey, Mexico)
- An integrated expert system (SEAPP) for well test analysis (SOFTTEK, Mexico)
- An expert system to help students select an undergraduate major (ITESM, Monterrey, Mexico)
- An expert system (RHUTA) to assign human resources to the planned substations and transmission lines of a power network (Electric Research Institute, Cuernavaca, Mexico)

Canada
- Diagnostic and administrative expert systems for network services (Bell Canada, Ontario, Canada)
- An expert system for configuration of local area networks (Northern Telecom, Toronto, Canada)
- An expert system (TRANSEPT) for the preliminary design of power networks (Hydro-Quebec, Montreal, Canada)
- An expert system for generative process planning (Northern Telecom, Alberta, Canada)
- An expert system that provides personalized information on how to reduce one's risk of developing cancer (Bell-Northern Research, Verdun, Quebec, Canada)
- A legal expert system as a nervous shock advisor (University of British Columbia, Vancouver, B.C., Canada)
- An expert system for proposed corporate name verification (Comdale Technologies, Toronto, Canada)
- An expert system (HIDES) for highway intersection design (Alberta Transportation and Utilities, Alberta, Canada)
- An expert system (VARMINT) for aiding maintenance and repair of machines on icebreakers (Transportation Development Center, Richmond, B.C., Canada)
- An expert resource system for public sector compensation and benefits personnel (Canadian Workplace Automation Research Center, Laval, Quebec, Canada)
- An expert assistant (STATEX) for statistical analysis (CWARC, Laval, Quebec, Canada)
- An expert system for automobile engine diagnosis (Simon Fraser University, Burnaby, B.C., Canada)

FIGURE 2.1   continued

```
Subject:
  Car engine diagnosis

Author
  Jay Liebowitz (Adapted from J. B. Shen and N. S. Tseng)

Starting text:
  Welcome. This expert system helps car users to diagnose
  some simple car problems on three parts: starting,
  transmission and steering, and wheels and tires. The system
  will ask you questions and prompt you answers which you
  should enter by typing in the number.

Ending text:
  Have a nice drive!

Uses all applicable rules in data derivations.


RULES:


─────────────────────────────────────────────────────────

RULE NUMBER: 1

IF:
      parts starting
  and symptoml is nothing happens when try to start
THEN:
      probleml is electricity is not going to the starter
  and clean and retighten disconnected cables, use jumper
      cables to start car or replace battery, or have a
      qualified mechanic check out the problem——
      Probability=9/10


─────────────────────────────────────────────────────────

RULE NUMBER: 2

IF:
      parts starting
  and symptoml is a click-click-click but nothing happens
THEN:
      probleml is enough electricity to activate the starter
      solenoid but not enough to turn the starter over
```

FIGURE 2.2   Simple Knowledge Base and Sample Run of an Engine Diagnosis ES Prototype Using Exsys. (Reprinted by permission from J. Liebowitz, *The Dynamics of Decision Support Systems and Expert Systems,* Dryden Press, Orlando, FL, 1990.)

```
          and clean and retighten corroded battery terminals and use
          jumper cable to start car, or have a mechanic check the
          defective starter--Probability=8/10


RULE NUMBER: 3

IF:
          parts starting
    and symptom1 is engine cranks slowly but won't start
THEN:
          problem1 is defective starter and weak battery
    and have a mechanic check the worn starter and the charging
          system--Probability=9/10


RULE NUMBER: 4

IF:
          parts starting
    and symptom1 is engine cranks briskly but won't start
THEN:
          problem1 is no spark or no fuel
    and remove the distributor cap and wipe dry the ignition
          path--Probability=9/10


RULE NUMBER: 5

IF:
          parts transmission and steering
    and symptom2 is chattering sound when first begin to move
THEN:
          problem2 is clutch is not engaging properly
    and check transmission fluid level or have a mechanic check
          the worn clutch or bands--Probability=10/10


RULE NUMBER: 6

IF:
          parts transmission and steering
    and symptom2 is pressing the accelerator and car doesn't
          respond while under way
THEN:
          problem2 is slipping clutch or low transmission fluid
    and check transmission fluid level or have a mechanic check
          and adjust the slipping clutch--Probability=9/10


RULE NUMBER: 7

IF:
          parts transmission and steering
```

FIGURE 2.2   continued

and symptom2 is a screeching noise when you are turning or
steering sharply at low speed
THEN:
    problem2 is the power steering belt is loose or worn or
    there is a leak in the power steering pump
and have the stretched power steering belt tightened or
    replaced, add steering fluid, or have a mechanic check
    the power steering pump or hose--Probability=9/10

RULE NUMBER: 8

IF:
    parts wheels and tires
and symptom3 is car's suspension bangs over bumps
THEN:
    problem3 is the suspension is hitting bottom
and replace the faulty shock absorbers or have a mechanic
    check out the problem as required--Probability=9/10

RULE NUMBER: 9

IF:
    parts wheels and tires
and symptom3 is car pulls in either direction when
    cruising along
THEN:
    problem3 is misaligned wheels, mismatched tires, or a
    partially deflated front tire
and check the front-end and wheel alignment, change one or
    both of the front tires so they will be identical, or
    check for tire damage then inflate the tire to its
    proper level--Probability=9/10

RULE NUMBER: 10

IF:
    parts wheels and tires
and symptom3 is tire wear is excessive in the middle
THEN:
    problem3 is the tire has been riding on its middle only
    due to over-inflation
and let the excess air out, check tire and replace if
    necessary--Probability=10/10

QUALIFIERS:

1 parts
   starting

FIGURE 2.2 continued

```
            transmission and steering
            wheels and tires

        Used in rule(s):  1  2  3  4  5  6
                          7  8  9 10

  2  symptom1 is
     nothing happens when try to start
     a click-click-click but nothing happens
     engine cranks slowly but won't start
     engine cranks briskly but won't start

        Used in rule(s):  1  2  3  4

  3  problem1 is
     electricity is not going to the starter
     enough electricity to activate the starter solenoid but not
       enough to turn the starter over
     defective starter and weak battery
     no spark or no fuel

        Used in rule(s):  ( 1)  ( 2)  ( 3)  ( 4)

  4  symptom2 is
     chattering sound when first begin to move
     pressing the accelerator and car doesn't respond while
       under way
     a screeching noise when you are turning or steering sharply
       at low speed

        Used in rule(s):  5  6  7

  5  problem2 is
     clutch is not engaging properly
     slipping clutch or low transmission fluid
     the power steering belt is loose or worn or there is a leak
       in the power steering pump

        Used in rule(s):  ( 5)  ( 6)  ( 7)

  6  symptom3 is
     car's suspension bangs over bumps
     car pulls in either direction when cruising along
     tire wear is excessive in the middle

        Used in rule(s):  8  9  10

  7  problem3 is
     the suspension is hitting bottom
     misaligned wheels, mismatched tires, or a partially
       deflated front tire
     the tire has been riding on its middle only due to
       over-inflation

        Used in rule(s):  ( 8)  ( 9)  ( 10)
```

FIGURE 2.2   continued

```
CHOICES:

1  clean and retighten disconnected cables, use
      jumper cables to start car or replace battery,
      or have a qualified mechanic check out the problem

      Used in rule(s):  (  1)


2  clean and retighten corroded battery terminals and use
   jumper cable to start car, or have a mechanic check the
   defective starter

      Used in rule(s):  (  2)


3  have a mechanic check the worn starter and the
   charging system

      Used in rule(s):  (  3)


4  remove the distributor cap and wipe dry the ignition path

      Used in rule(s):  (  4)


5  check transmission fluid level or have a mechanic check
   the worn clutch or bands

      Used in rule(s):  (  5)


6  check transmission fluid level or have a mechanic check
   and adjust the slipping clutch

      Used in rule(s):  (  6)


7  have the stretched power steering belt tightened or
   replaced, add steering fluid, or have a mechanic check
   the power steering pump or hose

      Used in rule(s):  (  7)


8  replace the faulty shock absorbers or have a mechanic
   check out the problem as required

      Used in rule(s):  (  8)


9  check the front-end and wheel alignment, change one or
   both of the front tires so they will be identical,
   or check for tire damage then inflate the tire to its
   proper level

      Used in rule(s):  (  9)


10 let the excess air out, check tire and replace
   if necessary

      Used in rule(s):  ( 10)
```

FIGURE 2.2   continued

```
┌─────────────────────────────────────┐
│          Car engine diagnosis        │
└─────────────────────────────────────┘

   by: Jay Liebowitz (Adapted from J.B. Shen
       and N.S. Tseng)




               Press any key to start:
```

```
   Welcome.  This expert system helps car users to diagnose
   some simple car problems on three parts: starting,
   transmission and steering, and wheels and tires.  The
   system will ask you questions and prompt you answers
   which you should enter by typing in the number.





               Press any key to start:
```

FIGURE 2.2   continued

```
parts
        1   starting
        2   transmission and steering
        3   wheels and tires
2
```

```
Enter number(s) of value(s), WHY for information on the
rule, (ESC) for edit mode or (H) for help
```

```
symptom2 is
        1   chattering sound when first begin to move
        2   pressing the accelerator and car doesn't respond
            while under way
        3   a screeching noise when you are turning or
            steering sharply at low speed
1
```

```
Enter number(s) of value(s), WHY for information on the
rule, (ESC) for edit mode or (H) for help

Have a nice drive!

              Press any key to display results:
```

FIGURE 2.2   continued

```
Values based on 0 - 10 system                          VALUE

1   check transmission fluid level or have a mechanic
    check the worn clutch or bands                        10
```

```
All choices (A), only if value> 1 <G>, Print <P>, Change
and rerun <C>, rules used <line number>, Help <H>,
Done <D>:
```

```
Values based on 0 - 10 system                          VALUE

1   check transmission fluid level or have a mechanic
    check the worn clutch or bands                        10
```

```
All choices (A), only if value> 1 <G>, Print <P>, Change
and rerun <C>, rules used <line number>, Help <H>,
Done <D>: 1
```

FIGURE 2.2   continued

```
RULE NUMBER: 5
IF:

    (1)   parts transmission and steering
and (2)   symptom2 is chattering sound when first begin
          to move

THEN:

          problem2 is clutch is not engaging properly
and       check transmission fluid level or have a
          mechanic check the worn clutch or bands —
          Probability=10/10




_____
IF line # for derivation, <K>—known data, <C>—choices or
— prev. or next rule, <J>—jump, <H>—help or
<ENTER> to continue:
```

FIGURE 2.2   continued

```
TOPSCO:  Training the ERBS spacecraft
analyst On Power Subsystem Contingency
Operations
```

```
                    by: Dr. Jay Liebowitz
```

```
                    Press any key to start:
```

```
This training aid will help the ERBS spacecraft analyst
in understanding what to do when faced with power
subsystem contingency operations. Hope you have fun.
```

```
                    Press any key to start:
```

FIGURE 2.3   Sample User Session Using TOPSCO

```
contingency id is
        1   analog alarm message
        2   discrete state colors in database
        3   performance and configuration checks
3




_____
Enter number(s) of value(s), WHY for information on the
rule, <ESC> for edit mode or <H> for help
```

```
contingency procedure responds to
        1   undervoltage or overcurrent condition on either
            the Non-Essential Bus or the Control System Bus
        2   battery overcharge
        3   battery high temperature and overtemperature
        4   battery rundown
        5   cell failure/cell balance greater than 0.6 volts
        6   SPRU has no output
        7   SPRU has reduced output
        8   28V instrument regulator failure
8




_____
Enter number(s) of value(s), WHY for information on the
rule, <ESC> for edit mode or <H> for help
```

FIGURE 2.3   continued

```
failure occurs in
      1  Regulator--1
      2  Regulator--2
      3  Regulator--3
      4  Regulator--4
WHY
```

```
Enter number(s) of value(s), WHY for information on the
rule, <ESC> for edit mode or <H> for help
```

```
RULE NUMBER: 35
IF:

      (1)  contingency procedure responds to 28V
           instrument regulator failure
and   (2)  failure occurs in Regulator-1

THEN:

           prior to switching regulators, the associated
           instrument is powered OFF first and powered
           back up again after the switch is complete--
           Probability=10/10
and        switch the ERBE-S to Reg.-2 (only if the
           regulator is still operational), the ERBE-
           NS to Reg.-3, and SAGE-II to NEB (only if
           SAGE-II is using Reg.-3)--
           Probability=10/10
```

```
IF line # for derivation, <K>-known data, <C>-choices
or--prev. or next rule, <J>-jump, <H>-help or
<ENTER> to continue:
```

FIGURE 2.3   continued

```
failure occurs in
        1   Regulator--1
        2   Regulator--2
        3   Regulator--3
        4   Regulator--4
2
```

```
Enter number(s) of value(s), WHY for information on the
rule, <ESC> for edit mode or <H> for help
```

```
ERBE-S is using Reg.-2 is
        1   yes
        2   no
1
```

```
Enter number(s) of value(s), WHY for information on the
rule, <ESC> for edit mode or <H> for help
```

FIGURE 2.3   continued

```
Thank you for using this training aid.  Have a good day.




















                    Press any key to display results:
```

```
              Values based on 0-10 system              VALUE
   1   action is call the observatory engineer and await
       direction  and concurrence                         10
   2   action is prepare an anomaly report and attach to
       applicable pass plan and file in Pass Plan Log      10
   3   action is look up parameter in the Telemetry List--
       Volume 2                                            10
   4   prior to switching regulators, the associated
       instrument is powered OFF first and powered back up
       again after the switch is complete                  10
   5   R2Fail procedure turns OFF Reg.-2 and
       the instrument                                      10




       _____
   All choices <A>, only if value> 1 <G>, Print <P>, Change
   and rerun <C>, rules used <line number>, Help <H>,
   Done <D>:
```

FIGURE 2.3   continued

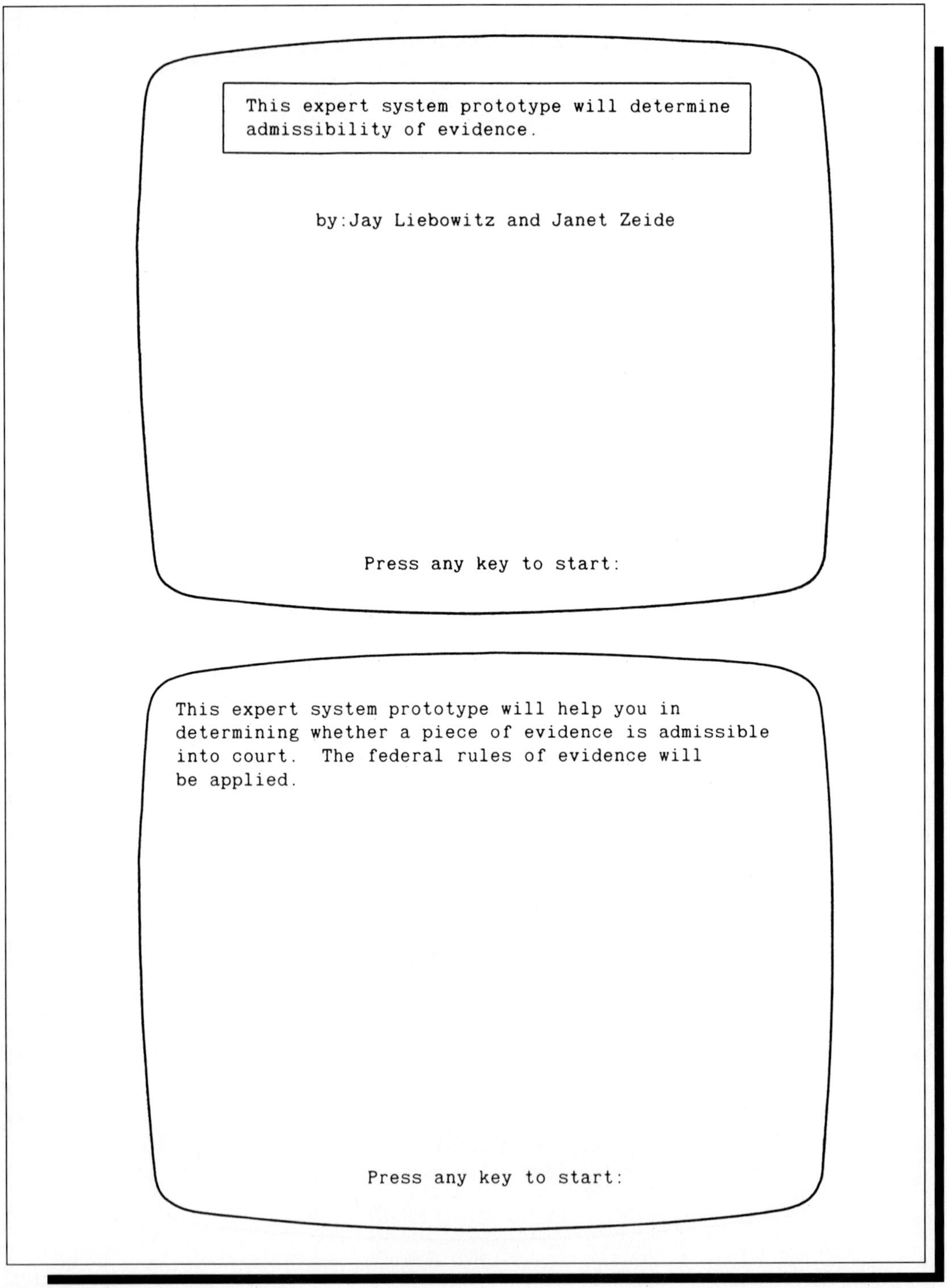

```
    ┌──────────────────────────────────────────────┐
    │  This expert system prototype will determine   │
    │  admissibility of evidence.                    │
    └──────────────────────────────────────────────┘



                  by:Jay Liebowitz and Janet Zeide








                    Press any key to start:
```

```
    This expert system prototype will help you in
    determining whether a piece of evidence is admissible
    into court.   The federal rules of evidence will
    be applied.









                    Press any key to start:
```

FIGURE 2.4   Sample User Session with EVIDENT

```
connection between evidence offered and issues before
the court is
     1   yes
     2   no
1
```

```
Enter number(s) of value(s), WHY for information on the
rule, <ESC> for edit mode or <H> for help
```

```
proffered evidence tends to prejudice jury is
     1   yes
     2   no
WHY
```

```
Enter number(s) of value(s), WHY for information on the
rule, <ESC> for edit mode or <H> for help
```

FIGURE 2.4   continued

```
RULE NUMBER: 3
IF:

      (1)   relevant is yes
and   (2)   proffered evidence tends to prejudice jury is no
and   (3)   evidence creates side issues and clouds main
            issue is no
and   (4)   evidence takes too much time to go into it is no
and   (5)   evidence causes unfair surprise which other
            side has no reasonable grounds to anticipate
            the offer of the evidence is  no

THEN:

            legal relevance is yes

ELSE:

            legal relevance is no
and         not admissible--Probability=10/10
and         stop
_____
IF line # for derivation, <K>-known data, <C>-choices
or--prev. or next rule, <J>-jump, <H>-help or <ENTER>
to continue:
```

```
proffered evidence tends to prejudice jury is
      1   yes
      2   no
2









_____
Enter number(s) of value(s), WHY for information on the
rule, <ESC> for edit mode or <H> for help
```

FIGURE 2.4   continued

```
evidence creates side issues and clouds main issue is
      1  yes
      2  no
2
```

```
Enter number(s) of value(s), WHY for information on the
rule, <ESC> for edit mode or <H> for help
```

```
evidence takes too much time to go into it is
      1  yes
      2  no
2
```

```
Enter number(s) of value(s), WHY for information on the
rule, <ESC> for edit mode or <H> for help
```

FIGURE 2.4   continued

```
evidence causes unfair surprise which other side has no
reasonable grounds to anticipate the offer of the
evidence is
      1  yes
      2  no
2
```

```
Enter number(s) of value(s), WHY for information on the
rule, <ESC> for edit mode or <H> for help
```

```
substantial bearing on the issues as contained in the
pleadings is
      1  yes
      2  no
1
```

```
Enter number(s) of value(s), WHY for information on the
rule, <ESC> for edit mode or <H> for help
```

FIGURE 2.4   continued

```
evidence offered to prove the truth of the matter
asserted is
      1  yes
      2  no
2
```

```
Enter number(s) of value(s), WHY for information on the
rule, <ESC> for edit mode or <H> for help
```

```
the evidence is a written instrument which is the
foundation of the legal act or transaction is
      1  yes
      2  no
WHY
```

```
Enter number(s) of value(s), WHY for information on the
rule, <ESC> for edit mode or <H> for help
```

FIGURE 2.4 continued

```
RULE NUMBER: 23
IF:

    (1)  hearsay doesn't apply
and (2)  relevant is yes
and (3)  material is yes
and (4)  legal relevance is yes
and (5)  evidence offered to prove the truth of the
         matter asserted is no
and (6)  the evidence is a written instrument which is
         the foundation of the legal act or transaction is yes
and (7)  original has been lost or destroyed without
         fault of the party offering the secondary
         evidence or is in the possession of the
         adverse party who refuses to produce it or
         is in the possession of a third person who
         refuses to produce it after being subpoenaed
         to do so or is voluminous and the opponent
         has been given adequate notice to examine
         the area represented by the abstract
and (8)  submitted a copy is yes

THEN:

         admissible--Probability=10/10

                  Press any key to continue:
```

```
the evidence is a written instrument which is the
foundation of the legal act or transaction is
     1  yes
     2  no
2

_____
Enter number(s) of value(s), WHY for information on the
rule, <ESC> for edit mode or <H> for help
```

FIGURE 2.4   continued

```
person wants to give opinions rather than facts is
     1  yes
     2  no
2
```

```
Enter number(s) of value(s), WHY for information on the
rule, <ESC> for edit mode or <H> for help
```

```
attack a witness' credibility is
     1  yes
     2  no
2
```

```
Enter number(s) of value(s), WHY for information on the
rule, <ESC> for edit mode or <H> for help
```

FIGURE 2.4   continued

```
a privilege exists which will allow the witness to not
testify is
     1   yes
     2   no
1
```

```
Enter number(s) of value(s), WHY for information on the
rule, <ESC> for edit mode or <H> for help
```

```
party offers parol evidence which would vary or
contradict a written instrument is
     1   yes
     2   no
2
```

```
Enter number(s) of value(s), WHY for information on the
rule, <ESC> for edit mode or <H> for help
```

FIGURE 2.4   continued

```
writings are involved is
     1  yes
     2  no
2
```

```
Enter number(s) of value(s), WHY for information on the
rule, <ESC> for edit mode or <H> for help
```

```
there involves
     1    spouse testifying against spouse
     2    anything said during marriage which is meant
          to be confidential
     3    client is not coming to attorney to seek advice
          on how to commit a crime
     4    information told/given by patient to physician
          to aid physician in diagnosis/treatment
     5    civil litigation and fifth amendment is not
          claimed on cross-exam once the witness
          elected to testify
     6    evidence of insurance coverage to show that
          a person acted negligently or wrongfully
     7    best evidence of insurance coverage is not
          used to show agency, ownership, control,
          bias, prejudice of a witness
     8    evidence of safety measures used to prove
          negligence or guilt but not used to prove
          ownership, control, feasibility of
          precautionary measures or impeachment

              Press any key for more values
```

FIGURE 2.4   continued

```
        9    evidence of offer to settle used to prove
             liability for or invalidity of the claim or
             its amount but not used to prove bias or
             prejudice of a witness
        10   evidence of furnishing, offering, or promising
             to pay medical expenses used to prove
             liability for the injury
  4




  _____
  Enter number(s) of value(s), WHY for information on the
  rule, <ESC> for edit mode or <H> for help
```

```
  Thank you for using this evidence "aid".










                  Press any key to display results:
```

FIGURE 2.4   continued

```
                    Values based on 0-10 system          VALUE
1   not admissible                                           9














_____
All choices <A>, only if value> 1 <G>, Print <P>, Change
and rerun <C>, rules used <line number>, Help <H>,
Done <D>:
```

```
                         Values based on 0-10 system    VALUE
1   not admissible                                           9














_____
All choices <A>, only if value> 1 <G>, Print <P>, Change
and rerun <C>, rules used <line number>, Help <H>,
Done <D>: 1
```

FIGURE 2.4   continued

```
RULE NUMBER: 31
IF:

    (1)   a privilege exists which will allow the witness
          to not testify is yes
and (2)   privilege might involve physician-patient
and (3)   there involves information told/given by patient
          to physician to aid physician in
          diagnosis/treatment

THEN:

          not admissible--Probability=9/10
and       stop

NOTE: Exception under physician-patient privilege.
_____

IF line # for derivation, <K>-known data, <C>-choices
or--prev. or next rule, <J>-jump, <H>-help or <ENTER>
to continue:
```

FIGURE 2.2   continued

Example Three: The Mass Market Expert System Application

Mass-marketed applications of expert systems will increase in number and variety. Already there are many mass-marketed expert systems, whose cost is low enough for many individuals. Examples of such applications are Tax Cut for providing tax advice, EXSAMPLE for determining the appropriate statistical analysis technique to use for a given situation, Family Care for diagnosing children's health problems, STS/Breakout for providing stock trading advice, WILLMASTER for drafting wills, and Root Directory for providing gardening advice. In the coming years, as expert systems become more widely recognized and more reasonably priced, applications will proliferate in law, medicine, home entertainment, business, and many other areas.

Example Four: Expert Systems in the Manufacturing Industry

Expert systems will continue to play a major role in the manufacturing industry. According to a survey by Battelle Memorial Institute, the top priority of worldwide research and development groups is developing expert systems for manufacturing process control. In the same study, the seventh priority item is building expert systems to aid design. It appears that expert systems will play an important role in these manufacturing activities. One major area in manufacturing that will use expert system technology is configuration management. DEC, IBM, Hitachi, Philips, Xerox, Motorola, and other manufacturing firms have already used expert systems for hardware configuration management. Other computer manufacturing companies are recognizing that expert systems are useful in configuration management, and are starting to explore these and other opportunities.

Example Five: Expert Systems in the Quest for Information

An important application of expert systems is intelligent information retrieval. With the proliferation of data in company databases, easier accessing techniques are needed for search and retrieval. One area that will continue to grow is expert database systems. In the future, books, journals, magazines, and reports will be on-line, so that individuals can readily access them. As more and more information is put on-line, the need for better methods of navigating through this barrage of information will grow. The use of expert systems in searching for and retrieving this information more intelligently will become especially important when such "electronic libraries" become commonplace. Additionally, expert systems might be used to help in the design and development of these database management systems.

Example Six: Expert Systems for the Military

The military has been the largest funder of AI/expert systems projects, and several expert systems have been developed for the military. These include such applications as diagnosing automated testing equipment, interpreting signals, and myriad command decision support applications. This trend will likely continue. Expert systems will be used to help interpret whether missiles are actual warheads, decoys, or debris. They will also be used to aid in operational planning activities, as well as other functional tasks. Training is another important area for expert systems, and the military will increasingly develop knowledge-based simulation systems to facilitate military training.

Example Seven: Expert Systems in the Classroom

Expert systems will be used in elementary and secondary schools. Interactive videodisc technology is now being used to teach history, geography, science, and other subjects. Expert systems could be linked with this videodisc technology to enhance education by tutoring students in selected subjects. For example, an expert system could be constructed for chemistry, and then simulated chemistry experiments could be shown via videodisc technology. An intelligent tutoring system would be able to adjust its questioning and tutoring according to the student's level of understanding. Intelligent tutors are now used in teaching foreign languages, geography, and other subjects. The main problem in constructing intelligent tutors is that it typically takes 5 person-years to incorporate 1 year of instruction in an intelligent tutoring system. As this technology matures and shells are developed to facilitate the construction of these tutors, more intelligent tutoring systems will be used in the classroom to supplement the teacher's lessons.

Example Eight: Expert Systems in Telecommunications

One of the fastest-growing industries is telecommunications. With the merging of computers and communications and the need to receive information on a timely basis, telecommunications is playing an increasingly important part in today's society. In order to fight network congestion and to quickly diagnose faults in telecommunications networks and equipment, expert systems have been used. Bell Labs, Bellcore, GTE Labs, Contel, MCI, British Telecom, and many other communications firms are already using expert systems. Their primary use in telecommunications has been in fault isolation and diagnosis. As the dependence on telecommunications grows and as the Integrated Services Digital Network (ISDN) becomes a reality, the need to respond quickly to network problems in real time will increase. Multiple cooperating expert systems might answer these needs. More research in expert systems is needed to develop better paradigms for handling data in a distributed environment.

Example Nine: Expert Systems as Clerical Aids

Expert systems will become more prevalent as clerical aids in the 1990s. They will be linked with speech understanding devices, so that one can dictate into a computer-like typewriter and the words will be typed out on paper based upon the dictation. Expert systems will be used in this sense to handle grammatical rules and to know, for example, if the dictated word is *to*, too, or *two*. Kurzweil's Voicewriter is an example of this type of device, and as the number of words that it can handle increases and the price decreases, this type of device will quickly penetrate the marketplace. Another such expert system is RightWriter. It is used to correct punctuation errors, grammar, and spelling, and it even gives the readability level of the writing being examined. This type of expert system would be beneficial at home, school, and the office.

Example Ten: Expert Systems at Home

Expert systems will become common in the home. Imagine a knowledge-based oven that describes the steps and the recommended way of making a particular kind of chicken, and then automatically adjusts the temperature in the oven to compensate for this recipe. Chef is an expert system that helps provide the best combinations of food for cooking. Other expert systems will be developed for home activities, such as gardening, room layouts (using knowledge-based computer-aided design/manufacturing systems), daily scheduling, and other activities. Who knows, maybe some day you will have a home robot preparing your dinners by interacting with an expert cooking system.

2.4 The Future Is Not Far Away

Expert systems will play an increasingly influential role in society. Such systems are already being woven into today's environment in many areas. They are being used in hospitals to diagnose and treat diseases; in gasoline stations to diagnose and repair automobile engine problems; and even by farmers in making planting and pesticide control decisions.

Even though there are advantages to using expert systems, there are also limitations. Future areas of expert systems development will consist of the following:

- Developing automated tools and better techniques for acquiring knowledge.
- Allowing expert systems to learn from previous experiences.
- Developing better debugging tools in building expert systems.
- Developing a structured methodology for validating expert systems.
- Improving explanation capabilities.
- Creating better expert system architectures and inference procedures.
- Incorporating in expert systems the ability to make assumptions and expectations.
- Developing better knowledge representation approaches.
- Improving methods of handling uncertain, incomplete, and inconsistent information.
- Developing better user interfaces.
- Creating parallel processing approaches.

- Developing techniques for embedding expert systems.
- Developing expert systems for generic tasks (i.e., for deep reasoning).
- Developing techniques for multiple, cooperating expert systems (i.e., distributed expert systems/AI).

If these research issues are addressed and resolved, then expert systems will become powerful and useful tools for many applications.

References

1. E. Rich, *Artificial Intelligence*, McGraw-Hill, New York, 1983.
2. J. Liebowitz, "Expert Systems and Telecommunications," *Telematics and Informatics*, Vol. 2, No. 3, Pergamon Press, New York, 1985.
3. J. Liebowitz, *Introduction to Expert Systems*, Mitchell Publishing, Santa Cruz, CA, 1988.
4. F. Hayes-Roth, D. A. Waterman, and D. B. Lenat, *Building Expert Systems*, Addison-Wesley, Reading, MA, 1983.
5. D. Michie, *Expert Systems in the MicroElectronic Age*, Edinburgh University Press, Edinburgh, 1979.
6. D. A. Waterman, *A Guide to Expert Systems*, Addison-Wesley, Reading, MA, 1986.
7. W. B. Rauch-Hindin, *Artificial Intelligence in Business, Science, and Industry*, Vol. I, *Fundamentals*, Prentice-Hall, Englewood Cliffs, NJ, 1986.
8. J. Liebowitz, "Problem Selection for Expert Systems Development," *Structuring Expert Systems: Domain, Design, and Development*, Yourdon Press, New York, 1989.
9. J. Liebowitz and D. A. DeSalvo (eds.), *Structuring Expert Systems: Domain, Design, and Development*, Yourdon Press, New York, 1989.
10. P. Harmon and D. King, *Expert Systems: Artificial Intelligence in Business*, John Wiley & Sons, New York, 1985.
11. B. G. Buchanan, "Expert Systems: Working Systems and the Research Literature," *Expert Systems*, Vol. 3, No. 1, January 1986.
12. J. Liebowitz (ed.), *Expert System Applications to Telecommunications*, John Wiley & Sons, New York, 1988.
13. Exsys, Inc., *Exsys: Expert System Development Package*, Albuquerque, NM, 1985.
14. T. Nagy, R. Gault, and M. Nagy, *Building Your First Expert System*, Ashton-Tate, Culver City, CA, 1985.
15. R. J. Mockler and D. G. Dologite, *An Introduction to Expert Systems*, Macmillan Publishing, New York, 1992.
16. J. Liebowitz, "Gazing Through the Crystal Ball in Predicting Future Developments in Expert Systems," *Journal CETTICO*, Universidad Politecnica de Madrid, No. 6, Spain, March 1992.
17. J. Liebowitz (series ed.), *Operational Expert System Applications Worldwide Book Series*, Pergamon Press, Tarrytown, NY, 1991.

Chapter 3

Overview of The Expert Systems Development Life Cycle: The Knowledge Engineering Process

3.1 Components of an Expert System   **3.3** Implementing an Expert System
3.2 Building an Expert System

Expert systems, as defined in Chapter 2, are built to capture the expertise of human experts in a well-defined, narrow area of knowledge. The early expert systems took 20 to 50 person-years to build; today's complex expert systems are still apt to take about 10 person-years. With the use of an expert system shell, however, expert systems can be built in 5 person-years and simple expert system prototypes in only 3 person-months.

This chapter briefly discusses the components of expert systems and their building process. More detailed explanation of each of these components and their development is provided in later chapters.

3.1 Components of an Expert System

The components of an expert system, as shown in Figure 3.1, can be described in terms of

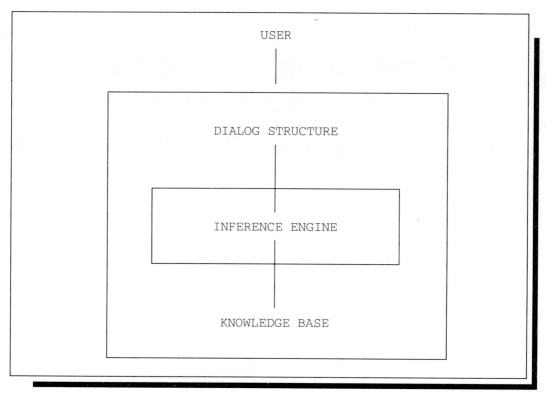

FIGURE 3.1   Components of an Expert System

- a user interface—the dialog structure;
- a control structure—the inference engine; and
- a fact base—the knowledge base.

Dialog Structure

The *dialog structure* is the language interface with which the user can access the expert system. Usually the user interacts with the expert system in a consultative mode. An explanation module is also included in the expert system. The explanation module allows the user to query and challenge the expert system and examine its reasoning process. According to Michie[1], there are three different user modes for an expert system:

1. Getting answers to problems—the user as client;
2. Improving or increasing the system's knowledge—the user as tutor; and
3. Harvesting the knowledge base for human use—the user as pupil.

Each of these three modes requires interaction through the dialog structure.

Inference Engine

The *inference engine* is a program that allows hypotheses to be generated based upon the information in the knowledge base. It is the control structure that manipulates the knowledge in the knowledge base to arrive at various solutions.

Three major methods are incorporated in the inference engine to search a space efficiently for deriving hypotheses from the knowledge base: forward chaining, backward chaining, and forward and backward processing combined. Later chapters will explain each of these methods in detail. *Forward chaining*, often described as *event-* or *data-driven reasoning*, is used for problem solving when data or basic ideas are a starting point. With this method, the system does not start with any particular goals defined for it. It works through the facts to arrive at conclusions, or goals. One drawback of forward chaining is that one derives everything possible, whether one needs it or not. Forward chaining has been used in expert systems for data analysis, design, and concept formulation.

Backward chaining, called *goal-directed reasoning*, is another inference engine technique. This method entails having a goal or a hypothesis as a starting point and then working backward along certain paths to see if the conclusion is true. A problem with backward chaining involves conjunctive subgoals in which a combinatorial explosion of possibilities could result. Expert systems employing backward chaining are those used for diagnosis and planning.

Forward and backward processing combined is another method used for search direction in the inference engine. This approach is used for a large search space, so that bottom-up and top-down searching can be appropriately combined. This combined search is applicable to complex problems incorporating uncertainties, such as speech understanding.

Most inference engines have the ability to reason in the presence of uncertainty. Different techniques have been used for handling uncertainty—namely, Bayesian statistics, certainty factors, and fuzzy logic. In many cases, one must deal with uncertainty in data or in knowledge. Thus, an expert system should be able to handle this uncertainty.

Knowledge Base

The *knowledge base* is the last and most important component of an expert system. It is composed of domain facts and heuristics based upon experience. According to Duda and Gaschnig[2], the most powerful expert systems are those containing the most knowledge.

3.2 Building an Expert System

Building an expert system typically involves the rapid prototyping approach[3]. This approach entails "building a little and testing a little" until the knowledge base is refined to meet the expected acceptance rate and users' needs. Expert systems development is an iterative process in which, after testing, knowledge is reacquired, represented, encoded, and tested again until the knowledge base is refined. A principal refinement for expert systems continues to be the need for effective filtering out of the biases created by the particular values and views of the experts who are the sources of the knowledge that constitute knowledge bases.

The first step in building an expert system is to select the problem, define the expert system's goal(s), and identify the sources of knowledge. The criteria for expert system problem selection can be broken down into three components: problem criteria, expert criteria, and domain area personnel criteria[4]. The following criteria should be followed when selecting an expert system problem:

Problem Criteria

- The task involves mostly symbolic processing.
- Test cases are available.
- The problem task is well bounded.
- The task must be performed frequently.
- Written materials exist explaining the task.
- The task requires only cognitive skills.
- The experts agree on the solutions.

Expert Criteria

- An expert exists.
- The expert is cooperative.
- The expert is articulate.
- The expert's knowledge is based on experience, facts, and judgment.
- Other experts in the task area exist.

Domain Area Personnel Criteria

- A need exists to develop an expert system for that task.
- The task would be provided with the necessary financial support.
- Top management supports the project.
- The domain area personnel have realistic expectations for the use of an expert system.
- Users would welcome the expert system.
- The knowledge is not politically sensitive or controversial.

Once these criteria are met and the problem is selected, the next step is to acquire the knowledge from the expert in order to develop the knowledge base. Knowledge acquisition is an iterative process in which many meetings with the expert are needed to gather all the relevant and necessary information for the knowledge base. Before being able to acquire the knowledge from the expert, however, the knowledge engineer must be familiar with the domain. Reading documentation and manuals and observing experts in the domain are needed to obtain a fundamental background on which the knowledge engineer's knowledge will be based. This background is needed so that the knowledge engineer can ask the appropriate questions and understand what the expert is saying.

Knowledge can be acquired by various methods. The most commonly used method is to have the knowledge engineer (i.e., the developer of the expert system) interview the expert. Various structured and unstructured techniques can be used for interviewing. Some of the methods are as follows[5]:

- Method of familiar tasks—analysis of the tasks that the expert usually performs.
- Limited information tasks—a familiar task is performed, but the expert is not given certain information that is typically available.
- Constrained processing tasks—a familiar task is performed, but the expert must do so under time or other constraints.
- Method of tough cases—analysis of a familiar task that is conducted for a set of data that presents a tough case for the expert.

When interviewing the expert, Olson and Rueter[6] suggest that the knowledge engineer should first enlist the expert's cooperation. Second, the knowledge engineer should ask free-form questions at the start, becoming more specific as the interview progresses. Third, the knowledge engineer should not impose his or her own understanding on the expert. Lastly, the knowledge engineer should limit the sessions to coherent tasks, recognizing fatigue and attentional limits.

Besides interviewing the expert to acquire knowledge, there are other techniques that can be used[6]:

- Questionnaires.
- Observation of the task performance.
- Protocol analysis—the expert thinks aloud while performing the task.
- Interruption analysis—the observer interrupts when unable to understand the expert's thought processes in performing a task.
- Inferential flow analysis—answers to particular questions about causal relations are used to build up a causal network among concepts or objects in the domain of expertise.
- Multidimensional scaling—the expert provides similarity judgments on all pairs of objects or concepts in the domain of inquiry.
- Repertory grid analysis—includes an initial dialog with the expert, a rating session, and analyses that cluster both the objects and the dimensions on which the items were rated.

Automated knowledge acquisition aids are being developed to help the knowledge elicitation process[7,8]. Meanwhile, these other techniques will be used, with interviewing as the major knowledge acquisition technique.

After the knowledge is acquired, the next step is to select a knowledge representation approach. These approaches include predicate calculus, frames, scripts, semantic networks, and production rules, as described earlier. According to Software Architecture and Engineering, Inc.[9], rule-based deduction would be an appropriate method to use if (1) the underlying knowledge is already organized as rules, (2) the classification is predominantly categorical, and (3) there is not much context dependence. Frames, scripts, and semantic networks are best used when the knowledge preexists as descriptions.

The next step consists of programming the knowledge by using a text editor in an expert system shell or by using LISP, Prolog, C, or some other appropriate programming language. An expert system shell contains a generalized dialog structure and an inference engine. A knowledge base can be designed for a specific problem domain and linked to the expert system shell to form a new expert system for a particular application. Some of the more popular expert system shells are these:

> ART—Inference Corporation
> KEE—Intellicorp
> Knowledge Craft—The Carnegie Group
> TIRS—IBM Corporation
> Nexpert Object—Neuron Data
> Level 5 Object—Information Builders, Inc.
> VP-Expert—Wordtech, Inc.
> Exsys—Exsys, Inc.
> KBMS/ADS—Trinzic Corporation
> G2—Gensym Corporation.

An expert system is not just a group of rules. It is a program that should be able to explain its reasoning, and human factors design should be incorporated into the system. Human factors should be designed into the expert system to include such features as messages, menus, free-text comments, rules against undesirable input, and high-level English-like representation language for encoding the knowledge. Explanation capabilities are needed so that the user can question and challenge the results of the expert system, as well as understand how the results were achieved. In MYCIN, an expert system designed to diagnose bacterial infections in the blood, explanation can be arrived at as shown here, with the user asking the questions[10]:

**HOW DID YOU DECIDE THAT ORGANISM-1 MIGHT BE AN E.COLI?
I used RULE021 to conclude that the identity of
ORGANISM-1 is e. coli. This gave a cumulative CF of (.47).
Then I used RULE084 to conclude that the identity of
ORGANISM-1 is e. coli. This gave a cumulative CF of (.55).
Finally, I used RULE003 to conclude that the identity of
ORGANISM-1 is e. coli. This gave a cumulative CF of (.74).

**DID YOU USE RULE163 TO FIND OUT ANYTHING ABOUT ORGANISM-1?
RULE163 was tried in the context of ORGANISM-1 but it failed
because it is not true that the patient has had a genito-
urinary tract manipulative procedure (clause 3).

**WHY DIDN'T YOU CONSIDER STREPTOCOCCUS AS A POSSIBILITY FOR ORGANISM-1?

The following rule could have been used to determine that the identity of
ORGANISM-1 was streptococcus: RULE033
But clause 2 ("the morphology if the organism is coccus") was already known
to be false for ORGANISM-1, so the rule was never tried.

The last step in the expert system building process consists of validating, testing, and evaluating the system. Validity assessment is necessary to check the
knowledge base and the expert system as a whole. Validity can be achieved by
running the knowledge base on past problems. Validity can also be confirmed by
other experts knowledgeable in the problem domain.

Testing is an important area to be examined because when the expert system
finally runs, it typically produces a variety of unexpected results. These unexpected results are summarized by Hayes-Roth et al[11]:

- Excess generality—special cases overlooked.
- Excess specificity—generality undetected.
- Concept poverty—useful relationships not detected and exploited.
- Invalid knowledge—misstatement of facts or approximations.
- Ambiguous knowledge—implicit dependencies not adequately articulated.
- Invalid reasoning—programmer incorrectly transforms knowledge.
- Inadequate integration—dependencies among multiple pieces of advice in-
  completely integrated.
- Limited horizon—consequences of recent, past, or probable future events
  not exploited.
- Egocentricity—little attention paid to the probable meaning of others'
  actions.

In order to correct these problems, knowledge refinement and maintenance are
needed. Also, many test cases involving hard and soft data, gray areas, and special cases must be used to refine the knowledge base.

After testing of the knowledge base and the resulting expert system, an evaluation of the expert system can be made by users and experts currently working in
the problem domain. This evaluation process is a post-audit to see if the expert
system meets the objectives for which it was developed. Evaluation criteria such
as input/output content, quality of advice, correct reasoning approach, cost effectiveness, and ease of use should be considered[12]. With these considerations
built into its design, the success of the expert system will be greatly enhanced[13].

3.3 Implementing an Expert System

After building the expert system, there are various implementation obstacles that
may have to be faced. There might be resistance to change in the organization, either because of the need to learn a new procedure/tool or the belief that "we have

been doing things all right so far, so why change?" Another obstacle might come from the expert who might think that he or she is being replaced. Still another obstacle might be a reluctance to use the expert system due to difficulty in learning how to operate it. A last major obstacle is that the expert system is unusable because it is not maintained and therefore not current.

There are several ways to overcome these barriers[14]. A resistance to change could be eliminated by incorporating users' comments into the development process. The users' inputs and feedback would be helpful in designing the user interface and determining how best to represent the output. Also, if the expert system is properly validated and tested, and proves to perform at the level of a human expert, then the system could be relied upon and confidence in using it would increase.

The obstacle of taking the competitive advantage away from the expert can be eliminated by recognizing that the expert system can free the expert's time to tackle other projects of interest that the expert never had time to do.

Reluctance to use the expert system can be overcome by training sessions, good documentation, and knowledge engineering consulting. If an expert system shell is used, the vendor usually provides training, documentation, a hot line, and knowledge engineering consulting. Even if a shell is not used, good user documentation and training should be provided by the developers to reduce the reluctance to use the expert system.

The last obstacle, not keeping the expert system current, is remedied by designating an individual or group of individuals to maintain the system. In most applications, a good percentage of the knowledge in the knowledge base is dynamic. It needs to be constantly refined and updated. For example, Digital Equipment Corporation has a group of people whose only task is to maintain XCON, an expert system for configuring VAX computer systems. New component descriptions and configuration knowledge need to be put into the system on a regular basis. Likewise, expert systems designed for tax planning need to be updated regularly, as the tax laws frequently change. Expert systems should be maintained, and their knowledge bases should be designed to facilitate change.

By employing these implementation strategies, the obstacles will be eliminated and expert systems will gain wide acceptance and usage.

References

1. D. Michie, *Knowledge-Based Systems* (Report 80-1001), University of Illinois at Urbana-Champaign, January 1980.
2. R. O. Duda and J. G. Gaschnig, "Knowledge Based Expert Systems Come of Age," *BYTE*, September 1981.
3. D. S. Nau, "Expert Computer Systems," *Computer*, IEEE, February 1983.
4. J. Liebowitz, "Problem Selection for Expert Systems Development," in *Structuring Expert Systems: Domain, Design, and Development*, ed. by J. Liebowitz and D. A. DeSalvo, Yourdon Press, New York, 1989.
5. R. R. Hoffman, "The Problem of Extracting the Knowledge of Experts," *AI Magazine*, Vol. 8, No. 2, Summer 1987.

6. J. R. Olson and H. H. Rueter, "Extracting Expertise for Experts: Methods for Knowledge Acquisition," *Expert Systems*, Vol. 4, No. 3, August 1987.

7. J. H. Boose, *Expertise Transfer for Expert System Design*, Elsevier, New York, 1986.

8. A. Hart, *Knowledge Acquisition for Expert Systems*, McGraw-Hill, New York, 1986.

9. Software Architecture and Engineering, Inc., *Knowledge Engineering System— Knowledge Base Author's Reference Manual*, Arlington, VA, November 1983.

10. B. G. Buchanan and E. H. Shortliffe, *Rule-Based Expert Programs: The MYCIN Experiments of the Stanford Heuristic Programming Project*, Addison-Wesley, Reading, MA, 1984.

11. F. Hayes-Roth, D. A. Waterman, and D. B. Lenat, *Building Expert Systems*, Addison-Wesley, Reading, MA, 1983.

12. J. Liebowitz, "Useful Approach for Evaluating Expert Systems," *Expert Systems*, Vol. 3, No. 2, April 1986.

13. J. Liebowitz, *Introduction to Expert Systems*, Mitchell Publishing, Santa Cruz, CA, 1988.

14. D. A. DeSalvo and J. Liebowitz (eds.), *Managing Artificial Intelligence and Expert Systems*, Prentice-Hall, Englewood Cliffs, NJ, 1990.

Chapter 4

Problem Selection for Expert Systems Development

Someone once said that there are three important rules in developing expert systems. The first rule is "pick the right problem," the second is "pick the right problem," and the third is "pick the right problem." In expert systems development, as in software development or scientific research, the most critical step is selecting the problem. Selecting too large a problem or one with few test cases could lead to disastrous results when building an expert system. Picking too trivial a problem could leave managers and users unimpressed. If the problem is not properly identified and researched, then complications will most likely occur later in the knowledge engineering (i.e., expert systems development) process. By spending time up front identifying the problem, time and money will ultimately be saved.

This chapter will discuss guidelines to use in selecting a problem for expert systems development. First, a description of expert systems and their building process will be presented. Then, after characteristics of problem selection are identified, some methodologies will be presented to help one select a problem suitable for expert systems development. Last, the application areas in which expert systems have been built and used will be reviewed[1,3].

4.1   Problem Selection Guidelines

The first step in building an expert system is to select the problem. This step can be discussed in terms of the type of problem, the expert, and the domain area personnel. Each of these areas will now be explained.

Type of Problem

The following guidelines might be followed by the knowledge engineering team in order to select an appropriate problem[4–15]:

- The task primarily requires symbolic reasoning.
- The task requires the use of heuristics.
- The task may require decisions to be based upon incomplete or uncertain information.
- The task does not require knowledge from a large number of areas.
- The purpose of development is either to create a system for actual use or to make major advances in the state of the art of expert system technology; however, it does not attempt to achieve both of these goals simultaneously.
- The task is defined very clearly: At the outset of the project, there should be a precise definition of the inputs and outputs of the system to be developed.
- A good set of test cases exists.
- Some small systems will be developed to solve problems that are amenable to conventional techniques simply because the users need the systems quickly and decide that they can develop workable solutions by themselves, using shells, rather than waiting for their data processing groups to help them.
- A few key individuals are in short supply.
- Corporate goals are compromised by scarce human resources.
- Competitors appear to have an advantage because they can perform the task consistently better.
- The domain is one where expertise is generally unavailable, scarce, or expensive.
- The task does not depend heavily on common sense.
- The outcomes can be evaluated.
- The task is decomposable, allowing relatively rapid prototyping for a closed, small subset of the complete task and then slow expansion to the complete task.

- The task solves a problem that has value but is not on a critical path.
- The task is neither too easy (taking a human expert less than a few minutes) nor too difficult (requiring more than a few days for an expert).
- The amount of knowledge required by the task is large enough to make the knowledge base developed interesting.
- The task is sufficiently narrow and self-contained: The aim is not to build a system that is expert in an entire domain, but a system that is expert in a limited task within the domain.
- The number of important concepts (e.g., rules) required is no more than several hundred.
- The domain is characterized by the use of expert knowledge, judgment, and experience.
- Conventional programming (algorithmic) approaches to the task are not satisfactory.
- There are recognized experts who solve the problem today.
- The experts are probably better than amateurs in performing the task.
- Expertise is not or will not be available on a reliable and continuing basis; that is, there is a need to capture the expertise.
- The completed system is expected to have a significant payoff for the corporation.
- Among possible application domains, the one selected is the one that best meets overall goals regarding project payoff versus risk of failure.
- The system can be phased into use gracefully: Incomplete coverage can be tolerated (at least initially), and it can be easily determined whether a subproblem is covered by the present system.
- The task is not all-or-nothing; some incorrect or nonoptimal results can be tolerated.
- The skill required by the task is taught to novices.
- There are books or other written materials discussing the domain.
- The task's payoff is measurable.
- Experts would agree on whether the system's results are good (correct).
- The need for the task is projected to continue for several years.
- The domain is fairly stable; expected changes utilize the strengths of expert systems (e.g., ease of updating or revising specific rules in a knowledge base) but will not require major changes in reasoning processes.
- At the outset of the project, the expert is able to specify many of the important concepts.
- Management is willing to commit the necessary human and material resources.
- The task requires only cognitive skills.
- The task is well understood.
- Expert systems could have great payoffs in mundane tasks, not necessarily heroic ones.
- Pick a task that you think is too small to handle; in all likelihood, that task will have to be narrowed even further.
- The task should be performed frequently.

The Expert

An essential part of expert systems development is having an expert to work with the knowledge engineering team. Here are some guidelines in selecting an expert[4–15]:

- There is an expert who will work with the project.
- The expert's knowledge and reputation must be such that if the system captures a portion of the expert's expertise, the system's output will have credibility and authority.
- The expert has built up expertise over a long period of task performance.
- The expert will commit a substantial amount of time to the development of the system.
- The expert is capable of communicating his or her knowledge, judgment, and experience, as well as the methods used to apply them to the particular task.
- The expert is cooperative.
- The expertise for the system, at least that pertaining to one particular subdomain, is to be obtained primarily from one expert.
- If multiple experts contribute in a particular subdomain, one of them should be the primary expert with final authority.
- It's always nice to have a backup expert.
- The expert is the person the company can least afford to do without.
- The expert should have a vested interest in obtaining a solution.
- The expert must also understand what the problem is and should have solved it quite often.
- Experts must agree on the solutions.

Domain Area Personnel

Besides the knowledge engineer who builds the expert systems and the domain expert whose knowledge and experiential learning are captured in the expert system, the domain area personnel must be considered when selecting a problem for expert systems development. The domain area personnel are the users and management. The following are guidelines relating to these when selecting a problem[11]:

- Personnel in the domain area are realistic, understanding the potential uses and limitations of an expert system for their domain.
- Domain area personnel understand that even a successful system will likely be limited in scope and, like a human expert, may not produce optimal or correct results all the time.
- There is strong managerial support from the domain area, especially regarding the large commitment of time by the expert(s) and their possible travel or temporary relocation, if required.
- The specific task within the domain is jointly agreed upon by the system developers and the domain area personnel.

- Managers in the domain area have previously identified the need to solve the problem.
- The project is strongly supported by a senior manager for protection and follow-up.
- Potential users would welcome the completed system.
- The system can be introduced with minimal disturbance of the current practice.
- The user group is cooperative and patient.
- The introduction of the system will not be politically sensitive or controversial.
- The knowledge contained by the system will not be politically sensitive or controversial.
- The results produced by the system will not be politically sensitive or controversial.

4.2 Methodologies for Expert System Problem Selection

To ensure proper problem selection for expert system development, the criteria and guidelines just presented should be carefully considered. One method that helps the knowledge engineer select and scope a problem is the Analytic Hierarchy Process (AHP)[16–18]. This method is helpful in quantifying subjective judgments used in decision making. A microcomputer software package called Expert Choice[19] embodies this process.

The AHP was developed by Saaty and has been applied successfully in numerous situations, ranging from selecting an appropriate expert system shell[20] to choosing the best house to buy. The AHP breaks down a problem into its constituents and then calls for simple pairwise comparison judgments to develop priorities in each hierarchy. The steps of the AHP are as follows[16]:

1. The problem is defined, and you determine what you want to know.
2. The hierarchy is structured from the top (the objectives from a general viewpoint) through the intermediate levels (criteria on which subsequent levels depend) to the lowest level (which is usually a list of the alternatives).
3. A set of pairwise comparison matrices is constructed for each of the lower levels—one matrix for each element in the level immediately above.
4. After all the pairwise comparisons have been made and the data entered, the consistency is determined using the eigenvalue.
5. Steps 3 and 4 are performed for all levels in the hierarchy.
6. Hierarchical composition is now used to weight the eigenvectors by the weights of the criteria, and the sum is taken over all weighted eigenvector entries corresponding to those in the next lower level of the hierarchy.
7. The consistency of the entire hierarchy is found by multiplying each consistency index by the priority of the corresponding criterion and adding them together.

Mathematically speaking, priorities are calculated by the process of principal eigenvector extraction and hierarchical weighting[21]. Suppose that we have a matrix of pairwise comparisons of weights that have n objects $A_1, \ldots, A_n$ whose vector of corresponding weights is $w = (w_1, \ldots, w_n)$. The problem $A_w = $ (maximum eigenvalue) (w) should be solved to obtain an estimate of the weights w. A pairwise comparison reciprocal matrix is used to compare the relative contribution of the elements in each level of the hierarchy to an element in the adjacent upper level[21]. The principal eigenvector of this matrix is then derived and weighted by the priority of the property with respect to which the comparison is made[21]. That weight is determined by comparing the properties in terms of their contribution to the criteria of a still higher level[21]. The weighted eigenvectors can next be added componentwise to obtain an overall weight or priority of the contribution of each element to the hierarchy. Bazaraa et al.[22] provide a further explanation, in terms of linear algebra, of the derivation of an eigenvalue.

The AHP has been rigorously tested and successfully applied in numerous diverse applications[17,18]. It provided remarkably accurate results when validated in situations where numerical measures are known[23]. In one experiment, four chairs were arranged in a straight line from a light source, and pairwise verbal judgments from subjects were then made about the relative brightness of the chairs[16,23]. The results, when analyzed, showed a remarkable conformity to the inverse square law of brightness as a function of distance, as seen by the following numbers[23]:

TRIAL 1	TRIAL 2	INVERSE SQUARE LAW
.61	.61	.61
.24	.22	.22
.10	.10	.11
.05	.06	.06

Another validation experiment involved estimating the relative areas of two-dimensional figures by using pairwise verbal judgments[19,23]. Subjects were asked to estimate the relative areas of five geometrically shaped objects by using Expert Choice. When different subjects provided verbal judgments in using Expert Choice, the accuracy of their results was amazing[23]:

FIGURE	ACTUAL PERCENTAGE	EXPERT CHOICE ESTIMATE
A	.47	.45
B	.05	.07
C	.23	.24
D	.15	.15
E	.10	.09

Expert Choice

Expert Choice[24,25] represents a significant contribution to the decision-making process, as it is able to quantify subjective judgments in complex decision-making environments[23]. This program enables decision makers to structure a multifaceted problem visually in the form of a hierarchy[23]. Expert Choice, which uses the AHP, is helpful in selecting an appropriate expert system problem.

In using Expert Choice, the user (i.e., decision maker) first constructs a hierarchy of the goal, criteria, and alternatives for the application. At the top level of the hierarchy, the goal is defined—which, in this case, is to select an expert system problem. At the next level, the criteria used in selecting an appropriate expert system problem are defined. These criteria are based on those discussed in Section 4.1. At this level, the criteria are as follows:

PRO TYPE—type of problem criteria
EXPERT—expert criteria
DOM PERS—domain area personnel criteria

Subcriteria under each of these headings can be defined at the next level of the hierarchy. These are:

PRO TYPE
    SYMBOLIC—task involves mostly symbolic processing
    TEST CAS—test cases are available
    WELL-BND—problem task is well bounded
    FREQUENT—task must be performed frequently
    WRIT MAT—written materials exist explaining the task
    COG SKLS—task requires only cognitive skills
    EXP AGRE—experts agree on the solutions

EXPERT
    EXP EXST—an expert exists
    COOPERTE—the expert is cooperative
    ARTICULT—the expert is articulate
    EXPERNCE—the expert's knowledge is based on
             experience, facts, and judgment
    OTHER EX—other experts in the task exist

DOM PERS
    NEED EXI—a need exists to develop an expert
             system for that task
    FIN SPRT—the task would be provided with the
             necessary financial support
    TOP MGMT—top management supports the project
    REAL EXP—the domain area personnel have realistic
             expectations for the use of an expert system

USERS WL—users would welcome the expert system
NOT POL—the knowledge is not politically sensitive or
controversial

The last level of the hierarchy consists of the alternatives—in this case, the possible problems (or tasks) to be worked on for expert systems development. In this example, there are three alternatives:

MACROECO—develop an expert system for determining
macro economic policy in the United States
NUCLEAR—develop an expert system for determining
what the United States should do in case of a
nuclear war
BID/NO—develop an expert system for determining
whether to bid on a request for proposal

Figure 4.1 shows the Expert Choice hierarchy before pairwise comparisons (i.e., before weighting takes place) for this expert system problem selection application.

After constructing this hierarchy, the evaluation process begins. Expert Choice will first question the user in order to assign priorities (i.e., weights) to the criteria. Expert Choice allows the user to provide judgments verbally, so that no numerical guesses are required (it also allows the user to give a numerical answer). Thus, the first question would be: "With respect to the goal of selecting an expert system problem, is criterion one (i.e., PRO TYPE) just as important as criterion two (i.e., EXPERT)?" If the user's answer to this question is "Yes," then criterion one is compared to criterion three (PRO TYPE vs. DOM PERS). If the answer is "No," as it is at the top of Figure 4.2, then Expert Choice will ask, "Is PRO TYPE more important then EXPERT?" and it will ask for the level of importance. The number of pairwise comparisons is shown in a triangle of dots, as displayed in the right-hand corner of Figure 4.2. The relative importance, as shown at the top of Figure 4.2, is moderately more important, strongly more important, very strongly more important, extremely more important, or a degree within the range. Based upon the user's verbal judgments, Expert Choice will calculate the relative importance on the following scale, based on Saaty's work[16–18]:

1 Equal importance
3 Moderate importance of one over another
5 Essential or strong importance
7 Very strong importance
9 Extremely important
2, 4, 6, 8 Intermediate values between the two adjacent judgments

This procedure is followed to obtain relative priorities of the criteria in which eigenvalues are calculated based upon pairwise comparisons of one criterion versus another, as discussed in the previous section. These pairwise comparisons are made for each of the criteria and subcriteria. Figures 4.2 and 4.3 show the priorities after the pairwise comparisons are made. Also, an inconsistency index is

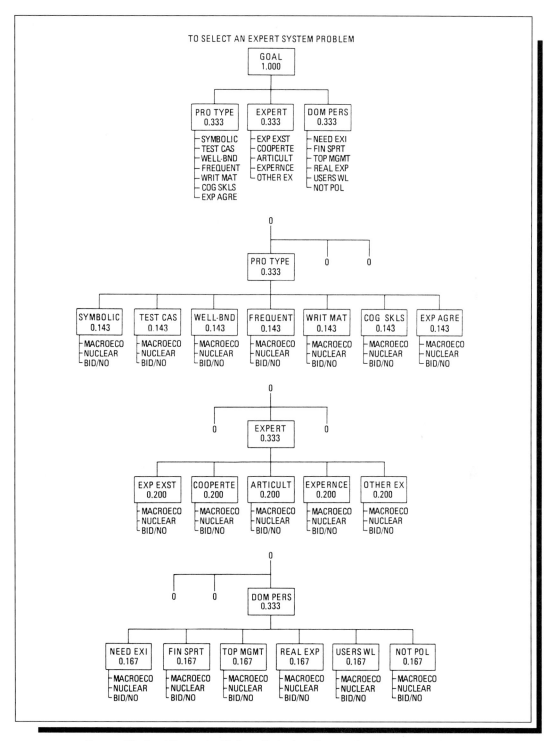

FIGURE 4.1 Expert Choice Hierarchy Before Pairwise Comparisons

```
      GOAL: TO SELECT AN EXPERT SYSTEM PROBLEM

                   With respect to
      GOAL OF TO SELECT AN EXPERT SYSTEM PROBLEM

   PRO TYPE
         is EQUAL to MODERATELY MORE IMPORTANT THAN
   EXPERT


      EXTREME---------------------
      VERY STRONG------------------
      STRONG-----------------------
      MODERATE---------------------
      EQUAL------------------------            ←
```

```
      PRIORITIES OF IMPORTANCE OF...... WITH RESPECT TO
           GOAL OF TO SELECT AN EXPERT SYSTEM PROBLEM

   0.500
   PRO TYPE

   0.250
   DOM PERS

   0.250
   EXPERT
             INCONSISTENCY RATIO = 0.000
```

FIGURE 4.2   Weighting of First-Level Criteria

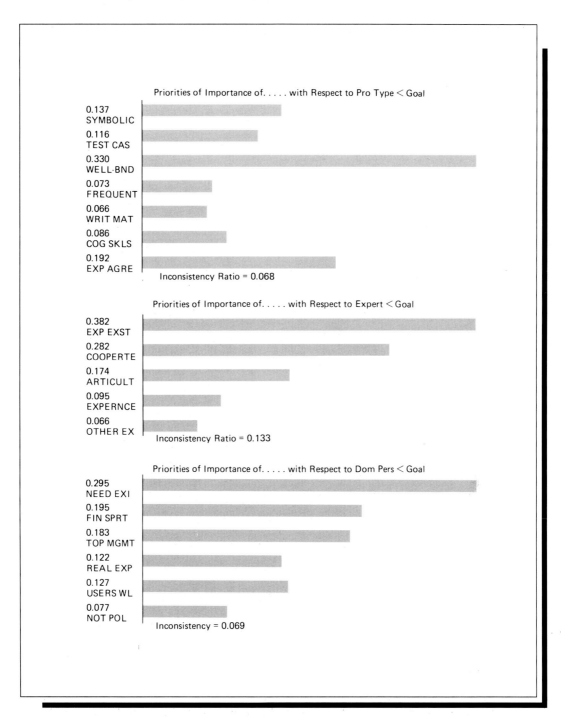

FIGURE 4.3 Weighting of Second-Level Criteria. (Reprinted by permission from J. Liebowitz, *The Dynamics of Decision Support Systems and Expert Systems,* Dryden Press, Orlando, FL, 1990.)

calculated after each set of pairwise comparisons to show how consistent the user's judgments are. An overall inconsistency index is calculated at the end of the synthesis as well. This measure is zero when all judgments are perfectly consistent with one another and becomes larger when the inconsistency is greater[23]. The inconsistency is tolerable if it is 0.10 or less[23].

After the criteria and subcriteria are weighted, the next step involves pairwise comparisons between the alternatives and the subcriteria. For example, one question would be: "With respect to SYMBOLIC, are MACROECO and NUCLEAR equally preferable?" After all the pairwise comparisons have been entered, Expert Choice performs synthesis by adding the global priorities (global priorities indicate the contribution to the overall goal) at each level of the tree hierarchy. Figure 4.4 shows the hierarchy after all the pairwise comparisons are made. Figure 4.5 shows the synthesis of the results and, finally, the ranking of the alternatives. In this example, after taking all the pairwise comparisons into account, the best problem to select for expert systems development is the BID/NO (i.e., develop an expert system for determining whether a company should bid on a request for proposal). Its priority is .578, followed by MACROECO (.266) and, last, NUCLEAR (.156). The overall inconsistency index is 0.06, which is within the tolerable range.

Through this methodology, the best problem for expert systems development, given these three alternatives, is to determine whether to bid or not on a request for proposal. Expert Choice also allows for sensitivity analysis if the user so desires.

Other Approaches for Expert System Problem Selection

If one does not want to use the AHP/Expert Choice approach to select an expert system problem, another technique is develop a checklist of important problem criteria, based on those in Section 4.1, and see how many of them fit the problem under consideration. This is an unsophisticated approach, but it is effective and is probably the one most knowledge engineers use when selecting a possible problem task for expert systems development.

Cost-benefit analysis should also be conducted to determine whether it is technically, economically, and operationally feasible and wise to develop an expert system for a particular problem. Costs include the expert's time, as well as that of the knowledge engineer[1,4]. Additional costs include possible acquisition of hardware, possible acquisition of software like expert system shells, overhead, the expert's travel and lodging expenses, and computing time. The benefits of an expert system might include reduced costs, increased productivity, increased training productivity and effectiveness, preservation of knowledge, enhanced products or services, or even the development of new products and services[4,26,27,28,29]. The costs and benefits between the status quo and the proposed expert system could then be compared. Expert Choice could even be used for this cost-benefit analysis to see if the expert system would be more cost-effective than the status quo.

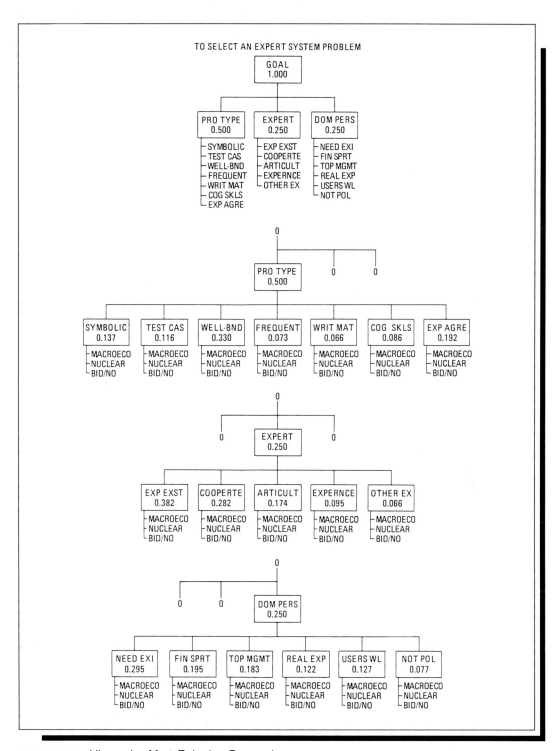

FIGURE 4.4 Hierarchy After Pairwise Comparisons

```
LEVEL 1          LEVEL 2          LEVEL 3          LEVEL 4          LEVEL 5
PRO TYPE =0.500

                 WELL-BND =0.165
    .                 .           BID/NO   =0.125
    .                 .           MACROECO =0.027
    .                 .           NUCLEAR  =0.012
    .            EXP AGRE =0.096
    .                 .           BID/NO   =0.075
    .                 .           MACROECO =0.013
    .                 .           NUCLEAR  =0.008
    .            SYMBOLIC =0.069
    .                 .           BID/NO   =0.042
    .                 .           NUCLEAR  =0.018
    .                 .           MACROECO =0.008
    .            TEST CAS =0.058
    .                 .           MACROECO =0.039
    .                 .           BID/NO   =0.015
    .                 .           NUCLEAR  =0.004
    .            COG SKLS =0.043
    .                 .           MACROECO =0.017
    .                 .           BID/NO   =0.017
    .                 .           NUCLEAR  =0.009
    .            FREQUENT =0.036
    .                 .           BID/NO   =0.025
    .                 .           MACROECO =0.009
    .                 .           NUCLEAR  =0.002
    .            WRIT MAT =0.033
    .                 .           BID/NO   =0.021
    .                 .           MACROECO =0.010
    .                 .           NUCLEAR  =0.002
EXPERT   =0.250
    .            EXP EXST =0.096
    .                 .           BID/NO   =0.071
    .                 .           MACROECO =0.017
    .                 .           NUCLEAR  =0.007
    .            COOPERTE =0.070
    .                 .           BID/NO   =0.050
    .                 .           MACROECO =0.015
    .                 .           NUCLEAR  =0.006
    .            ARTICULT =0.044
    .                 .           MACROECO =0.015
    .                 .           NUCLEAR  =0.015
    .                 .           BID/NO   =0.015
    .            EXPERNCE =0.024
    .                 .           MACROECO =0.011
    .                 .           BID/NO   =0.011
    .                 .           NUCLEAR  =0.002
    .            OTHER EX =0.017
    .                 .           BID/NO   =0.011
    .                 .           MACROECO =0.004
    .                 .           NUCLEAR  =0.001
DOM PERS =0.250
    .            NEED EXI =0.074
    .                 .           BID/NO   =0.036
    .                 .           MACROECO =0.023
    .                 .           NUCLEAR  =0.014
```

FIGURE 4.5 Synthesis of Results

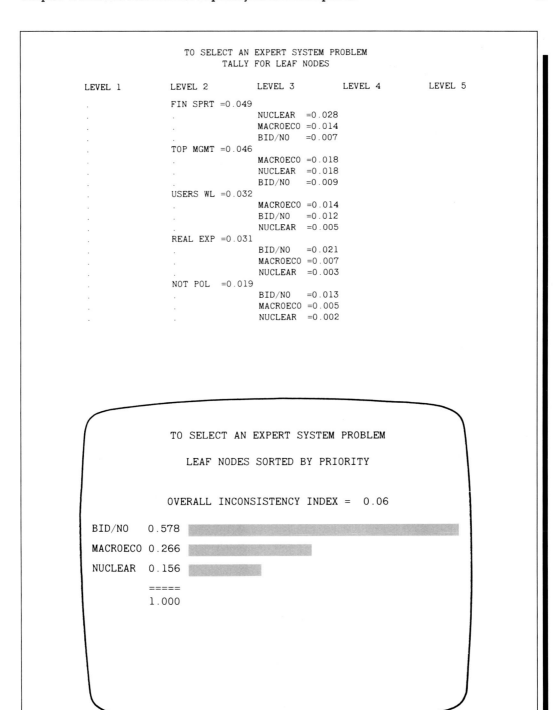

```
                    TO SELECT AN EXPERT SYSTEM PROBLEM
                        TALLY FOR LEAF NODES

   LEVEL 1           LEVEL 2          LEVEL 3          LEVEL 4          LEVEL 5

      .           FIN SPRT =0.049
      .                  .             NUCLEAR  =0.028
      .                  .             MACROECO =0.014
      .                  .             BID/NO   =0.007
      .           TOP MGMT =0.046
      .                  .             MACROECO =0.018
      .                  .             NUCLEAR  =0.018
      .                  .             BID/NO   =0.009
      .           USERS WL =0.032
      .                  .             MACROECO =0.014
      .                  .             BID/NO   =0.012
      .                  .             NUCLEAR  =0.005
      .           REAL EXP =0.031
      .                  .             BID/NO   =0.021
      .                  .             MACROECO =0.007
      .                  .             NUCLEAR  =0.003
      .           NOT POL  =0.019
      .                  .             BID/NO   =0.013
      .                  .             MACROECO =0.005
      .                  .             NUCLEAR  =0.002
```

```
              TO SELECT AN EXPERT SYSTEM PROBLEM

                 LEAF NODES SORTED BY PRIORITY


            OVERALL INCONSISTENCY INDEX =  0.06

  BID/NO    0.578
  MACROECO  0.266
  NUCLEAR   0.156

            =====
            1.000
```

FIGURE 4.5 continued

4.3 Conclusion

Problem selection is a critical step in the expert systems development process. Selecting the wrong problem or failing to reduce the problem to a manageable size will create problems later when constructing the expert system.

The guidelines for problem selection criteria presented in this chapter should be followed closely when considering the type of problem, domain expert, and domain area personnel. The AHP is a useful structured methodology for incorporating these criteria in selecting an expert system problem. Expert Choice easily facilitates the use of the AHP. Whether this structured methodology or some other approach is used in the problem selection process, the important point is to make sure that the method used will help to identify the right problem for expert systems development.

References

1. N. J. Bellord, "Information and Artificial Intelligence in the Lawyer's Office," *Artificial Intelligence and Legal Information Systems*, North-Holland, Amsterdam, 1982.
2. Software Architecture and Engineering, Inc., *Knowledge Engineering System— Knowledge Base Author's Reference Manual*, Arlington, VA, November 1983.
3. F. Hayes-Roth, P. Klahr, and D. J. Mostow, *Knowledge Acquisition, Knowledge Programming, and Knowledge Refinement*, Report R-2540-NSF, Rand Corporation, Washington, DC, May 1980.
4. P. Harmon and D. King, *Expert Systems: Artificial Intelligence in Business*, John Wiley and Sons, New York, 1985.
5. D. A. Waterman, *A Guide to Expert Systems*, Addison-Wesley, Reading, MA, 1986.
6. J. Liebowitz, *Introduction to Expert Systems*, Mitchell Publishing, Santa Cruz, CA, 1988.
7. J. Liebowitz (ed.), *Expert System Applications to Telecommunications*, John Wiley and Sons, New York, 1988.
8. S. K. Goyal, D. S. Prerau, A. V. Lemmon, A. S. Gunderson, and R. E. Reinke, "COMPASS: An Expert System for Telephone Switch Maintenance," *Expert Systems*, Vol. 2, No. 3, July 1985.
9. B. G. Buchanan, "Expert Systems: Working Systems and the Research Literature," *Expert Systems*, Vol. 3, No. 1, January 1986.
10. D. S. Prerau, "Knowledge Acquisition in Expert System Development," *AI Magazine*, Vol. 8, No. 2, Summer 1987.
11. D. S. Prerau, "Selection of an Appropriate Domain," *AI Magazine*, Vol. 7, No. 2, Summer 1985.
12. D. G. Bobrow, S. Mittal, and M. J. Stefik, "Expert Systems: Perils and Promise," *Communications of the ACM*, Vol. 29, No. 9, September 1986.
13. J. Liebowitz, "Expert Systems and Telecommunications," *Telematics and Informatics*, Vol. 2, No. 3, 1985.

14. J. Liebowitz, "Expert Systems in Law: A Survey and Case Study," *Telematics and Informatics,* Vol. 3, No. 4, 1986.

15. M. Freiling, J. Alexander, S. Messick, S. Rehfuss, and S. Shulman, "Starting a Knowledge Engineering Project: A Step-by-Step Approach," *AI Magazine,* Vol. 6, No. 3, Fall 1985.

16. T. L. Saaty, "Priority Setting in Complex Problems," *Proceedings on Second World Conference on Mathematics,* Las Palmas, Canary Islands, 1982.

17. T. L. Saaty, *The Analytic Hierarchy Process,* McGraw-Hill, New York, 1980.

18. T. L. Saaty, *Decision Making for Leaders,* Wadsworth Publishing, Belmont, CA, 1982.

19. Decision Support Software, Inc., *Expert Choice Manual,* McLean, VA, 1985.

20. E. H. Forman and T. J. Nagy, "EXSYS vs. TOPSI/OPS 5 vs. MICRO-PS: A Multicriteria Model to Select an Expert System Generator," *Telematics and Informatics,* Vol. 4, No. 1, 1987.

21. Y. Wind and T. L. Saaty, "Marketing Applications of the Analytic Hierarchy Process," *Management Science,* Vol. 26, No. 7, 1980.

22. M. S. Bazaraa and J. J. Jarvis, *Linear Programming and Network Flows,* John Wiley and Sons, New York, 1977.

23. E. H. Forman, "The Analytic Hierarchy Process as a Decision Support Systems," *IEEE Compcom 83 Proceedings,* IEEE, Washington, DC, 1983.

24. J. Liebowitz, "Useful Approach for Evaluating Expert Systems," *Expert Systems,* Vol. 3, No. 2, April 1986.

25. J. Liebowitz, "Structured Decision Making in Classroom Teaching: The Use of Expert Choice," *Collegiate Microcomputer,* Vol. 4, No. 3, August 1986.

26. W. T. Jones, and R. L. Samuell, "Strategic Assessment of Expert System Technology: Guidelines and Methodology," in *Expert System Applications to Telecommunications,* ed. J. Liebowitz, John Wiley and Sons, New York, 1988.

27. W. B. Rauch-Hindin, *Artificial Intelligence in Business, Science, and Industry, Vol. I, Fundamentals,* Prentice-Hall, Englewood Cliffs, NJ, 1986.

28. J. Liebowitz and P. Lightfoot, "Training NASA Satellite Operators: An Expert System Consultant Approach," *Educational Technology,* Educational Technology Publications, Englewood Cliffs, NJ, 1987.

29. J. Liebowitz and P. Lightfoot, "Expert Systems for Scheduling: Survey and Preliminary Design Concepts," *Applied Artificial Intelligence Journal,* 1987.

Chapter 5

Knowledge Acquisition

Acquiring knowledge from an expert for expert systems development is a difficult process. One reason is that an expert, talking continuously, will produce about 10,000 words a hour; this is equivalent to 300 to 500 pages of transcript from a single day's session with an expert[1]. This voluminous information must somehow be digested by the knowledge engineer and appropriately represented for expert systems development. In addition, the knowledge engineer, when interviewing the expert, must pay attention to the expert's intonation and use of words, which might influence the meaning of some of the information.

There are many problems in extracting information from an expert. This chapter will survey the problems that may be encountered during the knowledge acquisition process. Then some possible solutions to this problem will be presented.

5.1 Knowledge Acquisition Problems

Knowledge acquisition is the most difficult part of expert systems development. There are numerous problems associated with this process. The following are some of the major problems that may be incurred[2–7]:

- Human biases in judgment on the part of the knowledge engineer and expert which might inhibit transmission of the correct information. These biases include the following:
    - Recency—people are influenced by the most recent events.
    - Availability—people use only the information that is available to them.
    - Imaginability—people use information only in the form that is presented to them.
    - Correlation—people make correlations where none exist.
    - Causality—people assign causes where none exist.
    - Anchoring and adjustment—people use an anchor point and argue around that point.
    - Statistical intuition—people do not fully understand the effects of variance and sample size.
- The expert could cancel or defer knowledge acquisition appointments, fail to answer questions, or neglect to supply information.
- It is difficult for the knowledge engineer to extract and the expert to convey knowledge and heuristics that have been acquired over many years of professional experience; for example, information that the expert considers common sense may not be so to the knowledge engineer.
- The expert might, consciously or unconsciously, use the knowledge engineer to experiment with different models of the knowledge domain that he or she has developed.
- The process of knowledge elicitation requires many hours of an expert who is already busy and has many demands on his or her time.
- Some knowledge engineers may not be good at interviewing, causing them to interrupt, not listen to the way the expert uses knowledge, misinterpret information, or not ask the right questions.
- Some knowledge engineers might start feeling expert and then think that they are the experts.
- Even an expert may not be right 100 percent of the time.
- A knowledge engineer may not listen fully to the *language* that the expert uses to represent his or her experience; the knowledge engineer should be sensitive to auditory thoughts, visual thoughts, sensory memories, or feelings.
- The knowledge engineer may assume or project his or her favored modes of thinking into the expert's verbal reports.
- The knowledge engineer may not be cognizant of the body language that the expert is using.
- It might be difficult to uncover the expert's ability that is hidden at the gut level.

- The knowledge engineer may not be organized in his or her approach to eliciting knowledge from the expert.
- The knowledge engineer may not be skilled in or knowledgeable about the different methods that can be used to extract the expert's knowledge. Some these methods are as follows[4]:
  - Method of familiar tasks—analyze the tasks that the expert usually performs.
  - Structured and unstructured interviews—the expert is queried with regard to knowledge of facts and procedures.
  - Limited information tasks—a familiar task is performed, but the expert is not given certain information that is typically available.
  - Constrained processing tasks—a familiar task is performed, but the expert must work under time or other constraints.
  - Method of tough cases—analysis of a familiar task is conducted for a set of data that presents a tough case for the expert.
- Some knowledge engineers may not be very familiar with the domain, and may not know what questions to ask or understand what the expert is saying.
- The expert may not be cooperative or articulate.

These are typical problems that may surface during the knowledge acquisition process. One way to help ensure success during the knowledge acquisition process is to make sure that the problem selected is appropriate and well scoped for expert systems development. Additionally, the knowledge engineer should become knowledgeable about the domain before interacting frequently with the expert. The expert selected should be willing to participate, cooperative, and articulate.

The next sections survey solutions that are being developed to improve the knowledge acquisition process.

5.2 How to Reduce the Expert's Boredom

It is said that those closest to the technology may have a clouded view of where it is going. They may be too close to the technology to take a step back and distinguish the forest for the trees. The same situation may be true of the knowledge engineer during the sessions with the expert. The knowledge engineer may be caught up in questioning the expert, without realizing that the expert is bored with the process. This issue was recently raised by a domain expert who was being interviewed by a first-time knowledge engineer, who kept telling the expert to give him information in terms of IF-THEN rules. After about an hour of this exercise, the domain expert became bored and frustrated, and eventually withdrew from the project.

The question, then, is how to reduce the chance of the expert's becoming bored during the knowledge acquisition process. There are 10 methods that may be used:

1. The knowledge engineer needs to vary the methods used in acquiring knowledge. Alternatives include scenario building, observation, and limited information task interviewing, to allow flexibility on the part of the expert to explain his or her reasoning. Using a variety of methods should prevent the expert from getting into a rut.

2. Each knowledge acquisition session should last no more than 2 hours. Studies have shown that this time limit is optimal.

3. It is helpful to have two knowledge engineers present when interviewing the expert. Thus, during the questioning/listening process, the expert can bounce ideas off both of them, instead of dealing with the same person every day.

4. It might be helpful to deal with the expert away from the office, in an informal setting. Meeting at a restaurant or pub might make the expert more relaxed and at ease in answering the knowledge engineer's questions.

5. Let the expert explain his or her reasoning by running through typical scenarios. Asking about familiar tasks will make the expert feel more comfortable with the interviewing process. Later on, in order to obtain some of the heuristics, the method of tough cases, constrained time, or limited information tasks might be used.

6. Don't require or force the expert to reason or talk in a certain way, such as in the form of IF-THEN rules. This will be unnatural, awkward, and annoying to the expert. The knowledge engineer should listen to the way the expert is using his or her knowledge and should later determine the best way for representing it.

7. Early on, show the expert the interactive expert system in order to capture the expert's attention. In this manner, the expert can better visualize the expert system instead of looking at hard copies of rules. This will also show the expert that his or her time is not being wasted; there is a substantive result of the knowledge acquisition sessions. One caveat, however, is to be careful in showing the system to the expert too early. If there is not much in the system, the expert may consider it trivial and meaningless.

8. The knowledge engineer needs the expert to feel ownership of the expert system. One way to do this is to name the system after the expert or include the expert's name on the opening screen as the "expert con-101sultant."

9. According to Earl Sacerdoti at Copernican, let the expert do his or her normal daily activities, as well as spending up to 2 hours a session on knowledge acquisition. With this arrangement, the expert will not feel that the knowledge engineer is monopolizing his or her time.

10. As a corollary to the previous guideline, remember that, typically, 1 day of the expert's time for every 4 days of the knowledge engineer's time will be needed to develop the expert system. This formula should be kept in mind in projecting the expert's involvement in the expert system project.

Hopefully, by following these guidelines, the knowledge engineer will create a fruitful and enjoyable relationship with the expert. Ultimately, this should lead to an improved chance of building and implementing a successful expert system.

5.3 Possible Solutions to the Knowledge Acquisition Bottleneck

Traditional ways of acquiring knowledge have been based on interviewing techniques, scenario building, questionnaires, and protocol analysis[2,3,8,9]. Interviewing, that is, asking questions, is the most frequently used technique. Scenario building is a descriptive technique in which the knowledge engineer describes a scenario about the domain and then records how the expert solves the problem. Questionnaires are sometimes used to obtain specific information, particularly if the expert has limited time that day. Protocol analysis involves identifying phrases with high information content, grouping these phrases into areas of knowledge, showing the interrelationship between them, and then representing this knowledge[2].

Quinlan[10] claims that there are three general knowledge acquisition methods: descriptive, the intuitive, and observational. He explains each method and its weakness as follows:

- Descriptive method—the expert tells the knowledge engineer how he or she solves a problem, either one from past experience or a new one in the domain.
  - *Weakness*—the knowledge is so "compiled" that the expert cannot describe the process accurately.
- Intuitive method—through introspection, the expert tries to build theories about his or her own problem-solving methods and incorporate them directly into a computer system.
  - *Weakness*—frequently, the expert will, perhaps unknowingly, resort to the reconstructive method of creating plausible reasoning that may not reflect the actual technique.
- Observational method—as the expert works on a problem, the knowledge engineer records the expert's problem-solving method based on "thinking-aloud protocols," the expert talking to himself or herself while working.
  - *Weakness*—the expert frequently leaves huge gaps in the description of the process.

Quinlan[10] also describes the following specific knowledge acquisition techniques:

- On-site observation—staying in the background and watching as the expert handles real problems on the job; there is no interruption from the knowledge engineer.
- Problem discussion—an informal talk about a set of representative problems.
  - Problem description—the expert describes a typical case for each type of

problem that may arise; this is especially useful for diagnostic problems with relatively few solutions.

- Problem analysis—the expert solves problems while the knowledge engineer questions each step of the process.
- System refinement—the knowledge engineer solves problems based on the concepts and strategies learned from the expert; then the expert critiques the solutions to help in further refinement.
- System examination or inspection—the expert directly examines and critiques the prototype's rules and control strategies.
- System validation or review—comparing solutions achieved by the prototype system and by the expert to those developed by other experts.

Besides these direct methods for acquiring knowledge, there are also indirect methods. Olson et al.[11] describe some of them:

- Multidimensional scaling (MDS)—the expert provides similarity judgments on all pairs of objects or concepts in the domain of inquiry; these judgments are assumed to be symmetric and graded (i.e., A is as similar to B as B is to A), and the similarities are assumed to take on a variety of continuous values, not just 0 or 1.
- Johnson hierarchical clustering—this begins with a half-matrix of similarity judgments and assumes that an item is or is not a member of a cluster.
- General weighted networks—the expert gives symmetric distance judgments on all possible pairs of objects; these distances are assumed to arise from the expert's traversal of a network of associations.
- Ordered trees from recall—this technique is built on a model of how the data are produced by the expert; it assumes that people recall all items from a stored cluster before recalling items from another cluster.
- Repertory grid analysis—this includes an initial dialog with the expert, a rating session, and analyses that cluster both the objects and the dimensions on which the items are rated.

To improve these knowledge acquisition techniques, two main avenues of research have emerged. The first technique is an induction system in which expert system rules are inferred automatically from collections of data and facts or case histories. Quinlan's ID3/ID4 algorithms[12] follow this line of research. The second technique consists of automated knowledge acquisition aids or intelligent editors that the expert can use to elicit his or her own knowledge. An example of this approach is ETS (Expertise Transfer System)/AQUINAS[3,13], developed by Boeing Computer Services. This approach uses a rating/repertory grid technique based on personal construct theory to elicit knowledge from an expert. Based on this knowledge, ETS then constructs the knowledge base structure and will accordingly infer the rules. Other automated knowledge acquisition systems are currently being worked on, like KREME, KRITON, MOLE, KNACK, YAKYAK, SALT, and INFORM[14]. Still other aids are being developed that only partially involve the expert. This new version of the process, which involves intelligent text retrieval, has been worked on by companies such as ICF/Phase Linear, Inc[15].

ICF has developed the Knowledge Acquisition Module (KAM), a PC-based program that scans text and creates rules, relationships, IF-THEN statements, and heuristics based on constraints set by the user or expert. KAM can even scan the text of an interview with an expert by a knowledge engineer and create rules[15].

Work is also underway to develop knowledge acquisition tools based on learning by analogy. ThinkBack[16] is one such tool; its core is an analogical inference engine and its connecting control agent. ThinkBack is a convenient means of collecting verbal protocols and has helped human problem solvers during analogy sessions. Lenat's CYC[17] is being built as a large knowledge base of real-world facts and heuristics, as well as methods for reasoning efficiently about the knowledge base. Hopefully, it will be able to use commonsense knowledge and reasoning to draw analogies and overcome the knowledge acquisition bottleneck. Acquire (by Acquired Intelligence Inc., Canada) is another knowledge acquisition tool. It is commercially available, PC based, and acts as an interactive knowledge acquisition aid for certain kinds of tasks. Other automated knowledge acquisition tools are Nextra (Neuron Data), AC2 (ISoft, France), and KnAcq tool (England).

5.4 In the Future

Work will continue to develop methods and tools to overcome the knowledge acquisition bottleneck. There are two schools of thought on how to address the knowledge acquisition bottleneck. One side believes that the expert knows the problem area best and should therefore be the direct link to the software[15]. The other side believes that since so much of an expert's ability is hidden at the gut level, intense interviewing and probing by an informed outsider (i.e., the knowledge engineer) is needed to get to the heart of the matter[15]. Additionally, there is an overriding "knowledge engineering paradox" that states, "The more expert an expert is, the more compiled is his or her knowledge and the more difficult it is to extract this knowledge." This attitude emphasizes the knowledge engineer's role in eliciting knowledge from the expert. There is an ongoing debate on this issue.

This chapter has presented a survey of the problems in knowledge acquisition and possible solutions for overcoming them. With continued efforts in both basic and applied research, this problem will be greatly minimized in the future.

References

1. J. Naughton, "Precision Knowledge Acquisition Course," Expert Knowledge Systems, Inc., McLean, VA, 1988.
2. A. Hart, *Knowledge Acquisition for Expert Systems,* McGraw-Hill, New York, 1986.
3. J. H. Boose, *Expertise Transfer for Expert System Design,* Elsevier, New York, 1986.
4. R. R. Hoffman, "The Problem of Extracting the Knowledge of Experts," *AI Magazine,* Vol. 8, No. 2, Summer 1987.

5. J. Liebowitz, *Introduction to Expert Systems,* Mitchell Publishing, Santa Cruz, CA, 1988.

6. S. E. Evanson, "How to Talk to an Expert," *AI Expert,* Vol. 3, No. 2, February 1988.

7. J. Liebowitz, "The Need for Courses on Knowledge Acquisition in Expert Systems Curricula," *Interface: The Computer Education Quarterly,* Vol. 9, No. 4, Winter 1987–1988.

8. K. L. McGraw and K. Harbison-Briggs, *Knowledge Acquisition: Principles and Guidelines,* Prentice-Hall, Englewood Cliffs, NJ, 1989.

9. A. C. Scott, J. E. Clayton, and E. L. Gibson, *A Practical Guide to Knowledge Acquisition,* Addison-Wesley, Reading, MA, 1991.

10. J. R. Quinlan, "Knowledge Acquisition: The Key to Building Expert Systems," videotape, Addison-Wesley, Reading, MA, 1987.

11. J. Olson, J. Reitman, and H. H. Rueter, "Extracting Expertise from Experts: Methods for Knowledge Acquisition," *Expert Systems,* Vol. 4, No. 3, August 1987.

12. J. R. Quinlan, P. J. Compton, K. A. Horn, and L. Lazarus, "Inductive Knowledge Acquisition: a Case Study," in *Applications of Expert Systems,* ed. by J. R. Quinlan, Addison-Wesley, Reading, MA, 1987.

12. H. P. Newquist, "Braining the Expert," *AI Expert,* Vol. 3, No. 2, February 1988.

13. J. H. Boose and J. M. Bradshaw, "Expertise Transfer and Complex Problems: Using AQUINAS as a Knowledge Acquisition Workbench for Expert Systems," *Proceedings of Knowledge Acquisition for Knowledge-Based Systems Workshop,* Banff, Canada, November 1986.

14. American Association for Artificial Intelligence, *Proceedings of Knowledge Acquisition for Knowledge-Based Systems Workshop,* Banff, Canada, November 2–7, 1986.

16. L. B. Eliot, "Investigating the Nature of Expertise: Analogical Thinking, Expert Systems, and ThinkBack," *Expert Systems,* Vol. 4, No. 3, August 1987.

17. D., Lenat, M. Prakash, and M. Shepherd, "CYC: Using Common Sense Knowledge to Overcome Brittleness and Knowledge Acquisition Bottlenecks," *AI Magazine,* Vol. 7, No. 5, Winter 1986.

Chapter 6

Knowledge Representation and Inferencing

After acquiring knowledge from the expert, the next step in building an expert system is deciding on the knowledge representation approach. According to Duda and Gaschnig[1]:

> The power of the expert system lies in the specific knowledge of the problem domain, with potentially the most powerful systems being the ones containing the most knowledge.

This suggests that the knowledge base, which is the set of domain facts and heuristics, is probably the most important component of the expert system.

In deciding which knowledge representation method to incorporate in the expert system, a good rule of thumb is to select the one that seems most natural to the expert. In other words, the knowledge should be represented in the expert system in the same way the expert uses it when explaining a domain or task to the knowledge engineer. For example, suppose that an expert system is being developed to determine whether one has a cold. In an interview, the expert on colds, presents some knowledge in the following manner:

> If one has a runny nose, watery eyes, and a sore throat, then there is a very good likelihood that the individual has a cold. Of course, this is not certain, as the person might have an allergy.

This description suggests two conclusions. One conclusion is that the expert is thinking of IF-THEN or SITUATION-ACTION kinds of rules. Thus, the use of production rules, which will be explained later, might be an appropriate way of representing the knowledge for that expert system. The other conclusion is that the expert is thinking in terms of probability or possibility. Such terms as "a very good likelihood" suggest that the expert system should incorporate uncertainty in this case. It turns out that, in most cases, expert system tasks involve uncertainty.

There are five major ways of representing knowledge in an expert system: predicate calculus, production or inference rules, frames, scripts, and semantic networks. Each of these methods will be discussed.

6.1 Predicate Calculus

Predicate calculus is one way of representing knowledge in an expert system. This is a reasoning approach built on formal logic that incorporates mathematical properties (transitive and associative laws). It is made up of constants (called *terms*), predicates (called *atomic formulas*), functions (called *mappings*), and logical connectives (^ for *and*, v for *or*, ---> for *implies*, and ~ for *not*). For example, the statement "All football players are big" can be expressed in predicate calculus as follows:

(ALL (X) (IF IS-A X FOOTBALL PLAYER) (BIG X))

This means that for all x, if x is a football player, then x is big.

Let's take another example, derived from Rich and Knight[2] and Kaisler[3], which uses predicate calculus to represent knowledge in a knowledge base. Suppose that we have the following facts, with their predicate calculus representations:

1. Harry is a man.
   MAN(HARRY)
2. Harry is a tennis player.
   TENNISPLAYER(HARRY)
3. All tennis players are athletes.
   (FORALL X) [TENNISPLAYERS(X)--->ATHLETE(X)]

4. Bob is a coach.
   COACH(BOB)
5. All athletes either obey or disobey the coach.
   (FORALL X) [ATHLETE(X)--->OBEYS(X,COACH) OR
   DISOBEY(X,COACH)]
6. Everyone is loyal to someone.
   (FORALL X) (EXISTS Y) LOYALTS(X,Y)
7. Athletes only disobey coaches they aren't loyal to.
   (FORALL X) (FORALL Y) [ATHLETE(X) AND COACH(Y) AND
   DISOBEY(X,Y)] ---> NOT LOYALTS (X,Y)
8. Harry was disobedient to Bob.
   DISOBEDIENT(HARRY,BOB)

If we want to prove "Is Harry loyal to Bob?", the following proof could be done using predicate calculus:

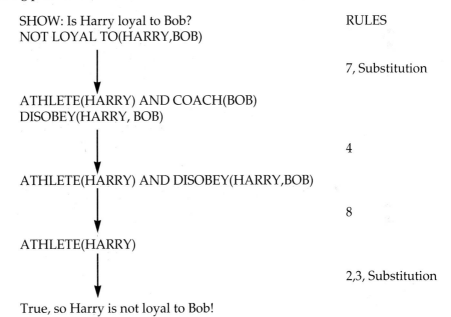

SHOW: Is Harry loyal to Bob?   RULES
NOT LOYAL TO(HARRY,BOB)

                                                      7, Substitution

ATHLETE(HARRY) AND COACH(BOB)
DISOBEY(HARRY, BOB)

                                                      4

ATHLETE(HARRY) AND DISOBEY(HARRY,BOB)

                                                      8

ATHLETE(HARRY)

                                                      2,3, Substitution

True, so Harry is not loyal to Bob!

A major drawback to predicate calculus is that it provides only a skeleton of a representation scheme. Its main disadvantage is that the relevant information is not collected together, as it is under frames or semantic networks.

6.2 Production Rules

Another technique for representing knowledge is through production rules. This is probably the most popular approach for knowledge representation in expert systems. Production rules were popularized by Newell and Simon[4] and by Davis and King[5]. They are used for procedural representation—knowledge that can be executed. Production rules take the form IF (antecedent) THEN (consequent) or SITUATION-ACTION. The rules also can have some measure of uncertainty associated with them, as will be explained in the next chapter. They have been used extensively in expert systems, particularly those created for diagnosis and planning.

A typical production rule in MYCIN, an expert system used to diagnose bacterial infections in the blood, is as follows:

IF: 1. The site of the culture is blood, and
         2. The identity of the organism is not known with certainty, and
         3. The stain of the organism is gramneg, and
         4. The morphology of the organism is rod, and
         5. The patient has been seriously burned,
Then: There is weakly suggestive evidence (.4) that the identity of the organism is pseudomonas.

In order for the consequent of this rule to be true, each of the antecedents must be true. If one of the antecedents is false, then the consequent, using this rule, would not be concluded. Another production rule from R1, an expert system used to configure VAX computers (now called XCON), is as follows:

IF: 1. The current context is assigning devices to unibus, and
         2. There is an unassigned dual port disc drive and
         3. The type of controller it requires is known and
         4. There are two such controllers
         5. Neither of which has any devices assigned to it and
         6. The number of devices that these controllers can support is known
Then: Assign the disc drive to each of the controllers and note that the two controllers have been associated and that each supports one device.

According to Reggia and Perricone[6] and Software Architecture and Engineering[7], there are three criteria to use in selecting a knowledge representation approach: (1) preexisting format of the knowledge, (2) type of classification desired, and (3) context dependence of the inference process. Production rules are usually used when the preexisting format of the knowledge is already organized as rules or expressed in terms of rules when the expert is explaining the task to the knowledge engineer. In this case, by using production rules, the knowledge can be kept in the same form presently used, thus creating intuitive appeal[7]. Production rules are also used when the classification of knowledge is predominantly categorical. If most of the decisions in the expert system task can be answered by "yes" or "no," then production rules would be appropriate. Last, if the knowledge has little context dependence, then production rules are a good form for representing it because there is not much descriptive knowledge. For descriptive knowledge, other knowledge representation methods, such as frames, are better.

There are several advantages to using production rules. First, rules are a natural expression of what-to-do knowledge, that is, procedural knowledge[3]. Second, all knowledge for a problem is uniformly presented as rules. Third, rules are comprehensible units of knowledge. Fourth, rules are modular units of knowledge that can be easily deleted or added. Last, rules may be used to represent how-to-do knowledge, that is, metaknowledge. *Metaknowledge* refers to knowledge about knowledge and can be represented as metarules. A *metarule* is a production rule that controls the application of object-level knowledge. It gives another layer of sophistication to the expert system because it adds additional layers of space to a search space to help decide what to do next[8]. A disadvantage of production rules is that there is a limit to the amount of knowledge that can be expressed conveniently in a single rule[9]. This is not a severe limitation because even when using microcomputer-based expert systems shells like Exsys[10], a rule can have up to 126 conditions in the IF part and up to 126 conditions in its THEN part.

6.3 Frames

A third knowledge representation method used in expert systems is frames. Frames, developed by Minsky[11] and Kuipers[12], are used for declarative knowledge. *Declarative knowledge,* in contrast to procedural knowledge, is knowledge that can't be immediately executed but can be retrieved and stored. Frames were developed because there was evidence that people do not analyze new situations from scratch and then build new knowledge structures to describe those situations[2]. Instead, people use analogical reasoning and take a large collection of structures, available in memory, to represent previous experience with objects, locations, situations, and people[2]. Frames[2] (1) contain information about many aspects of the objects or situations they describe; (2) contain attributes that must be true of objects that will be used to fill individual slots; and (3) describe typical instances of the concepts they represent. Frames are used in situations where there is a large amount of context dependence, implying the use of descriptive knowledge. Frames are represented like cookbook recipes, where "slots" are filled with the ingredients needed for the recipe, and then procedural attachments (e.g., if-added, if-needed, and to-establish procedures) are used to manipulate the data (i.e., to fill the slots) within and among the frames, such as going through the steps on how to actually "prepare" the "recipe." Default values may be provided with frames.

Each frame corresponds to one entity and contains a number of labeled slots for things pertinent to that entity[13]. Slots, in turn, may be blank, or may be specified by terminals referring to other frames, so that the collection of frames is linked together in a network[13]. This allows the knowledge to be useful for modularity and accessible[14]. Attempts to design general knowledge structures based on the frame concept were made by Bobrow and Winograd via the Knowledge Representation Language and by Roberts and Goldstein via the Frame Representation Language.

6.4 Scripts

A special kind of frame is sometimes called a *script*. Clusters of facts can have useful special-purpose structures that exploit specific properties of their restricted domains[2]. A script, developed by Schank and Abelson[15] in 1977, is such a structure that describes a stereotyped sequence of events in a particular context. The components of a script include the following[2,15]:

- Entry conditions.
- Results—conditions that will generally be true after the events described in the script have occurred.
- Props—slots representing objects.
- Roles—slots representing people.
- Track—specific variation on a more general pattern represented by a particular script.
- Scenes—actual sequences of events that occur.

In part of a Restaurant Script[15], the track can be a coffee shop. The entry conditions are given where the customer is hungry and has money. The scenes of entering the coffee shop, ordering, eating, and exiting are displayed. The results of this script are that the customer has less money, is not hungry (hopefully!), and is pleased (optional). Another result is that the owner of the coffee shop has more money. Scripts are helpful in situations there are many causal relationships between events[2]. Figure 6.1 shows examples of the knowledge representation methods discussed.

6.5 Semantic Networks

The last major way of representing knowledge in an expert system is by semantic networks. Semantic networks were discovered by Quillian[16] and Raphael[17] in 1968 and are used to represent declarative knowledge. With semantic networks, knowledge is organized around the objects being described, but objects are represented as nodes on a graph and relations among them are represented by labeled arcs[2]. A semantic network is a collection of nodes and arcs where the following conditions occur[2]:

- Nodes represent classes, objects, concepts, situations, events, and so on.
- Nodes have attributes with values that describe the characteristics of the thing they represent.

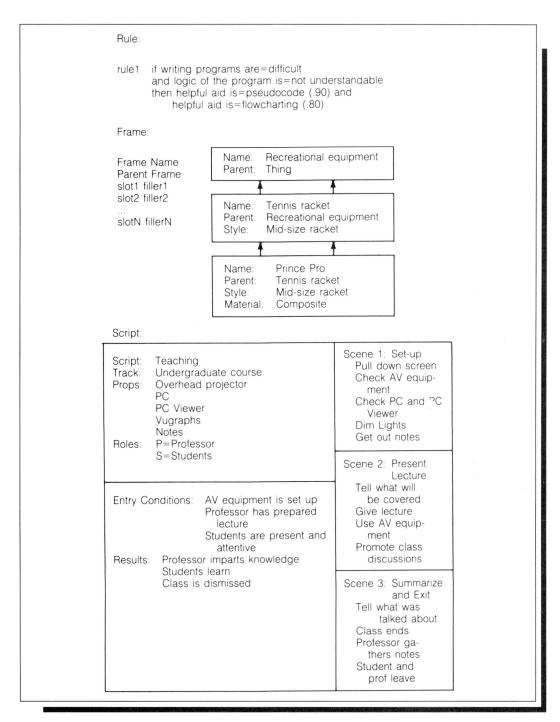

FIGURE 6.1 Examples of Knowledge Representation Methods. [Reprinted by permission from J. Liebowitz, *The Dynamics of Decision Support System and Expert Systems,* Dryden Press, Orlando, FL, 1990.]

- Arcs represent relationships between nodes.
- Arcs allow us to organize knowledge within a network hierarchically.

For example, Figure 6.2 shows a fragment of a semantic network on computers. This figure shows the following associations:

MICROCOMPUTER	Isa	COMPUTER
DISK DRIVE	Ispart	MICROCOMPUTER
IBM PC	Isa	MICROCOMPUTER
IBM PC	Color	BEIGE
IBM PC	Isattached	OKIDATA 192
IBM PC	Owner	ME
OKIDATA 192	Isa	PRINTER
ME	Isa	PERSON

FIGURE 6.2   Fragment of a Semantic Network on Computers

This is only a fragment of a semantic network because we haven't included all the relevant nodes and arcs relating to microcomputers, nor have we indicated those nodes and arcs associated with other kinds of computers, like minicomputers, mainframes, superminicomputers, supercomputers, and lap-size computers.

The reasoning in a semantic network depends on the procedures used to manipulate the network[2]. The following steps are usually accomplished[2]:

- Basically, match patterns against one or more nodes to retrieve information; heuristics may be needed to tell where to begin matching.
- Inference—derive general properties by examining a set of nodes for common features and relations.
- Deduction—follow paths through a set of nodes to derive a conclusion.

The main advantage of using semantic networks is that for each object, event, or concept, all the relevant information is collected together[2]. Semantic networks are used to represent specific events or experiences, as well as for tasks that have a large amount of context dependence.

6.6 Case-Based Reasoning

Another paradigm of increasing interest is called *case-based reasoning*. Case-based reasoning is built on the premise of analogical reasoning, whereby one relies on past episodes or experiences and modifies an old plan to fit the new situation. It assumes a memory model for representing, indexing, and organizing past cases and a process model for retrieving and modifying old cases and assimilating new ones[21]. Many computer programs use case-based reasoning for problem solving or interpretation: MEDIATOR and PERSUADER use cases to resolve disputes, CLAVIER and KRITIK use case-based reasoning for design, HYPO uses cases for legal reasoning, and MEDIC utilizes case-based reasoning for diagnosis[22]. With today's growing interest in case-based reasoning, several case-based reasoning shells are being sold commercially. These include ReMind (Cognitive Systems), Esteem (Esteem Software, Inc.), and CBR Express (Inference Corporation). Many research issues still need to be resolved to advance case-based reasoning. These include the representation of episodic knowledge, memory organization, indexing, case modification, and learning[21].

6.7 Object-Oriented Programming

Object-oriented programming (OOP) is another popular paradigm that is gaining worldwide interest. Object-oriented representation of knowledge can be used in expert systems. Some of the main features of OOP involve the use of objects, inheritance and specialization, and methods and message passing. An *object* is a data structure that contains both data and procedures. The data structures contained within an object are called *attributes* (or *slots* or *variables*). *Inheritance* is the technique that ensures that the child of any object will include the data structures and methods associated with its parents. Inheritance means that a developer does not have to re-create slots or methods that have been created[23]. *Specialization* is the idea that one can specialize (or override) information that is inherited[23]. A *method* is a function or procedure attached to an object. A method is activated by a message sent to the object[23]. *Message passing* (or *binding*) is the process involved in sending messages to objects.

Pure object-oriented languages include Smalltalk, Simula 76, and Eiffel. Hybrid object-oriented languages, which are built on an existing high-level language, include C++, Turbo Pascal 5.5, and CLOS. It is expected that object-oriented languages and development tools, expert system tools, and current CASE (computer-aided software engineering) tools will all merge into a single product by the mid-1990s.

6.8   Control Structure in an Expert System—Inference Engine

An expert system has a control structure to manipulate and generate hypotheses in its knowledge base[18,19,20]. The control structure is called the *inference engine*. There are various inferencing mechanisms, namely, search strategies, that are used to generate hypotheses from the knowledge base—a set of facts and rules of thumb (heuristics) about a specific task in a problem domain.

Three major methods can be incorporated into the inference engine to search a space efficiently to derive hypotheses from the knowledge base. These solution direction techniques are backward chaining, forward chaining, and forward and backward processing combined.

Backward chaining, also called *goal-directed reasoning,* as discussed in Chapter 3, is an inference engine technique. This method entails having a goal or hypothesis as a starting point and then working backward along some paths to see if the conclusion is true. For example, suppose that an expert system is being developed for determining an appropriate tennis strategy to use for a particular kind of tennis player on a specific court surface. After talking with a tennis professional, eight major tennis strategies emerge that could be used:

1. Hit kick serve and angled net shots and deep ground strokes.
2. Hit spin serve and angled net shots and drop shots.
3. Hit spin serve and angled net shots and lobs.
4. Hit slice serve and angled net shots and drop shots.
5. Hit flat serve and angled net shots and slice ground strokes.
6. Hit spin serve and angled net shots and slice ground strokes.
7. Hit slice serve and angled net shots and shorten backswing.
8. Hit slice serve and angled net shots and slice ground strokes.

From discussions with the tennis professional, the following 10 rules are developed in relation to tennis strategies on a particular court surface:

Rule 1
IF: material is grass
or   material is clay
THEN: surface is soft

Rule 2
IF: material is cement
or   material is indoor synthetic
THEN: surface is hard

Rule 3
IF: surface is soft
and   player is serve and volleyer
and   opponent is serve and volleyer

THEN: hit kick serve and angled net shots and deep ground strokes

Rule 4
IF: surface is soft
and   player is serve and volleyer
and   opponent is baseliner
THEN: hit spin serve and angled net shots and drop shots

Rule 5
IF: surface is soft
and   player is baseliner
and   opponent is serve and volleyer
THEN: hit spin serve and angled net shots and lobs

Rule 6
IF: surface is soft
and   player is baseliner
and   opponent is baseliner
THEN: hit slice serve and angled net shots and drop shots

Rule 7
IF: surface is hard
and   player is serve and volleyer
and   opponent is serve and volleyer
THEN: hit flat serve and angled net shots and slice ground strokes

Rule 8
IF: surface is hard
and   player is serve and volleyer
and   opponent is baseliner
THEN: hit spin serve and angled net shots and slice ground strokes

Rule 9
IF: surface is hard
and   player is baseliner
and   opponent is serve and volleyer
THEN: hit slice serve and angled net shots and shorten backswing

Rule 10
IF: surface is hard
and   player is baseliner
and   opponent is baseliner
Then: hit slice serve and angled net shots and slice ground strokes

Backward chaining could be used in this example. It would work in the following manner:

1. The expert system starts with a goal or hypothesis to be proved. The first goal in the knowledge base appears in rule 3. It is in the THEN part (consequent) of the rule—hit kick serve and angled net shots and deep ground strokes.

2. To see if this goal is true, the IF parts (antecedents) of rule 3 must be true. Backward chaining then continues, whereby the truth of the first antecedent of rule 3—surface is soft—is determined. The expert system looks for other rules in its knowledge base to infer the value for "surface is." Indeed, there are two rules—rule 1 and rule 2—that can determine the value for "surface is." In order to determine the value for "surface is," the value for "material is" in the IF part of those two rules must be determined. Since there are no rules to deduce the value for "material is," the expert system will ask the user to enter one of the values for "material is"—namely, grass, clay, cement, or indoor synthetic. If the user enters grass or clay, then the inferred value for "surface is" would be soft (according to rule 1). If the user enters cement or indoor synthetic, then the inferred value for "surface is" would be hard (according to rule 2). If the user types in clay in this example, then the first antecedent of rule 3 is true.

3. Next, in rule 3, the second antecedent is tested to prove the truth of the goal in rule 3. Since there are no rules to infer the value for "player is," the expert system will ask the user to input one of the values for this attribute—namely, serve and volleyer or baseliner. If the user enters serve and volleyer, then according to rule 3, the value for "opponent is" would be determined. Again, since there are no rules to infer this value, the expert system would ask the user to answer by giving one of the possible values (already supplied in the knowledge base by the knowledge engineer) for "opponent is"—namely, serve and volleyer or baseliner. If the user types in serve and volleyer, then the three antecedents in rule 3 are true. Thus the truth of the goal—hit kick serve and angled net shots and deep ground strokes—is true.

4. The expert system will then examine the other goals in rules 4 to 10 to see if other tennis strategies could be reached. In this example, the goal in rule 3, as stated previously, would be the only tennis strategy concluded by the system.

5. If the material of the court had been cement or indoor synthetic, then the surface would have been "hard", and rules 7 to 10 would have been applied in the same manner previously explained.

A problem with backward chaining concerns conjunctive subgoals, in which a combinatorial explosion of possibilities could result. Examples of expert systems using backward chaining are those used for diagnosis and classification.

Forward chaining, often described as *data-driven* or *event-driven reasoning*, as described in Chapter 3, is used for problem solving when data or basic ideas are a starting point. In this method, the system does not start with any particular defined goals. It works from facts to conclusions. It reasons forward, starting with data supplied by the user, and applies all rules whose "if" part is satisfied[18].

In the previous tennis example, the user would first type in any known facts, such as that the material is grass, the player is a serve and volleyer, and the opponent is a serve and volleyer. Using rule 1, a soft court surface would be inferred. Then, according to rule 3, the tennis strategy of "hit kick serve and angled net shots and deep ground strokes" would be concluded.

One possible drawback of forward chaining is that one would derive everything possible, whether one needed it or not. Forward chaining has been used in expert systems for telecommunications[19], data analysis, mathematical formulation, and design.

Another example of backward chaining and one of forward chaining is shown in a traveling example. The situation here is to fly from Washington, D.C., to San Diego with a connecting stop. Backward chaining or forward chaining could be applied as inferencing techniques. With backward chaining, you would check the flights arriving in San Diego, trace backward to see which cities they are arriving from, and then see if any of these flights originate from Washington, D.C. Forward chaining could also be employed by checking the flights departing Washington, D.C., and finding their destination cities. Then you would check the flights leaving those cities, and so on, until you find San Diego[20].

Forward and backward processing combined is another method for searching direction in the inference engine. This approach is used for a large search space, so bottom-up and top-down search can be appropriately combined. This combined search is applicable to complex problems incorporating uncertainties, such as speech understanding.

6.9 Conclusions

Representing knowledge and using the appropriate inferencing mechanism are important elements in building an expert system. The knowledge engineer should not try to force-fit the knowledge representation and inferencing strategies to the expert system. Instead, the knowledge engineer should establish the requirements needed to represent the knowledge and the inferencing technique for the expert system's domain, so that the representation and inferencing approaches match the way the expert is using his or her knowledge and reasoning through it.

References

1. R. O. Duda and J. G. Gaschnig, "Knowledge-Based Expert Systems Come of Age," *BYTE*, September 1981.
2. E. Rich and K. Knight, *Artificial Intelligence*, McGraw-Hill, New York, 1991.
3. S. M. Kaisler, *Expert Systems Tutorial*, ACM Professional Development Seminar, College Park, MD, 1984.

4. A. Newell and H. A. Simon, *Human Problem Solving,* Prentice-Hall, Englewood Cliffs, NJ, 1972.

5. R. Davis and J. J. King, "An Overview of Production Systems," in *Machine Intelligence,* Vol. 8, E. Elcock and D. Michie, eds., Horwood, Chichester, England, 1977.

6. J. A. Reggia and B. T. Perricone, *KMS Manual,* Department of Mathematics, University of Maryland, College Park, MD, January 1982.

7. Software Architecture and Engineering, Inc., *Knowledge Engineering System: Knowledge Base Author's Reference Manual,* Arlington, VA, March 1984.

8. F. Hayes-Roth, D. A. Waterman, and D. B. Lenat, *Building Expert Systems,* Addison-Wesley, Reading, MA, 1983.

9. R. Davis, "Knowledge Acquisition in Rule-Based Systems: Knowledge about Representation as a Basis for System Construction and Maintenance," in *Pattern-Directed Inference Systems,* Academic Press, New York, 1978.

10. EXSYS, Inc., *EXSYS: Expert System Development Package Manual,* Albuquerque, NM, 1985.

11. M. Minsky, "A Framework for Representing Knowledge," in *The Psychology of Computer Vision,* P. Winston, ed., McGraw-Hill, New York, 1975.

12. B. J. Kuipers, "A Frame for Frames," in *Representation and Understanding,* D. G. Bobrow and A. Collins, eds., Academic Press, New York, 1975.

13. J. R. Quinlan, "Fundamentals of the Knowledge Engineering Problem," in *Introductory Readings in Expert Systems,* D. Michie, ed., Gordon and Breach Science Publishers, 1984.

14. D. S. Nau, "Expert Computer Systems," *IEEE Computer,* February 1983.

15. R. C. Schank and R. P. Abelson, *Scripts, Plans, Goals, and Understanding,* Erlbaum, Hillsdale, NJ, 1977.

16. R. Quillian, "Semantic Memory," in *Semantic Information Processing,* M. Minsky, ed., MIT Press, Cambridge, MA, 1968.

17. B. Raphael, "A Computer Program for Semantic Information Retrieval," *Semantic Information Processing,* M. Minsky, ed., MIT Press, Cambridge, MA, 1968.

18. R. Davis, "Knowledge-Based Systems," *Science,* Vol. 231, February 28, 1986.

19. J. Liebowitz, ed., *Expert System Applications to Telecommunications,* John Wiley and Sons, New York, 1988.

20. K. Parsaye and M. Chignell, *Expert Systems for Experts,* John Wiley and Sons, New York, 1988.

21. S. Slade, "Case-Based Reasoning: A Research Paradigm," *AI Magazine,* Vol. 12, No. 1, Spring 1991.

22. J. L. Kolodner, "Improving Human Decision Making Through Case-Based Decision Aiding," *AI Magazine,* Vol. 12, No. 2, Summer 1991.

23. P. Harmon and J. Aikins, "Tutorial Notes on Object-Oriented Programming and Expert Systems," *The World Congress on Expert Systems,* Pergamon Press, Orlando, FL, December 1991.

Chapter 7

Knowledge Encoding

7.1 Introduction

After representing the knowledge, the next step is to encode the knowledge. Knowledge encoding[1–4] involves programming the expert system, typically using an expert system shell or programming from scratch, and then incorporating the proper human factors features to ensure the expert system's usability. Most knowledge engineers employ a rapid prototyping approach to building expert systems. This "build a little, test a little" approach involves encoding a set of prototypical cases that relate to the domain and then iteratively expanding the coverage of the cases in enlarging the knowledge base of the expert system. There are many expert system shells on the market, ranging from microcomputers to mainframes to workstations to specialized AI hardware. Many knowledge engineers, even when using a shell, tailor the user interface and other design features

119

(like the explanation facility of the expert system) to customize the expert system for the intended users.

This chapter will discuss some criteria to use in selecting from among appropriate expert system shells in encoding the expert system. The knowledge engineer should remember that "for every shell, there is a perfect task; but for every task, there is not a perfect shell." The chapter will also explain some important human factors features that should be considered in designing the expert system.

7.2   Criteria for Expert System Shell Selection

In selecting an appropriate expert system, there are several problem-oriented and user-oriented criteria that should be considered. The most important step is for the knowledge engineer to perform a thorough analysis to determine the system's requirements. If this is done, the knowledge engineer will not have to force-fit requirements to a shell; rather, the problem requirements will be outlined first, and then the knowledge engineer will see whether an expert system shell is available that meets all or most of the requirements.

The problem-oriented and user-oriented criteria that should be considered will now be briefly discussed.

Problem-Oriented Criteria

Knowledge Representation In deciding whether an expert system shell is appropriate, the knowledge engineer should determine how the knowledge is being used by the domain expert. If the knowledge is being expressed procedurally, in terms of IF-THEN rules, then a production rule format may be the most natural way of representing the knowledge in the expert system. If the knowledge is more context dependent and descriptive, then a frame-based approach may be appropriate. A combination of knowledge representation techniques may also be feasible. The knowledge engineer should determine how the domain expert is expressing and using the knowledge, and then see if an expert system shell exists that allows for that knowledge representation scheme.

Uncertainty Another problem-oriented criterion is how uncertainty is used in the problem domain. The knowledge engineer, through interactions with the domain expert, can determine if uncertainty should be factored into the expert system. If so, the knowledge engineer can assess the best way to handle uncertainty in the system—fuzzy logic, certainty factors, probabilistic techniques, or other methods. Some expert systems, like ACE for diagnosing telephone cable problems, do not need to include uncertainty. However, most expert systems do use uncertainty, so the knowledge engineer must select a shell that has the appropriate way of handling uncertainty to solve the problem.

Inferencing The knowledge engineer should determine how the domain expert is reasoning through the knowledge. If the expert is using a goal-directed technique, this suggests the use of backward chaining. If the expert is using a data-driven reasoning method, then forward chaining is appropriate. The expert may also use both chaining techniques to arrive at a solution. The knowledge engineer should consider a shell that allows the appropriate chaining technique to be used.

Integration with Other Systems (External Interfaces) Most expert systems need to interface with existing databases, information systems, spreadsheets, and other systems/programs. Some expert system shells have built-in direct links to such programs as dBase or Lotus 1-2-3. Other shells have direct links to optimization routines, like LINDO for linear programming, and other methods. Exsys Professional even has an interface with the neural network development tool NeuralWorks Professional II/Plus for building hybrid systems. The knowledge engineer should consider a shell that interfaces easily with the systems/programs required to solve the problem. These external interfaces are extremely important in moving the expert system from the prototype stage to the full production mode.

Debugging/Verification and Validation Methods An important part of the knowledge engineering process is the ability to verify and validate easily the expert system, as will be explained in the next chapter. Debugging facilities are very useful for refining the knowledge base. Many expert system shells have limited capabilities for debugging the knowledge base, such as checking for redundant and inconsistent rules, checking for "unclosed" paths, and other debugging features. Some expert system shells, like Exsys, has an automatic expert system validation feature to allow for either systematic or random testing of possible user input. Errors such as failure to derive needed data, loop errors, values outside of bounds, or user-defined custom tests are reported. The testing, using this feature in Exsys, also produces a tree diagram that shows all the possible combinations of input and the resulting output of the system, which is ideal for system documentation. The knowledge engineer should select an expert system shell that facilitates the debugging and testing of the expert system.

Ability to Maintain/Update the System If an expert system is to be used, maintenance is vital. The ability to learn how to use the expert system shell is an important criterion in choosing an appropriate shell. Good documentation, tutorials, and training programs are necessary to ease development using the shell. The shell should provide tracing features in order to show the paths of rule firings. The expert system's knowledge base should also be designed in a modular way so that maintenance is facilitated. In other words, the system should be designed for easy maintenance in order to ensure its continued use.

Customizable User Interfaces One of the most important features of the expert system is a properly designed user interface. Many expert systems have failed due to a poorly designed interface. The knowledge engineer should understand who the user is when designing the interface and the expert system. Some user interfaces may need to include graphical displays, touch screens, light pens, and other pertinent features. A customizable user interface gives the knowledge engineer great flexibility. The use of custom screens in designing the user interface may be important in building the expert system. The expert system shell should be considered partly in terms of the ability to design a proper user interface.

Explanation Facility An important part of most expert systems is their ability to explain their reasoning. Most expert systems can respond to queries regarding how and why conclusions were reached. Many rule-based systems simply show the rules that were fired to arrive at a conclusion. Other expert systems and associated shells are more sophisticated and let the knowledge engineer tailor the explanation facility to better suit the users' needs. Customizing the explanation facility may be important in inducing the user to accept the expert system. In selecting an expert system shell, the knowledge engineer should pay close attention to the explanation capability and what kind of explanation the users expect.

Human Factors Features As will be explained later in this chapter, an expert system is not simply a set of rules. The ability to make the expert system user-friendly is extremely important. The ability to provide hypertext to allow definitions or fuller descriptions of terms may be very useful. The ability to back up to previous questions during a user session, instead of exiting from the session and restarting, may be another vital feature. A properly designed user interface, good messages, useful report generation facilities, and a host of other human factors considerations will help ensure adequate technology transfer of the expert system. The knowledge engineer should carefully consider these human factors features and examine the capabilities of the expert system shell.

Ability to Run on Different Platforms The knowledge engineer may want to use the expert system on different hardware platforms to accommodate users. In selecting an expert system shell, this requirement should be kept in mind.

User-Oriented Criteria

Besides the criteria related to problem domain requirements, there are user-oriented characteristics that should be considered in selecting the expert system shell. These user-oriented criteria will be described next.

User Interface Some studies have indicated that the user interface of an expert system accounts for up to 70 percent of the expert system code. If a user interface is not acceptable to the users, the expert system will most likely not be used. Bethelem Steel encountered this problem: Their expert system for assembly line workers was not utilized because of the inappropriately designed user interface. In selecting the expert system shell, the ability to customize the user interface may be one of the most important criteria to consider.

Ability to Use the Shell The expert system should be easy for the user to operate. Even if the shell is sophisticated, the knowledge engineer should design the expert system to minimize its complexity. The expert system and its shell should not require a great deal of training to be operated by the user. For the team that is maintaining the expert system, however, a significant amount of training will be necessary to understand the workings of the shell and how to update the knowledge base. For the user's perspective, though, the expert system should be relatively easy to use.

Vendor Existence With increasing competition in the AI/expert systems market worldwide, social Darwinism—survival of the fittest—is becoming common. In determining which expert system shell may be appropriate, an important factor is whether the vendor will be in business 3 to 5 years from now. Periodically, there are updates to shells to improve their capabilities and expand their functions. These updates are necessary to keep the shell current with the state of the art. If the vendor is likely to go out of business in the near term, the users of the shell may be at an extreme disadvantage. In selecting a shell, the knowledge engineer should try to determine if its manufacturer is likely to be financially viable in the near term.

User Support If an expert system is not properly institutionalized, it may be a technical success but a technology transfer failure. The user should have access to such support services as help desks, documentation, online tutorials, hotlines to vendors, and access to the shell's technical support team. In assessing which expert system shell may be appropriate, these factors are important for the user.

"Hooking" Features In order for the user to be eager to accept the expert system, he or she needs to be hooked. *Hooking* refers to building features into the system that will attract the user. These features are usually what the user always wanted but was never able to have, such as a report generation facility that produces a particular report. Another hook may be the ability to back up to several questions and reenter a response during a sample session with the expert system. Still another may be a particular graph generated by the expert system that shows dynamic changes in values. Whatever the hooks may be, the knowledge engineer should select an expert system shell that will incorporate these user-desired features.

Runtime Licenses Another important user-oriented criterion is the arrangement and cost of the runtime license to use and distribute the expert system shell. Some vendors charge a set price for the runtime license, which allows the developer to make multiple copies of the shell and the associated expert system for distribution within the organization. Other vendors will charge per copy for a runtime license. With some shells, like Exsys, there is a small, one-time license fee that allows unlimited noncommercial distribution of the expert system. If the developer markets the expert system, there may be a very reasonable commercial distribution license policy. The knowledge engineer should determine up front how the expert system is to be distributed and to whom, and should consider this in looking at the runtime license policies of various vendors.

Security One of the most overlooked issues in expert systems development is security. Security should be established so that the knowledge base is updated and edited only by the maintenance team. Some shells support password protection. Exsys, for example, has two levels of password protection: one to run a system and another to allow editing. With Exsys, it is even possible to lock a system so that a user can run it but not examine the rules with the "how" or "why" commands. Security should be carefully considered by the knowledge engineer when determining which shell is appropriate.

7.3 Human Factor Features

The previously discussed problem-oriented and user-oriented criteria will help the knowledge engineer evaluate which shell will facilitate the knowledge encoding process of the expert system. To make the expert system more attractive and usable, the knowledge engineer should use good human factors design in building it.

Menus are typically used in representing the possible responses to expert system—-generated questions. Menus allow the user to recognize the appropriate answers rather than having to recall them. This factor is related to the limitation of short-term memory. For this reason, no more than seven possible choices should be listed in a menu (as Miller's 7+/-2 model suggests). If the knowledge engineer uses menus, program shortcuts should be built in for knowledgeable users. The knowledgeable or frequent user may not want to go through all levels of the menus to get to the desired location. Thus, the knowledge engineer should design the expert system to facilitate movement through the menu hierarchy.

Besides menus, proper messages should also be used within the expert system. The messages should provide constructive, specific guidance and should have the appropriate physical format (e.g., blinking, bleeping, different colors) for the message. Messages should not be in the imperative form (e.g., use "Ready for command" instead of "Enter command"). In this way, the user feels that he or she is in control of the expert system.

Hypertext is a very useful technique that should be considered for improving the human factors design of the expert system. *Hypertext* refers to associated links whereby the user can obtain textual descriptions or definitions of terms to clarify the questions or terms used in the system. In many shells, like Exsys and KnowledgePro, hypertext can be used to increase understanding of the questions being asked. A user can ask for a hypertext keyword anytime during the run, and will be provided with a custom help system incorporating hypertext for hierarchical references. In some shells, like Exsys, since hypertext screens are created with the screen definition language, the knowledge engineer can include external programs and graphics within the help systems. Figure 7.1 shows the use of hypertext using KnowledgePro.

As we have previously discussed, the user interface and explanation facility should be designed with human factors in mind. The user interface may need to include graphical icons, preformatted forms, links to spreadsheets, and other fea-

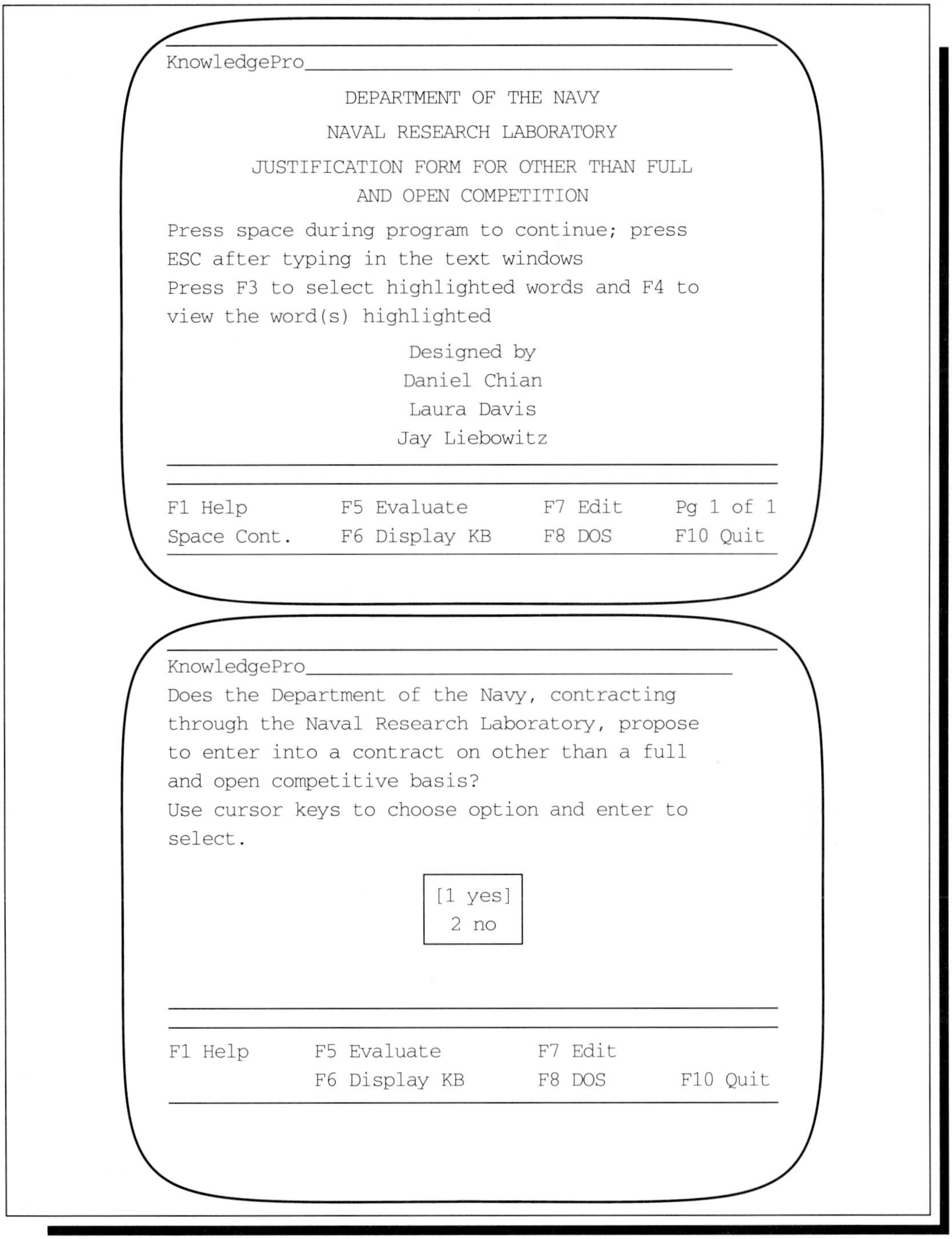

```
KnowledgePro_____

                    DEPARTMENT OF THE NAVY

                    NAVAL RESEARCH LABORATORY

            JUSTIFICATION FORM FOR OTHER THAN FULL
                    AND OPEN COMPETITION

Press space during program to continue; press
ESC after typing in the text windows
Press F3 to select highlighted words and F4 to
view the word(s) highlighted

                        Designed by
                        Daniel Chian
                        Laura Davis
                        Jay Liebowitz
_____

F1 Help          F5 Evaluate        F7 Edit        Pg 1 of 1
Space Cont.      F6 Display KB       F8 DOS         F10 Quit
```

```
KnowledgePro_____
Does the Department of the Navy, contracting
through the Naval Research Laboratory, propose
to enter into a contract on other than a full
and open competitive basis?
Use cursor keys to choose option and enter to
select.

                        [1 yes]
                         2 no

_____

F1 Help          F5 Evaluate        F7 Edit
                 F6 Display KB       F8 DOS         F10 Quit
```

FIGURE 7.1   Sample Hypertext screens for completing a justification and approval form. Reprinted by permission from J. Liebowitz, *Institutionalizing Expert Systems: A Handbook for Managers* (Prentice-Hall, Englewood Cliffs, NJ, 1991).

```
 KnowledgePro _____
 State the nature and/or description of the
 [supplies/services required] to meet the
 needs of the Naval Research Laboratory and the
 estimated value including all options.
 Example for question 3.

     ┌Example: Requirements ─────────────────────
     │ NRL requires that this hardware be
     │ operational to the fullest extent possible
     │ and the hardware and software be current
     │ with the latest revisions from the
     │ manufacturer.
     └

 _____

 F1 Help          F5 Evaluate        F7 Edit     Pg 1 of 1
 Space Cont.      F6 Display KB      F8 DOS      F10 Quit
```

```
 KnowledgePro _____
 State the nature and/or descriptions of the supplies/
 services required, to meet the needs of the Naval
 Research Laboratory and the estimated value including all
 options.[Example for question 3]

 ┌Requirements: press ESC when done ─────────────────
 │ NRL requires that this hardware be operational to the
 │ fullest extent possible and that the hardware and soft-
 │ ware be current with the latest revisions from the manu-
 │ facturer. NRL needs a service contract in place to
 │ repair broken equipment and to provide the latest hard-
 │ ware and software revisions and
 │ upgrades as released by XYZ Corp.
 └

 _____

 F1 Help   F3 Select   F5 Evaluate   F7 Edit Page
 Esc Exit F4 View      F6 Disp. KB   F8 DOS    F10 Quit
```

FIGURE 7.1   continued

KnowledgePro _____

You must have an identification of the statutory
authority permitting other than full or open
competition (See FAR 6.302) usually 10 U.S.C. 2304(c) (1)
and FAR 8.302-1—Only one responsible source or
Unsolicited Proposal; -or- 10 U.S.C. 2304(c) (2) and FAR
6.302-2—[Unusual and Compelling Urgency]

┌ Urgency ──────────────────────────────────────┐
│ If urgency is used, describe in paragraph 5 what harm │
│ would come to the government if the date is missed. │
│ Note that failure to plan and the length of the pro- │
│ curement process are not justification.   │
└──┘

F1 Help   F5 Evaluate   F7 Edit   Pg 1 of 1
Space Cont.   F6 Display KB   F8 DOS   F10 Quit

KnowledgePro _____

You must have an identification of the statutory
authority permitting other than full or open
competition (See FAR 6.302) usually 10 U.S.C.
2304(c) (1) and FAR 6.302-1—Only one responsible
source or Unsolicited Proposal; -or- 10 U.S.C. 2304(c)
(2) and FAR 6.302-2—Unusual and Compelling Urgency.

      [1 10 U.S.C. 2304 (c) (1) and FAR 6.302-1]
      ┌───┐
      │ 2 10 U.S.C. 2304 (c) (2) and FAR 6.302-2 │
      │ 3 other   │
      └───┘

F1 Help   F3 Select   F5 Evaluate   F7 Edit
           F4 View   F6 Disp. KB   F8 DOS   F10 Quit

FIGURE 7.1   continued

tures to win the approval of the user. Similarly, the explanation facility may have to be tailored to fit the particular user's needs. The explanation may have to be different in terms of the level of detail, depending upon whether the user is the knowledge engineer, domain expert, novice user, or knowledgeable user.

Other important human factors features that should be considered in the design of the expert system include providing a help function; guarding against undesirable input, such as the use of multiple versus single answers; minimizing memorization on the part of the user; providing a program action for each user input; engineering for errors; and other related human factors features.

7.4 Summary

Knowledge encoding is an important step in the knowledge engineering life cycle. This process includes selecting an appropriate expert system shell, or programming from scratch, and incorporating good human factors in the system. The knowledge encoding step is revisited iteratively throughout the expert system's development. After knowledge encoding, verification and validation are performed. This process will be discussed in the next chapter.

References

1. D. Dologite, *Developing Knowledge Based Systems Using VP-Expert,* Macmillan, New York, 1993.
2. T. Luce, *Using VP-Expert in Business,* McGraw-Hill, New York, 1992.
3. R. Mockler and D. Dologite, *An Introduction to Expert Systems*, Macmillan, New York, 1992.
4. E. Turban, *Expert Systems and Applied Artificial Intelligence*, Macmillan, New York, 1992.

Chapter 8

Issues and Methods in Verification and Validation of Expert Systems

8.1 Introduction

As expert systems technology has matured and as expert system applications have become more common, there has resulted an increasing need to develop structured, standardized methodologies for verifying and validating expert systems. Whether the expert system is designed for diagnosing medical problems or for aiding in military warfare, the critical nature of verification and validation (V&V) is readily apparent. According to a Price Waterhouse study on the management of information technology[1], one of the major problems preventing widespread use of expert systems is the concern about validating the system's results.

Verification refers to getting the expert system right, and *validation* means getting the right expert system[2]. With verification, the knowledge engineer is test-

129

ing the implementation of specifications. With validation, the major concern is the accurate performance of the system. Without proper V&V procedures, current commercial expert systems that underwrite insurance policies, monitor alarms in nuclear power plants, make medical diagnoses, or schedule factories can cause dramatic adverse impacts on human lives and corporate bottom lines[3].

8.2 Survey Results on V&V Activities During Expert System Development

There have been several surveys on the level of V&V during expert system development. One such survey is that of Hamilton et al.[4], performed by IBM Corporation and NASA Johnson Space Center. Sixty-six percent of the respondents used functional testing, and 44 percent used structural testing. Typically, 25 percent of the development effort involved V&V. The recommendations based on the survey include developing requirements for expert system V&V, addressing common issues, recommending a life cycle for expert systems development, addressing readability and modularity issues, and investigating the applicability of analysis tools.

Another survey on V&V activities of expert systems was conducted by O'Leary[5]. He found that the expert who provided the knowledge performs validation (29.57 percent), with a different expert, knowledge engineer, end user, project sponsor, and independent validator following in sequence. The survey indicated that about 48 percent of the time, testing with actual and test data was used for validation; about 30 percent involved direct examination by the expert or a nonexpert; about 18 percent parallel use of the system by the expert or nonexpert; and about 4 percent decision/contingency tables and other methods. In terms of when validation is typically performed, most respondents answered "continuously," followed by "after each major phase." It was also reported that about 20 percent of the total development and implementation budget goes to validation of the expert system application.

A third important study, by Terano et al. from Japan[6], was based on a three-year project on expert system evaluation. The study identified a class of expert systems to be critically evaluated, defined an expert system development life cycle model, proposed a checklist for evaluation covering the expert system class and the life cycle model, and presented a framework in which to use the checklist for expert system development. The comprehensive checklist for V&V of expert systems has about 350 items.

8.3 Expert System V&V Issues

The Need to Allocate More Resources to V&V

A major issue in V&V of expert systems is lack of resources. According to a 1989 survey by O'Leary and O'Keefe on the V&V of expert systems, (1) validation rarely exceeds the budget and generally is allocated significantly less of the total than is normally planned; (2) validation efforts are often driven out of the life cycle by the production process; and (3) further development and enhancements are perceived as more important than validation[7]. These results indicate that inadequate attention is given to V&V and testing in expert systems development. Lance Miller further substantiates these views, saying that experiences at Science Applications International Corporation (SAIC) indicate that V&V and testing can consume as much as half of the budget and is usually one of the first areas to be cut when budgets get tight[8].

The Need to Incorporate V&V Early in the Expert System Life Cycle

Another central issue is the need to incorporate V&V early in the expert system life cycle. Rapid prototyping should facilitate this objective. By incorporating V&V early in the life cycle, the expert system's specifications may become better defined early on. According to a U.S. Army study[8], one of the major difficulties with V&V of expert systems was testing issues were not raised early enough in the development process. According to Bellman and Walter[9], "preparing for testing begins with system design." Building a testable, knowledge-based system involves building a model, and requires specifying acceptable performance ranges up front and a sound development methodology[8]. "Rapid prototyping is not an excuse for poor plans and task analysis, quick fix or kludges[9]."

The Need for More V&V Tools

Another important issue is the need for more tools to facilitate V&V. Both static and dynamic testing are useful. For example, to investigate consistency, static testing could be used via contingency tables, dependency charts, or incidence matrices in graph theory. According to Constantine and Ulvila[8], the lack of tools for static analysis is a major problem. Few testers have access to such tools, most shells do not provide extensive utilities for static analysis, and most developers do not have sufficient time or resources for an extensive manual analysis of the knowledge base[8]. CRSV (Cross Reference Style and Verification Tool), an exception, has been made available and is distributed with CLIPS[8]. Dynamic testing, according to O'Keefe and Lee[2], could be used to treat the system as a "simulation," randomly generating inputs and tallying outputs into a distribution. Other verification tools are needed to evaluate the consistency and completeness of rules. EVA, developed at the Lockheed AI Center, is used to check such areas as the expert system's structure, logic, semantics, rules, uncertainty, and rule satisfiability[10]. Validation tools are also needed for expert systems. According to O'Keefe and Lee[2], the major expert system validation techniques include test cases, Turing tests, simulation, sensitivity analysis, and line of reasoning. Expert system validation tools need to be constructed to facilitate this process. Tools are also needed to test the V&V of other expert system tools, like knowledge-based simulation tools.

The Need for More Standards and Methodologies to Ensure Testability and Traceability

Since expert systems is a relatively new field, the creation of standards for expert systems development, particularly V&V, is just beginning. Various groups including ANSI, IEEE, and the International Association of Knowledge Engineers are trying to create standards for expert system development, testing, and implementation. For example, medical expert systems in the United States must adhere to the same Food and Drug Administration regulations required of other medical software. Thus, V&V of the expert system must be at least as comprehensive as those steps required for V&V of conventional software. According to Rushby[11], "the best way to develop credible and effective quality assurance and evaluation techniques for AI software will be to identify the facets of such software that are inherently, or essentially, different from conventional software, and to distinguish them from those facets that are only accidentally or inessentially different." To maintain high quality in software, this must be built into the product right from the start[13]. Expert system development methodologies that support V&V need to be created. Culbert et al[12] suggest a panels approach. That is, a panel consisting of the expert system developers, the domain experts, the system users, and managers with system responsibility should represent all applicable viewpoints. Verification of both design and purpose would be provided by regular panel review. Bellman[13] believes that building an expert system is like building a model. She claims that not only is the modeling analogy helpful, since it use of the associated methodology and perspective, but it is also vital to the design, V&V, and testing of expert systems.

8.4   Methods for V&V of Expert Systems

Verification Techniques

Verification applies to the process of expert system development[14]. All components of the system are subject to verification: the knowledge base, inference engine, user interface, database interface, and other system interfaces. Face and subsystem validity need to be established. Face validity requires the domain expert to certify that the problem has been correctly identified, that the essential concepts have been included, and that the domain expert's knowledge has been correctly interpreted and represented[14]. Face validation is accomplished by examining the code using a three-party team: domain expert, knowledge engineer, and independent validator. Focus is on the procedures that model the expert's reasoning process and knowledge. Subsystem validity serves to identify deficiencies within the prototype. The code is divided into sets of modules (e.g., rules with common sets of inputs), and module inputs are exercised and outputs observed.

In verifying rule-based systems, the knowledge engineer should make checks for the following[14,15]:

- Rules with the same name.
- Rules with incorrect syntax.
- Redundant rules (rules are redundant if they can be fired using the same set of conditions and provide the same set of results as other rules).
- Isolated rules (rules are isolated if the set of conditions through which they may be fired can never be achieved or if the results they achieve do not affect any other knowledge element or cannot otherwise be used).
- Subsumed rules (rules are subsumed within other rules when the premise contains a larger set of conditions but yields the same results as other rules).
- Conflicting rules (rules conflict when their results do not agree when presented with the same set of conditions).
- Circular rules (rules are circular when their results directly or indirectly establish the set of conditions which fire the rule).

Most of today's commercial expert system shells provide simple checking for syntax and naming conventions. Additionally, automated rule checkers are available with some systems to check for other problems with rules. Capabilities for visual mapping of rules, knowledge groups, and other knowledge base elements are typically available within many shells[14]. For frame-based systems, verification should be conducted to check for illegal slot values, frames with the same name, unresolved slot inheritance conflicts, and circular inheritance paths.

Inference engine verification is a critical part of the V&V process. In practice, when using a commercially available inference engine and development environment (expert system shell), the shell and its inference engine typically have a proven track record of reliability and support. Newly developed inference engines, as well as enhancements and modifications to existing inference engines, should be thoroughly tested prior to release[14]. The inference engine should be tested using black box and conventional software testing techniques. Likewise, the user interface, database interface, and other system interfaces can be verified using conventional software techniques. One interesting way to verify the expert system's functionality is to run the system over a library of cases to which the system is linked, detecting erroneous functioning and then proceeding to refinement of the knowledge expressed in the knowledge base in order to eliminate the malfunction[16].

Validation Techniques

Validation applies to the expert system product itself. As with verification, all components of the expert system are subject to validation. According to Prerau[17], one method of validation utilizes three techniques that may be used alone or in combination, depending upon the application: absolute validation, validation against expert performance, and validation by field testing.

In some domains, one can obtain absolute confirmation of the correctness of the expert system. The competence of the system may be determined without the need to compare it against human results[14,17]. Examples of such domains include equipment diagnosis problems (the part is replaced and the system now works correctly) and prediction problems (performance can be compared to historical data to determine correctness).

In domains where there is no clear agreement among experts on the correctness of any one particular solution, an alternative approach is to achieve consensus among the experts that a decision is good, reasonable, or acceptable (e.g., medical diagnosis, forecasting). Validation against expert performance can be achieved by comparing the expert system against operational expert judgments (see how the system fared when compared against prior expert decisions); comparing test case results (comparing the results of the expert system against the performance of human experts using the same test cases); or comparing against project expert judgments (showing that the expert system performs close to the level of the project domain expert)[17]. Validation using multiple experts or independent experts reduces potential for bias in the results and lends credibility to the validation process.

Validation by field testing involves running the program in the field under actual or equivalent operational conditions. The field trial may be conducted either during initial production use or in parallel[17].

O'Leary[15] identifies the usual methods of expert system validation. The most common method involves the use of test cases. Cases previously solved by an expert are run through the system or new cases are presented to both. This is a good approach if done objectively and if guidelines are followed: The problem presented to the system should be reflected in the cases; the coverage of the cases is important; the range of the problems to be encountered should be considered; and expert decisions may precipitate the actual outcome. A major problem with the test case approach is that synthetic cases can be dangerous.

A second popular approach to expert system validation is the Turing test. This test involves giving the solutions of both the expert and the machine to a third party who is blinded), who assesses both[15]. This approach is particularly appropriate when the developer cannot assess a solution, when validation against multiple experts is necessary and when those experts differ. Two problems with this approach are that it requires more expert time, and comparison against multiple experts can be difficult to measure.

Simulation is a third approach used for validation of some expert systems. For systems with a time component (e.g., real-time control systems), connection to a simulation model is analogous to using test cases.

Control groups is another method used for validating expert systems. Where a system cannot be validated alone, its use can be compared against a control group; each group gets the same cases. Two problems with this approach are identifying significant differences between groups and making sure that the system is properly implemented and institutionalized[15].

If no case studies exist, sensitivity analysis or comparison against other methods may be used for system validation. Through sensitivity analysis, by systematically altering inputs, one can analyze changes in the output. If no case studies exist, one can also compare the system against another model, either built or already existing[15].

Statistical methods can be used to validate an expert system. In these situations, the null hypothesis can be tested—the expert system is valid for the acceptable performance range under the prescribed input domain. Useful methods include confidence intervals, chi-square tests, regression analysis, consistency methods, and other nonparametric approaches[15].

8.5 Conclusions

In order for expert systems usage to increase, it is important that standardized, structured methodologies for V&V be developed and used[18–20]. Additionally, V&V should be incorporated early in the system's development life cycle. According to Rossomando[21], although knowledge-based system V&V tools can assist with the engineering of these systems, they alone cannot guarantee complete knowledge-based system correctness. To do so requires systems that have themselves been designed from the start with testability in mind: Knowledge-based systems are not inherently transparent and explainable; they must be so engineered[21]. Lastly, the necessary resources and tools must be allocated to allow proper V&V of the expert system.

References

1. Price Waterhouse, "Managing Information Technology," *International Journal of Computer Application Technology,* Vol. 2, No. 3 (1989).
2. R. M. O'Keefe and S. Lee, "An Integrative Model of Expert System Verification and Validation," *Expert Systems with Applications: An International Journal,* Vol. 1, No. 3 (1990).
3. P. Chapnick, "Software Quality Assurance," *AI Expert,* February 1990.
4. D. Hamilton, K. Kelley, and C. Culbert, "State of the Practice in Knowledge Based System Verification and Validation," *Expert Systems with Applications,* Vol. 3, No. 4 (1991).
5. D. O'Leary, "Survey Results on Verification and Validation of Expert Systems," Workshop on V&V of Expert Systems, AAAI Conference, Menlo Park, CA, 1991.
6. T. Terano, H. Kongoji, K. Kaji, and K. Yamamoto, "Development of a Guideline for Expert System Evaluation—A Report on a Three Year Project," Presented at the AAAI '91 Workshop on Verification, Validation, and Testing of Knowledge Based Systems, American Association of Artificial Intelligence, CA, 1991.
7. D. O'Leary and R. O'Keefe, "Verifying and Validating Expert Systems," Tutorial at the 11th International Joint Conference on AI, AAAI, Menlo Park, CA, August 21, 1989.
8. M. M. Constantine and J. W. Ulvila, "Testing Knowledge-Based Systems: The State of the Practice and Suggestions for Improvement," *Expert Systems* with *Applications,* Vol. 1, No. 3 (1990).
9. K. L. Bellman and D. O. Walter, "Designing Knowledge-Based Systems for Reliability/Performance," notes for a one-day tutorial course, The Aerospace Corporation, April 20, 1989.

10. C. L. Chang, J. B. Combs, and R. A. Stachowitz, "A Report on the Expert Systems Validation Associate (EVA)," *Expert Systems with Applications*, Vol. 1, No. 3 (1990).

11. J. Rushby, "Quality Measures and Assurance for AI Software, SRI International, Menlo Park, CA, 1989.

12. C. Culbert, G. Riley, and R. T. Savely, "An Expert System Development Methodology Which Supports Verification and Validation," Fourth IEEE Conference on AI Applications, Los Alamitos, CA, IEEE, 1987.

13. K. L. Bellman, "The Modeling Issues Inherent in Testing and Evaluating Knowledge-Based Systems," *Expert Systems with Applications*, Vol. 1, No. 3 (1990).

14. R. G. Wright, "Tutorial Notes on Expert System Verification and Validation," IEEE Managing Expert System Programs and Projects Conference, IEEE Computer Society, Bethesda, MD, September 10–12, 1990.

15. D. O'Leary, "Tutorial Notes on Verification and Validation of Expert Systems," International Symposium on Artificial Intelligence, Cancun, Mexico, November 1991.

16. L. Brunessaux, J. P. Vaudet, S. Petitjean, and M. N. Jullion, "An Attempt to Improve the Knowledge-Based Systems Validation: The VALID Project," internal report, Cognitech, Paris, 1991.

17. D. Prerau, *Developing and Managing Expert Systems*, Addison-Wesley, Reading, MA, 1990.

18. J. Liebowitz and D. A. DeSalvo (eds.), *Structuring Expert Systems: Domain, Design, and Development*, Prentice-Hall/Yourdon Press, Englewood Cliffs, NJ, 1989.

19. D. A. DeSalvo and J. Liebowitz (eds.), *Managing AI and Expert Systems*, Prentice-Hall, Englewood Cliffs, NJ, 1990.

20. Liebowitz (ed.), *Expert Systems for Business and Management*, Prentice-Hall, Englewood Cliffs, NJ, 1990.

21. P. J. Rossomando, "Knowledge Based Systems Verification and Validation: A GE Astro Perspective," Briefing for the NASA Space Station Program, Reston, VA, May 25, 1989.

Chapter 9

Strategies for Successful Expert System Inception, Management, and Institutionalization

9.1 Introduction

The commercialization of expert systems technology has now existed for about a decade[1]. Even though many advances are still to come, a major deterrent in applying the technology now involves management and institutionalization. Often expert systems are wonderfully designed and developed but never used. The barriers to implementation include maintenance strategies, legal and distribution considerations, documentation standards, institutionalization considerations, integration, and other issues. Additionally, Price Waterhouse's Managing Information Technology study[2] discovered, in surveying 4,000 information technology executives, that the greatest barrier to the widespread use of expert systems worldwide is management's unawareness of such systems. All these issues focus on the process of developing and implementing expert systems within an organization[3]. As Randy Shumaker, former director of the Navy Center for Applied Research in Artificial Intelligence at the Naval Research Laboratory, points out[4]:

> Expert systems technology has matured to the point where technical concerns are no longer the driving issue in a successful expert system implementation. While many early efforts focused on advancing technology, leading to improvements in shells and tools for development, more recent work has focused on the process of development. Issues of project selection, use of tools, planning and documentation, integration into the work environment, maintenance and long term support have rarely rated much attention . . ., yet these are now the primary risk factors for expert systems development efforts. (p. vi)

This chapter will address strategies to help managers introduce, manage, and institutionalize expert systems in their organizations.

9.2   Strategies for Introducing Expert Systems into an Organization

There are several methods for building an AI/expert system capability within an organization. Vedder and Turban[5] and Liebowitz and DeSalvo[6,7] summarize the major strategies for introducing expert systems within an organization. These include the following:

- Do it yourself.
- Hire an outside developer.
- Form a joint venture.
- Attack on all fronts.
- Wait (do nothing).

The do-it-yourself strategy can employ several approaches. One approach, used by DuPont, is to use expert system development as a part of end-user computing. Here, the experts or users are trained to use expert systems shells, and they develop their own expert systems for their applications. This is a grass-roots arrangement. Another strategy is to use a centralized group or department that is designated as the AI or advanced technologies group. Boeing and FMC use this approach. The Internal Revenue Service has also used this method in developing their AI Laboratory staff. A decentralized development/centralized control strategy could also be used. Here, AI specialists might be placed in different departments within the organization. These specialists would be the points of contact within their respective groups for developing, implementing, and promoting AI/expert systems technology. Another strategy is to develop an expert systems group whose main function is to train others in expert systems and related technologies. Lockheed has adopted this approach[5].

Hiring an outside developer is another strategy for developing an AI/expert systems capability within the organization. Hiring a consulting firm, vendors, or contractors either to develop the expert system or to train the client organization's staff in expert systems development may be a useful approach for some organizations[5,6].

The third major strategy, the joint venture,[5l] is to align the organization with either a company specializing in expert systems or a university with a strong AI/expert systems capability. DEC has used this approach, developing strong ties with Carnegie Mellon University. American Cimflex used a variation of this strategy by merging with Teknowledge, an expert systems consulting firm, to form American Cimflex-Teknowledge.

The fourth strategy, attacking on all fronts, employs a hybrid of these strategies for building an AI/expert systems capability within the organization. The Air Force Logistic Command (AFLC) is an example of this strategy; an AI unit has been created to disseminate AI training and expertise to all AFLC sites worldwide[5]. This controlled grass-roots effort has led to over 250 expert system projects of all sizes completed or under development worldwide[5].

The last strategy, doing nothing, may also be used. If an organization does not desire to be seen as a technological leader in expert systems, it could wait for a commercial, ready-made version of the expert system[5]. ExperTax and its variants, marketed by Coopers & Lybrand, is an example of this approach, whereby small firms can buy ready-made expert systems from developers[5].

Creating an Awareness of Expert Systems

One of the first steps in building an AI/expert systems capability within a firm is to create an awareness of the technology. The next few paragraphs describe how this awareness was created at Encore Computer Corporation[8].

Encore is a manufacturer of minicomputer systems that acquired Gould Computer Systems. Encore manufactures a variety of computer families for use in real-time simulation, software development, computer architecture research, and a host of other applications. A critical component of Encore's operations is configuration management. *Configuration management* or, more appropriately, *configuration control* refers to configuring the hardware (and software) correctly for a customer's order. Encore wanted to reduce the number of times needed to configure an order correctly. The former vice president of development and the vice president/general manager of manufacturing and customer service wanted to explore the feasibility of developing a Configurator, using expert systems technology for configuring an order and providing a quotation correctly the first time. With such a system, it was thought that the amount of time spent in contracts/configuration control could be reduced, thereby freeing up time for the customer's system to be built and shipped well within the delivery date. Additionally, an automated Configurator could facilitate the creation of forecasting reports, improve customer relations, and provide timely and accurate configuration information to the analysts and sales representatives in the field. It was also felt that an expert system might be a good vehicle for building up the corporate memory of the firm so that valuable knowledge and experiential learning would not be lost.

The next few sections explain how an awareness was created for an expert configuration system at Encore.

The Initial Step   The first step in starting an expert systems project is to create an awareness of the technology. Fortunately, at Encore, the vice president of development and the vice president/general manager of manufacturing and customer service had some familiarity with expert systems, and they thought it would be useful to see how expert systems technology could help improve Encore's operations. They then hired a consultant specializing in expert systems to write a feasibility study on whether and how such systems could be used in configuration management at Encore.

The initial step, creating an awareness of expert systems technology, was thus facilitated because some top executives were backing the study. Unfortunately, the vice president of development left the company about a week after the consultant arrived. This event was not a major hindrance because the other sponsor of the project (i.e., the vice president/general manager of manufacturing and customer service) was a supporter of this feasibility study. However, an awareness and understanding of expert systems still had to be created within the organization at all operating levels.

To do this, it was necessary to use a variety of methods. These included a top-down approach, a bottom-up approach, and an introductory seminar approach.

Top-down Approach   In order to develop the feasibility study, the company's operations had to be understood. This involved speaking with the vice presidents of the various departments (customer service, manufacturing, engineering and development, sales, marketing, information systems, etc.). By enlisting the support of some top management executives, it was easy to gain access to other individuals in the company in order to make them aware of this study and of expert systems. In speaking with individuals throughout Encore, the purpose was to determine their needs if an expert configuration system were built and what practices and policies at Encore would have to change to successfully build and use such a system. The 35 individuals who were interviewed felt comfortable knowing their comments would be incorporated into the feasibility study, which would be sent to all members of top management.

An essential player in these efforts was the proposed expert. It was vital to obtain input and advice from this expert in regard to the need to have such an expert system. Additionally, it was important to gain the expert's support, so that this project would not seem forced upon her. The expert was kept abreast of the work during this effort so that there would be no surprises at the end.

Another innovative idea to create a better awareness of expert systems at the top management level was to give a pad to each top management executive, each page of which was embossed with the saying "Artificial Intelligence/Expert Systems Is for Real at Encore." As top management used these pads to write short notes, they were constantly reminded of expert systems.

Bottom-up Approach In addition to a top-down approach, a bottom-up approach was utilized. This involved working with the actual users of the proposed expert configuration system to obtain their views and requirements. The consultant and a member of the information systems department at Encore took the three-day sales/analysts training course. Most of the analysts and sales representatives at Encore took part in this course. We were able to have a round table discussion with about 16 analysts (the primary users of the expert configuration system) and to speak with several sales representatives (secondary users). The analysts were very interested in the project and offered valuable comments and insights. Additionally, as an outgrowth of our meeting, four analysts from various areas throughout the country were designated to assemble a list of their requirements for an expert configuration system. This information was very helpful in formulating the feasibility study.

Almost everyone in the company was excited about the prospect of having a better way of configuring orders. The consultant and members of the information systems department were particularly careful to make sure that expectations were kept under control.

Introductory Seminar Another method used to create an awareness of this project and of expert systems throughout the company was an introductory seminar on AI/expert systems to key individuals. This one-hour presentation increased the interest of those who attended and familiarized them with expert systems technology and applications. Even though the attendance at this seminar was less than expected, we were able to gain further support for this project.

Before Gaining Full Support, Make Sure You do Your Homework After interviewing many individuals throughout Encore and analyzing the results, the feasibility study was written and sent to all top management executives. The study included the following sections:

EXECUTIVE SUMMARY
1.0 Does a Need Exist for Developing an Aid for Facilitating Encore's Configuration Management Function?
2.0 Can Expert Systems Technology Solve the Configuration Need?
   2.1 Survey of Expert Systems for Configuration Management
   2.2 Can Expert Systems Technology be Used at Encore?
      2.2.1 Expert System Problem Selection Criteria
      2.2.2 Alternatives for Using Expert Systems Technology for Encore's Configuration Management
      2.2.3 The Analytic Hierarchy Process as an Evaluation Methodology
      2.2.4 The Best Alternative Based on the Analytic Hierarchy Process and Expert Choice
      2.2.5 Cost-Benefit Analysis Associated with the Best Alternative
3.0 Building an Expert System Prototype for Configuring a Specific Product Line at Encore

3.1 Next Steps
REFERENCES
APPENDICES

As part of the feasibility study, a thorough survey of existing expert configuration systems worldwide was included. It showed that companies like IBM, Xerox, Honeywell, Philips, Hitachi, and DEC have been successfully using expert systems for configuration management. This demonstrated to Encore officials that expert systems have proved successful for configuration management. A separate summary of the recommendations based upon this feasibility study was also circulated to top management.

Setting the Stage Other groundwork was laid to set the stage. A functional requirements document for an expert configuration system was prepared and sent to top management. This document included the following sections:

1.0 Purpose of Expert System
2.0 Reference Documents
3.0 User Information
4.0 Functional Requirements
        4.1 Database Access
        4.2 User Interface
        4.3 Input/Output Content
        4.4 Control Structure (Inference Engine)
        4.5 Knowledge Representation
        4.6 Hardware
5.0 Documentation
6.0 Training
7.0 Maintenance Requirements

This document showed top management that we had gone one step further by generating requirements for an expert configuration system instead of merely stating that such a system was feasible for Encore. We also lined up a local company with expertise in developing expert configuration systems to develop the proposed system at Encore and provide technology transfer in order to familiarize the information systems staff with expert systems. In addition, we arranged for a major local university to provide education/courses on expert systems on site at Encore for designated individuals. Finally, we enlisted the support of the expert.

Final Approval from Top Management The stage was set, and a meeting was scheduled with top management in order to get the go-ahead on developing the expert system. We quickly learned that timing is a critical element in any business decision. Unfortunately, the meeting was canceled due to emergency budget planning sessions, and it became apparent that it would be difficult to reschedule. Additionally, the project's approval became clouded due to other timing issues, such as a transition in information systems management and a new company-wide hiring freeze. Coupled with these events, Encore was trying to cut back new projects in order to help ensure profitability.

What did these events mean for the expert configuration system project? Principally, the decision to go ahead was delayed until new management felt comfortable about funding new projects.

Epilogue The birth of a new technology at Encore (i.e., expert systems) was a slow process. It took about three months from the first time the phrase "expert systems" was uttered at Encore to top management's complete familiarity with the notion. The best outcome thus far of this project was the creation of an awareness of expert systems throughout the company. Encore has taken this first step in bringing in expert systems technology. The hybrid approaches used to get the project underway were very successful in terms of introducing the systems technology to the company's employees and management. The need to become familiar with the corporate climate and culture was an important lesson learned from this experience. This case study hopefully illuminates some useful techniques that may be used to create an awareness of expert systems within other organizations for eventual funding and support.

9.3 Management Considerations Regarding Expert Systems Development

The previous sections have described strategies for creating an awareness of expert systems within an organization. After stimulating this interest, there are important considerations in securing successful management of an expert systems project. This section will present a checklist of these considerations, gleaned from lessons learned from many managers and knowledge engineers[9–18].

People Issues

- People must be adequately trained to understand the expert system.
- Involvement in the planning process as it relates to their jobs is critical.
- The system's creators must have credibility.
- System developers must be familiar with the potential users of the system and their environment.
- The user is the real customer.
- Involve the user in all aspects of development.
- Pay attention to all users' suggestions, no matter how trivial they might seem.
- User acceptance will make or break your application.
- Insufficient user involvement will ensure failure.
- Involve an accredited person from the inside or outside the organization who favors the technology.
- Obtain commitment from experts, knowledge engineers, and operational groups.

- Use a project leader and staff that have a good track record with the user area.
- Staff project teams with motivated individuals having complementary skills.
- The knowledge engineer should have an a priori understanding of the problem domain.
- Domain experts provided by the customer are valuable assets and are on the critical path for software development.

Management Issues

- Try to use hooking—adding capabilities to your system that management and/or potential users would like to have but are unable to obtain easily by any other means.
- Ensure high-level administrative support to obtain the required resources and accept the risk involved in introducing the technology.
- Present successful systems developed elsewhere and working prototypes that demonstrate the kinds of things expert systems do so that misunderstandings can be avoided.
- Obtain middle management support and clearly identify the benefits of the system.
- Identify champions of the expert system technology within the company and get them involved.
- Training and orientation of middle management are essential for widespread success of expert system implementation in an organization.
- Seek project support from management at least two levels above the point of project application.
- Maintain close coordination with the operational group throughout all phases of the project; the operators should believe that this particular decision aid is their own.

Application Issues

- Use KISS (keep it simple but significant).
- Pick applications that are real; fit in with your organization's future directions and plans; are of manageable size; are doable; have sources of knowledge and experts willing to cooperate; and have measurable benefits.
- Propose problems with acceptable risks and appropriate paybacks; then let the client select the problem the expert system will solve.
- Perform a cost/benefit analysis to measure the impact of the expert system; be sure to include both tangible and intangible benefits.
- Have a methodology for selecting an expert system application.
- Achieve critical mass in an organization, for example, in the utilization of expert systems for end-user development; there must be a plan for the development of critical mass in the organization.
- If the domain expert cannot define the target domain, the first step should be a requirements study.

- High-technology applications should not be limited to AI; other technologies, such as decision analysis, are also powerful decision-aiding tools.

Development Issues

- Use rapid prototyping to develop the expert system;
- As you design the system, keep users' needs in mind.
- Don't forget to prepare system documentation.
- Use shells, if appropriate.
- Use a hardware platform familiar to your users.
- Don't be afraid to ask for help.
- Prepare time and resources estimates, a chart of activities and a critical path calculation, checkpoints, and structured walkthroughs including prototype presentations.
- Maintain a high level of motivation, and convince experts and users that the expert system will not displace them.
- Develop a methodology for evaluating expert system tools/shells.
- Shape the expectations of executive management; expert systems should be viewed not only as a way to cut costs in the short term, but also as a means of capturing and distributing expertise in the long term.
- Successfully implemented innovations are compatible with the currently installed technology base; testable piecemeal; observable as implemented at some other site so that potential users can see the innovation in operation; and simple to understand, install and use;
- Balance the factors of technology, people, and dollars.
- Breaking issues into manageable pieces and communicating the time frames for resolution can prevent roadblocks.
- Use structured methodologies and tools for designing, developing, testing, and evaluating the expert system.
- Knowledge-based software development includes several checkpoints for making go/no-go decisions.
- Knowledge-based software development provides an early proof-of-concept operating model (the prototype).
- The test/evaluation phase of the project will identify the strengths and weaknesses of the expert system; the weaknesses should not be concealed (the search for their solutions can easily lead to follow-on efforts to strengthen the expert system).

9.4 Institutionalization Issues

Much of the success of an expert systems project lies in its follow-through. Just as a golfer's or tennis player's shot is largely dependent on the follow-through of the club or racket, the manager of an expert system project must have follow-through in implementing the system in the organization.

Follow-through, in terms of expert system implementation or institutionalization, means providing the capabilities and services to ensure the expert system's use now and in the future. The project manager should do the following to lead to successful expert system usage:

- Have a maintenance team in place to help transfer the technology and ultimately to maintain/update the expert system.
- Provide training for the users and the maintenance team.
- Incorporate user support services, such as a help desk or information center for answering questions relating to the expert system's use.
- Deliver good documentation/on-line tutorials to the users and the maintenance team.
- Anticipate any legal or distribution problems resulting from the expert system's usage and prepare in advance.
- Keep tabs on the users' comments to make sure that their requests regarding the use and future development of the expert system are satisfied.

Many beautifully designed and accurate expert systems do not move into operational use because of a lack of institutionalization measures[19]. To ensure that the system will be used, carefully incorporate users' comments throughout the expert system's development, and have well-thought-out plans for institutionalizing the expert system within the organization.

9.5 Conclusions

Proper management of an expert systems project is critical for the success of the system. This chapter has presented some guidelines, examples, and helpful hints to aid the manager in the inception, management, and implementation of the expert system project. In the years ahead, as more manufacturing firms adopt AI/expert systems technology, management of the technology will become even more crucial. DEC offers short courses for its employees on managing expert system projects. With awareness of these management issues, successful use of the expert systems will be assured.

References

1. J. Liebowitz, "Strategies for Successful Expert System Inception, Management, and Institutionalization," *ISA Transactions,* Instrument Society of America, North Carolina, 1992.
2. Price Waterhouse, "Survey Results of Managing Information Technology Study," *International Journal on Computer Applications in Technology,* Inderscience Enterprises/UNESCO, Geneva, Switzerland, 1988.
3. D. A. DeSalvo and J. Liebowitz (eds.), *Managing Artificial Intelligence and Expert Systems,* Prentice-Hall, Englewood Cliffs, NJ, 1990.
4. R. Shumaker, "Foreword from the Program Chairman," *Proceedings of the IEEE Conference on Managing Expert System Programs and Projects* (J. Liebowitz, J. Feinstein, and R. Shumaker, eds.), IEEE Computer Society Press, Los Alamitos, CA, 1990.
5. R. G. Vedder and E. Turban, "Strategies for Managing Expert Systems Development," *Proceedings of the IEEE Conference on Managing Expert* System

Programs and Projects (J. Liebowitz, J. Feinstein, and R. Shumaker, eds.), IEEE Computer Society Press, Los Alamitos, CA, 1990.

6. J. Liebowitz and D. A. DeSalvo (eds.), *Structuring Expert Systems: Domain, Design, and Development,* Prentice-Hall, Englewood Cliffs, NJ, 1989.

7. J. Liebowitz, "Expert Configuration Systems: A Survey and Lessons Learned," *Expert Systems with Applications: An International Journal,* Vol. 1, No. 2, 1990.

8. J. Liebowitz, C. Rogan, D. Disch, D. Quara, and D. Edberg, "Creating an Awareness of Expert Systems at Encore Computer Corporation: A Case Study," *Proceedings of the IEEE Conference on Managing Expert System Programs and Projects,* (J. Liebowitz, J. Feinstein, and R. Shumaker, eds.), IEEE Computer Society Press, Los Alamitos, CA, 1990.

9. D. Smith, "Implementing Real World Expert Systems," *AI Expert,* Miller Freeman Publications, San Francisco, CA, December 1988.

10. F. Cantu-Ortiz, "A Strategy for Transferring Expert Systems Technology to Industry," *Proceedings of the IEEE Conference on Managing Expert System Programs and Projects* (J. Liebowitz, J. Feinstein, and R. Shumaker, eds.), IEEE Computer Society Press, Los Alamitos, CA, 1990.

11. R. Crittenden, "Building on Success—Lessons Learned," *Proceedings of the IEEE Conference on Managing Expert System Programs and Projects* (J. Liebowitz, J. Feinstein, and R. Shumaker, eds.), IEEE Computer Society Press, Los Alamitos, CA, 1990.

12. N. M. Goldsmith, "Beyond Technology: Managing Expert System Projects at American Express Company," *Proceedings of the IEEE Conference on Managing Expert System Programs and Projects* (J. Liebowitz, J. Feinstein, and R. Shumaker, eds.), IEEE Computer Society Press, Los Alamitos, CA, 1990.

13. B. Procaccini and G. Lynn, "Expert System Project Management Issues," *Proceedings of the IEEE Conference on Managing Expert System Programs and Projects* (J. Liebowitz, J. Feinstein, and R. Shumaker, eds.), IEEE Computer Society Press, Los Alamitos, CA, 1990.

14. K. H. Gates, "Project Management Techniques for Knowledge Based Systems Development," *Proceedings of the IEEE Conference on Managing Expert System Programs and Projects* (J. Liebowitz, J. Feinstein, and R. Shumaker, eds.), IEEE Computer Society Press, Los Alamitos, CA, 1990.

15. J. Feinstein, "Tutorial notes on Managing Expert System Programs and Projects," IEEE Conference on Managing Expert System Programs and Projects, Bethesda, MD, 1990.

16. R. T. Greene, *Implementing Japanese AI Techniques,* McGraw-Hill, New York, 1990.

17. E. Turban and J. Liebowitz (eds.), *Managing Expert Systems,* Idea Group Publishing, Harrisburg, PA, 1992.

18. K. Wiig, *Expert Systems: A Manager's Guide,* Geneva, International Labor Organization, 1990.

19. J. Liebowitz, *Institutionalizing Expert Systems: A Handbook for Managers,* Prentice-Hall, Englewood Cliffs, NJ, 1991.

Chapter 10

Summary and Analysis of Expert System Technology

As we have seen, expert systems technology is a powerful method for capturing human expertise in computing systems. Many applications are now in use, and a whole profession, knowledge engineering, has developed to incorporate expert systems into computerized systems development[1].

Yet, as with any technology, the expert systems approach has limitations and needs to be used carefully, mindful of the appropriate areas of application. This situation has two aspects. On the one hand, the inappropriate use of expert systems can lead to excessive development times or a failed project if the developer forces the technology to work. On the other hand, a system can be more efficient and effective if all or part of it uses the appropriate technologies for the functions for which they are best suited.

This chapter summarizes the strengths and weaknesses of the expert system approach. With this background, we then look at other technologies to see where they might be appropriate alternatives or supplements to expert systems. Among these complementary technologies is the neural network, which we introduce in this chapter and discuss in the remainder of the book.

10.1 Expert System Strengths

Expert systems perform reasoning, using previously established rules for a well-defined, narrow domain. They combine knowledge bases of rules and domain-specific facts with information from clients or users about specific instances of problems in the knowledge domain of the expert system.

An important advantage of expert systems is the ease with which knowledge bases can be modified as new rules and facts become known. This is a result of the architecture that separates the knowledge base from the inference engine. The result is that changing the knowledge base does not require programming; it can be done via word processing or an editor. This feature makes knowledge engineering accessible to a wider variety of analysts, end users, and experts.

Ideally, reasoning can be explained. Most expert system development systems allow the creation of explanation systems to help the user understand questions being asked or conclusions. Thus, the system can function more like human experts who explain the reasoning processes behind their recommendations. This capability is especially useful for interacting with the client/user to define a specific problem and bring in facts peculiar to the problem being solved.

Expert systems are especially good for closed-system applications for which inputs are literal and precise, leading to logical outputs. For stable applications with well-defined rules, expert systems can be easily developed to provide good performance. Such systems can take advantage of the efficient, systematic techniques developed in expert systems research to perform different types of reasoning. Thus, people are able to inspect and understand these systems because they have familiar structures similar to the logical frameworks humans use.

Another advantage of expert systems is the number and variety of commercial development systems that have become available over the last several years. These tools and associated techniques allow exploratory studies and rapid prototyping for use in knowledge engineering. Prototypes are especially useful in gaining the interest and attention of experts so that the knowledge acquisition process is more productive and amicable.

10.2 Expert System Limitations

A fundamental limitation of the expert system approach arises from the fact that experts do not always think in terms of rules. In these cases, an expert system does not mimic the actual reasoning process of human experts. The computerized system is an attempt to produce a performance that resembles human reasoning in some limited domain. The mechanism, however, may or may not resemble the actual biological or cognitive process. Thus, extensions of any expert system technique may not carry over into behavior that is similar to that of a human. Cognitive science, AI, and expert system research are still needed to produce a fundamental approach that models actual human reasoning.

In the meantime, a variety of approaches have been developed to address deficiencies in current expert system techniques, and many of these approaches show improvement in those limited areas. The major techniques of current interest are surveyed in the next section of this chapter. A comprehensive technique based on a good understanding of human reasoning is still needed.

A specific problem with expert systems is what is referred to as the *knowledge acquisition bottleneck.* That is, while development tools have become very sophisticated and effective, expert systems still require extensive effort for eliciting knowledge from humans as well as from written material. Knowledge acquisition is still primarily a human-intensive activity requiring the usual system analysis abilities plus additional interviewing and interpersonal skills that are tailored to interacting with human experts. Furthermore, human experts may be too busy or otherwise difficult to deal with, so that a whole project may be threatened or delayed. Research and development efforts are focusing on understanding and automating the knowledge acquisition process to the extent possible. However, this activity remains a serious problem for the rapid and pervasive development of large expert systems.

Another difficulty with expert systems is in the area of large systems development. For real-world applications, the development process becomes difficult to manage. Working with experts and dealing with the complexity of large systems leads to prolonged, expensive development and long delivery times. Furthermore, V&V of systems becomes difficult, if not impossible, as many lines of reasoning must be checked.

Other limitations involve fundamental uncertainties about the expert system approach. For example, more work is needed on how to represent common knowledge, which humans deal with so well and so often. Also, expert systems do not automatically benefit from experience with their use and thus do not learn from failures or from their use with novel examples.

While research and development are proceeding to improve expert system technology, some researchers question the underlying philosophy, at least in terms of the deficiencies previously described. The alternate technologies discussed next address many of these concerns and may, while solving certain practical problems, give insight into fundamental research questions that need to be answered before the goals of expert systems are fully realized.

10.3   Alternate and Complementary Technologies

Some technologies that precede the commercialization of expert systems are still useful as alternate approaches or as components of an integrated system. In this section, we present an overview of current technologies that are important to include, along with expert systems, in making design decisions.

Database Systems

Database is a well-established field with commonly available products that can provide two broad areas of support related to expert systems. One is the use of database management systems (DBMS) to store rules and facts efficiently for use in the expert system. Another is integrated expert database systems that combine rules with the query facilities of the DBMS to make an improved system.

Examples of systems that combine intelligent processing of information stored in databases are computer-aided design/manufacturing, military, and telecommunications systems. The expert system component provides flexibility and powerful inferencing, while the DBMS provides superior performance in dealing with large amounts of data.

A DBMS is software for creating applications that need access to shared data by multiple users. The DBMS provides many services to users, including protection of data, consistency of shared data, security, and insulation from the details of physical storage of data. The DBMS provides users with different views and models of the common database.

Expert systems and database systems can interact in a loosely coupled manner in which information is exchanged. For large knowledge bases, the expert system can require a more sophisticated system for storing, manipulating, and retrieving facts and even rules. Intermediate results from an expert system, or from various expert system components of a complex system, may also be stored in the database for subsequent use. In conjunction with databases, expert systems can use selected facts, for example, from tables of engineering or business data. A DBMS may also be useful in the knowledge acquisition process, collecting and manipulating information to be structured into a knowledge base.

Expert system components can also act as an intelligent front end to a database. The expert system can assist the user in formulating queries to the database, thereby making the database more accessible and useful. An intelligent interface can be more forgiving of user errors and inaccuracies in formulating requests for data.

Recent interest has focused on intelligent databases as a more integrated way to combine databases with expert systems. The DBMS is used to combine data from several sources and focus it for analysis with intelligent software. Historically, humans have been essential for analyzing data by filtering, viewing, and interpreting data to find trends or patterns. The DBMS is necessary to make large volumes of data manageable for human processing.

Either the human or the expert system performs several important functions. Interpretation of data involves forming mental models or structuring the problem in order to understand the data. Diagnoses may be needed or causal relationships may need to be established. Focusing and organizing data includes selecting important features and deleting unnecessary information.

Increasingly, ways are being found to substitute intelligent software for human functions. Additional benefits have gone beyond the performance improvements and the opportunity to reduce staff. Intelligent databases have a greater ability to associate related pieces of information and the ability to present data from different perspectives and in different contexts. One application area that is emerging is database mining, in which large volumes of corporate data can be explored, perhaps in the background or overnight, to find interesting features or connections between data that could be pursued in more depth.

Decision Support Systems (DSS)

DSS technology has for many years been an important ingredient in information systems that assist managers and other users in making decisions[2]. This technology deals with tools and techniques that aid decision makers, especially at the middle and top levels of management. The domain of applicability includes dynamic, open systems subject to considerable uncertainty and risk. Problems tend not to be well structured, and exact solutions and data requirements are difficult to anticipate.

Data and DBMS are essential to DSS and to organizations that need to make business and strategic decisions. These decisions are often prompted by unexpected problems or opportunities and may require looking at data in a different form than was originally anticipated. The DSS needs to provide flexible analysis for a broad range of problems and *ad hoc* analyses. This type of task is often a one-time activity that cannot await expensive and time-consuming application development. In practice, a decision maker or, more likely, his or her staff puts together a particular DSS task from a suite of modeling techniques and database and graphics tools. The outcome is information derived from a central database and manipulated at a workstation to focus on information relevant to a needed decision.

Traditional DSS provide immediate access to and flexible analysis of data, including access to a variety of databases and models as required. The components of such systems include DBMS, model base management systems, and facilities for generating dialogue interfaces. Tools must enable decision makers to estimate the consequences of proposed actions and model situations for finding optimal solutions.

The graphical and interactive aspects of DSS are important features. The overall decision system, in effect, is both the computer system and the human decision maker. Human intervention provides judgments during the process to follow certain lines of investigation and reasoning. This is the aspect that expert systems are often intended to replace; however, human interaction will always be needed to some extent, or totally in some cases. The ability to have flexible access and to make ad hoc queries are major features of DSS.

One important DSS tool is fourth-generation languages (4GLs) associated with modern database systems. 4GLs allow people to use computers more easily by requesting information in more everyday language. Rather than having to be a programmer, the user can formulate requirements for a report or another database inquiry in terms of human conversation and the language of the application area. Recent technologies that enhance this aspect are graphical user interfaces (GUI) and natural language interfaces, which eventually will be able to handle spoken input well.

Increasingly, expert system applications have played a role along with traditional DSS in providing tools that are adaptable to the needs of individual managerial decision makers. Current extensions of conventional DSS are group DSS and executive information systems. As a replacement for or supplement to DSS, expert systems provide a more automated approach to aspects of decision making that were previously provided by humans.

Neural Networks

Neural networks rely on training data to program the systems. Thus, neural network components can be useful for hybrid systems by using an appropriate training set that allows the system to learn and generalize for operation on future input data. Inputs exactly like training data are recognized and identified, while new data (or incomplete and noisy versions of the training data) can be matched as closely as possible to patterns learned by the system.

Neural network components can be useful when rules are not known, either because the topic is too complex or because no human expert is available. If training data can be generated, the system may be able to learn enough information to function as well as or better than an expert system. This approach also has the benefit of easy modification to a system by retraining with an updated data set, thus eliminating programming changes and rule reconstruction. The data-driven aspect of neural networks allows system adjustment as a result of changing environments and events. Another advantage of neural network components is the speed of operation after the network is trained, which will be enhanced dramatically as neural chips become readily available.

The two technologies in many ways represent complementary approaches. Neural network components can be the best solutions for some of the problems that have proven difficult for expert system developers, and can allow system developers to address problems not amenable to either approach alone. The integration of these and other intelligent systems components with conventional technologies promises to be an important area for research and development in the 1990s.

The state of the art in neural computing is inspired by our current understanding of biological neural networks; however, after all the research in biology and psychology, important questions remain about how the brain and the mind work. Advances in computer technology allow the construction of interesting and useful artificial neural networks that borrow some features from the biological systems. Information processing with neural computers consists of analyzing patterns of activity, with learned information stored as weights between neurode connections.

A common characteristic is the ability of the system to classify streams of input data without the explicit knowledge of rules and to use arbitrary patterns of weights to represent the memory of categories. Together the network of neurons can store information that can be recalled in order to interpret and classify future inputs to the network. Because knowledge is represented as numeric weights, the rules and the reasoning process in neural networks are not readily explainable.

Neural networks have the potential to provide some of the human characteristics of problem solving that are difficult to simulate using the logical, analytical techniques of expert system and standard software technologies. For example, neural networks can analyze large quantities of data to establish patterns and characteristics in situations where rules are not known and can in many cases make sense of incomplete or noisy data. These capabilities have thus far proven too difficult for the traditional symbolic/logic approach.

The immediate practical implications of neural computing are its emergence as an alternative or supplement to conventional computing systems and AI techniques. As an alternative, neural computing offers the advantage of rapid execution speed once the network has been trained. The ability to learn from cases and train the system with data sets, rather than having to write programs, may be more cost effective and more convenient when changes become necessary. In applications where rules are not known, neural computers may be able to represent rules, in effect, as stored connection weights.

Fuzzy Systems

Fuzzy systems are based on fuzzy set theory and associated techniques pioneered by Lotfi Zadeh[3]. A goal of this approach is to mimic an aspect of human reasoning by doing approximate reasoning. In this way, fuzzy systems are less precise than conventional systems but are more like our everyday experience as human decision makers. We tend to talk in fuzzy terms such as *tall, large,* and *rarely.* These terms are not precise but they are meaningful, and they allow us to describe our world and reason about it.

Fuzzy systems allow users to give input in these imprecise terms and use them to derive fuzzy or precise advice. The internal logic system is designed to deal with fuzzy terms and give useful conclusions, much as humans do. This technique can broaden the usefulness of expert systems, allowing operation in gray areas where precise values may not be know or may not be necessary for drawing conclusions. Fuzzy systems can be developed to use alone or as parts of other software such as an expert system. They can provide a more familiar fuzzy interface to the system or allow the user to make educated guesses[4]. Fuzzy logic uses the concept of membership in a set of values. For example, a confidence factor of 0.95 that someone is poor does not mean that the person's chance of being rich is 5 percent. Rather, the value is an indication of how poor the person is believed to be. In everyday life we might say "very poor," but the quantitative measure is necessary in the logic process to combine that information with other facts to draw a conclusion about a larger question. Fuzzy systems allow reasoning to take place even when certain facts are not completely established. Rules can be executed with different strengths, depending on the certainty of the antecedents.

A number of applications of fuzzy logic have recently appeared in consumer products, especially in Japan. Examples include autofocusing cameras, washing machines, and microwaves. Also, special software packages for developing fuzzy systems are becoming available and should markedly increase the number of such systems in use.

Object-oriented Techniques

Object-oriented techniques have recently become very popular as a general approach to automated problem solving, including the development of expert systems. The relationship with expert systems is very strong because of the connection with the knowledge representation techniques using frames and semantic networks.

The object-oriented approach to programming, and the design of systems in general, is a nonconventional way of modeling situations. The approach is gaining much attention as a useful way to describe data, relationships, and processes that are associated with reasoning.

In using object-oriented techniques, the application area is viewed as a set of objects with associated attributes, including procedures and processes. Interaction between objects is accomplished by sending and receiving messages. The abilities to define objects and pass messages can be added to a programming language or a design tool.

Knowledge can in some cases be viewed successfully as a set of objects with associated behaviors. Objects can represent physical entities or concepts, and properties and behaviors can be associated with the objects. The hierarchical arrangement of these objects influences our understanding of knowledge and the way we reason about the knowledge. Object-oriented systems allow the user to focus on particular properties of a context or problem at hand. For example, a television may be treated in one case as an entertainment center and in another case as an object to be arranged in a room.

Object-oriented techniques provide a programmer or designer additional functions that make their work easier and more effective. As an alternative or addition to an expert system, object-oriented features may provide more human-like aspects. For example, in some reasoning processes, we think of physical or conceptual objects with both general and specific properties. Cars have tires and motors common to the general class of objects we call cars. When we think of specific cars, additional characteristics are involved. The assumed aspects are efficiently handled in object-oriented systems by the mechanism called *inheritance*. This is the ability of the design or development tool to store hierarchical information that can be accessed efficiently when needed. Object-oriented techniques thus foster modular systems that are easier to design and maintain.

Object-oriented systems thus provide a clear way of representing a problem in a framework familiar to humans. The hierarchical design or program translates readily into a physical model that simulates our understanding of situations we experience.

Smalltalk is the name of an object-oriented development environment with a long history[1]. Recently, many more programming languages and environments have become available. These include C++, Object Pascal, and CLOS. Expert system shells are also beginning to include object-oriented features. Examples are Level5 Object, an educational version of which is included with this book.

Case-based Reasoning (CBR)

CBR, a relatively new field, started in the mid-1980s and is based on the idea of using solutions to previous problems for solving new ones. Development systems are now available to help analyze historical information and put it into a form that is useful for subsequent problem solving.

CBR was conceived as a technique that may be similar to an aspect of human reasoning—namely, the tendency to refer to past experiences for guidance in solving current problems. A CBR tool assists the developer in storing solutions to previous problems and determining the differences from new problems. This process involves finding many relevant cases, finding the best matches to the current problem, and analyzing the input characteristics. The differences compared to the problem at hand are then used to modify the old solutions.

A technique from AI that is used in CBR is *scripts,* which is a way of describing a sequence of events in a particular case. An example of the use of scripts is the analysis a trip to a restaurant. The experience can be divided into a sequence of events, each of which is separately described in more detail—for example, enter the restaurant, order the meal, eat the meal, and pay. If we know what script to apply in a new situation, we do little hard reasoning but instead just follow the script. The main reasoning involves choosing the best script.

Applied to CBR, we try to describe reasoning from experience. For example, we may want to describe the series of steps we used to lead to decisions in similar situations. In those cases, CBR can be better than an expert system because the availability of the previous experience avoids the effort required for a more general solution when it is not necessary.

CBR can be used by itself or as part of another intelligent or conventional system. CBR is especially indicated when rules for the knowledge domain are difficult to discern and/or the number and complexity of rules are too large for the normal knowledge acquisition process. Some domains have particularly rich histories of precedents. Examples are legal applications and medical and other diagnostic systems.

In the area of knowledge acquisition, CBR can be used to automate the analysis of cases and to store the information as a script. In this regard, many CBR tools have become available, such as ReMind from Cognitive Systems, CBR Express from Inference Corporation, and Esteem from Esteem Software Inc. With CBR, past failures as well as successes can be used, and once the script is chosen, processing can be fast.

Genetic Algorithms (GA)

GA systems represent intelligent systems by mimicking biological systems that self-organize and adapt to their environments[5]. Modeling after concepts of biological evolution, GA systems use feedback from interaction with the environment. Weak or negative feedback causes certain possible solutions to a problem to be dropped from consideration, while other feedback causes better candidate solutions to survive.

GA can also be considered a search technique that is an alternative to those in traditional AI. GA can find a local optimum solution that is adequate, thereby avoiding an exhaustive search. This technique is good for complex situations in which the search space would be prohibitively large for AI techniques.

Problems to be solved with GA need to be posed in a way that allows solutions to be described as a string of numbers or characters. Each symbol can represent more complex operations. For example, the string ADHBEC could represent the order in which a solution to a problem could be implemented. This string is called a *chromosome*. This particular solution has certain properties or consequences that give it a relative worth as a solution to a particular problem. An evaluator function produces a numerical value that represents the chromosome's ability to solve the problem. The GA approach uses genetic operators described generally as follows:

Reproduction	Produce a new generation of potential solutions and select two of them to be the parents of other possible solutions, for example, ADHBEC and CDHAFE.
Crossover	Choose segments of the parent solutions to exchange for the purpose of creating new potential solutions, for example, ADHBEC + CDHAFE --> CDHBEC and ADHAFE.
Mutation	Occasional arbitrary changes in candidate solutions may be necessary if the algorithm becomes stuck and does not proceed toward a useful solution.

A generator function uses the crossover and mutation operators to randomly reconfigure parents into new candidate solutions. The result of the evaluator function is used to weed out solutions below a threshold and create a new pool of candidate solutions.

GA has potential to solve scheduling and other resource allocation problems. Rather than using the systematic AI approach, GA can jump around, searching for possible solutions, and find one that is good enough for the situation at hand. In the case of scheduling, the chromosome consists of tasks that could be scheduled. A particular order of tasks will have certain consequences in terms of the total time needed to complete the job and other resource considerations. These factors are used by the evaluator function to give an overall rating of each solution.

Example: Scheduling Scheduling problems are computationally difficult and can involve exhaustive searches through many possible solutions. The GA approach gives the user the advantage of hopping around to test different potential solutions without getting trapped in dead-end searches[5].

In the case of scheduling applications, a chromosome can represent a sequential ordering of tasks to be done. Various resources (people, materials, machines, and money) are associated with the tasks and therefore represent varying costs for each possible sequence or schedule. Each task that is a part of the schedule has associated data such as the name of the task, priority, time required, and resources used. For example, one of the tasks for a construction project could be "prepare cement," which requires 1 hour and three resources (people, truck, and a cement machine).

With GA for scheduling, a creator operator first produces an initial pool of chromosomes (schedules), restricted to permissible patterns allowed by the particular application being addressed. An evaluator operator then rates the ability of each chromosome to solve the scheduling problem and produces information (such as the time needed to complete the schedule) to determine which chromosomes should be used in the rest of the procedure. A generator then uses mutate and crossover operators to reconfigure the solutions for repeating the evaluation step. These steps are repeated until an acceptable schedule is found. For further reading, see [5].

GA is an interesting technique that is receiving considerable attention in research and development laboratories. Two advantages of GA over expert systems is the ability to learn from experience and to use information to identify inferior and preferred solutions.

10.4 Summary

In this chapter, we have reviewed the advantages and disadvantages of using expert system technology. The appropriate use of expert systems leads to useful systems with improved performance or other characteristics that cannot be achieved through other methods. The developer should not be tempted, though, to use expert systems when another technology would be better, either as an alternative or as a supplement in an integrated system.

A theme characterizing these alternatives is the attempt to make up for deficiencies in the expert system approach. In some cases, the goal is more efficient and more effective intelligent systems. Another theme is the need to provide additional features associated with human intelligence, such as learning and the ability to generalize from current knowledge.

Although intelligent systems of the future will integrate many if not all of the technologies described in this chapter, neural networks are currently receiving the most attention and appear to be the most promising in terms of commercial applications. The focus of the remainder of this book is also appropriate because of the natural synergy and complementary nature of neural network and expert system approaches.

References

1. Efraim Turban, *Expert Systems and Applied Artificial Intelligence*, Macmillan, New York, 1992.
2. D. L. Olson and J. F. Courtney, Jr., *Decision Support Models and Expert Systems*, Macmillan, New York, 1992.
3. L. Zadeh, "Fuzzy Logic," *Computer*, Vol. 21 (April 1988).
4. B. Kosko, *Neural Networks and Fuzzy Systems*, Prentice-Hall, Englewood Cliffs, NJ, 1992.
5. George Lawton, "Genetic Algorithms for Schedule Optimization," *AI Expert*, Vol. 7 (May 1992).

Chapter 11

Introduction to Neural Networks

A different approach to intelligent systems is to construct computers with architectures and processing capabilities that mimic those of the human brain. This requires different knowledge representations based on massive parallel processing, fast retrieval of large amounts of information, and the ability to recognize patterns based on experience. Research into these brain-style computers is currently focused on *artificial neural networks (ANNs),* which are collections of simple, highly connected processing elements that respond (or "learn") according to sets of inputs. Most of the applications today use software simulations; however, specialized hardware implementations are starting to appear.

After falling into disfavor in the 1970s, the field of neural networks experienced a dramatic resurgence in the 1980s. The renewed interest was due to the need for brain-like information processing, advances in computer technology, and progress in neuroscience in better understanding the mechanisms of the brain. Declared the "decade of the brain" by the U.S. government, the 1990s seem to be extremely promising in making progress toward understanding the brain and the mind. Neural computing should have an important role in this research area.

In some cases, neural computing systems are taking the place of expert systems and other AI solutions. In other applications, neural networks provide features not possible with conventional AI systems, and they may be able to provide aspects of intelligent behavior that have thus far eluded the AI symbolic/logical approach.

This chapter surveys the fundamentals of neurocomputing and the biological foundations of ANN. Note that ANNs are not nearly as complex as biological neural networks, nor do they necessarily closely mimic the way real neural networks operate. Nevertheless, ANNs are proving to be useful computing methods and have some properties analogous to biological systems. A discussion of the structures and learning mechanisms of ANNs are included in this chapter.

11.1   Biological Basis

Biological Neural Networks

The brain is composed of over 100 different kinds of special cells called *neurons*. The number of neurons in the brain is estimated to range from 50 billion to over 100 billion. Neurons are divided into interconnected groups called *networks* and provide specialized functions. Each group contains several thousand neurons that are highly interconnected with each other. Thus, the brain can be viewed as a collection of neural networks. A portion of a network composed of two cells is shown in Figure 11.1.

Thinking and intelligent behavior are believed to be controlled by the brain and the rest of the central nervous system. The ability to learn from and react to changes in our environment requires intelligence. An example is the optical path in visual systems. External stimuli are transformed via cone cells and rod cells into signals that map features of the visual image into internal memory. Human intelligence is then used to understand the various visual features that are extracted and stored in memory.

An *artificial* neural network (ANN) is a *model* that emulates a biological neural network. The nodes in an ANN are based on the simplistic mathematical representation of what we think real neurons look like. Today's neural computing uses a limited set of concepts from biological neural systems to implement software simulations of massively parallel processes involving processing elements (also called *artificial neurons* or *neurodes*) interconnected in a network architecture. The neurode is analogous to the biological neuron, receiving inputs that represent the electrical impulses that the dendrites of biological neurons receive from other neurons. The output of the neurode corresponds to a signal sent out from a biological neuron over its axon. The axon of the biological neuron branches to the dendrites of other neurons, and the impulses are transmitted over synapses. A synapse is able to increase or decrease its strength, thus affecting the

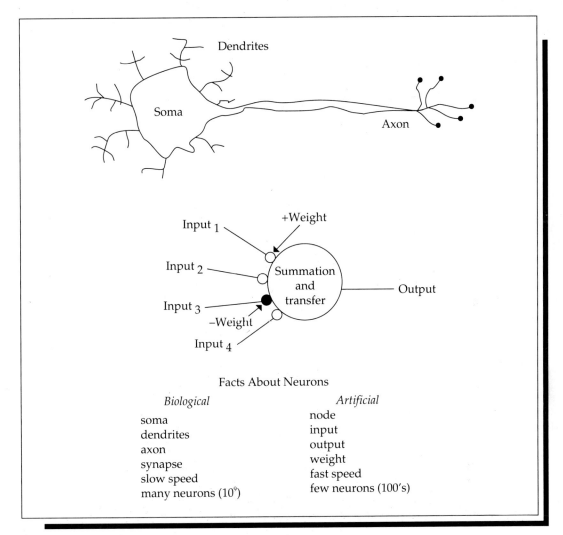

Facts About Neurons

Biological	*Artificial*
soma	node
dendrites	input
axon	output
synapse	weight
slow speed	fast speed
many neurons (10^9)	few neurons (100's)

FIGURE 11.1   A biological neuron versus an artificial neuron.

level of signal propagation, and is said to cause *excitation* or *inhibition* of a subsequent neuron.

Artificial Neural Networks

The state of the art in neural computing is inspired by our current understanding of biological neural networks. However, despite the extensive research in neurobiology and psychology, important questions remain about how the brain and the mind work. This is just one reason why neural computing models are not very close to our current understanding of biological systems.

Research and development in the area of ANN is producing interesting and useful systems that borrow some features from the biological systems, even though we are far from having an artificial brain-like machine. The field of neural computing is in its infancy, with much research and development required in order to mimic the brain and mind. However, many useful techniques inspired by the biological systems have already been developed and are finding use in real-world applications.

11.2   History of Neurocomputing

The history of ANN can be broken into an early period and decline in interest and then the recent period of intense research and development that has given rise to the neurocomputing field. In 1949, Donald Hebb[l] wrote about early theories of neural learning that were soon applied to parallel distributed processing (PDP) networks. In the late 1950s, Frank Rosenblatt[2] developed the perceptron model; however, Minsky and Pappert[3] in the late 1960s showed that the single-layer perceptron is useless for a large class of problems. Recently, obstacles have been reduced by adding hidden layers and using learning algorithms such as back error propagation (back propagation). However, right after the publication of Minsky's work, research interest and funding dropped off and the neural network field essentially lay dormant, while the field of AI flourished.

A few neural network researchers continued their work, however, and by the early 1980s the technological environment was ripe for a resurgence of interest. Hardware advances allowed fast processing, theoretical advances had been made in algorithms and computing techniques, and the prospects for parallel processing systems were good. Scientists and engineers such as Hopfield[4], Grossberg[5], Widrow[6], and Kohonen[7,8] discovered interesting ANN architectures and applications that demonstrated the potential of ANN technology. In the 1980s, rapid changes in research and development and the increasing appearance of applications led to the creation of neural network organizations, conferences, and journals. More recently, neural network development systems and tools have become commercially available. As with expert systems, the availability of a convenient development method is allowing the spread of neurocomputing and is putting neurocomputing on the road to becoming part of the standard repertoire of systems developers.

11.3   Neurocomputing Fundamentals

The key concepts needed to understand artificial neural networks will now be discussed.

Neurode

An ANN is composed of basic units called *artificial neurons,* or *neurode*s, that are the processing elements (PEs) in a network. Each neurode receives input data,

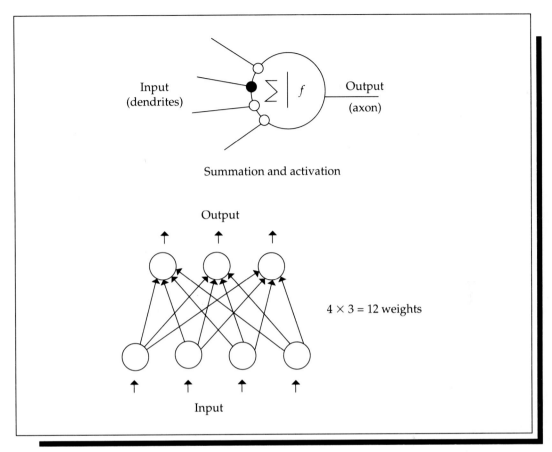

FIGURE 11.2 Models of the artificial neurode and network.

processes it, and delivers a single output. This process is shown in Figure 11.2. The input can be raw data or output of other PEs. The output can be the final product or it can be an input to another neurode.

Network

An ANN is composed of a collection of interconnected neurons that are often grouped in layers; however, in general, no specific architecture should be assumed. The various possible neural network topologies are the subject of research and development. In terms of layered architectures, two basic structures are shown in Figure 11.3. In part (a) we see two layers: input and output. In part (b) we see three layers: input, intermediate (called *hidden*), and output. An input layer receives data from the outside world and sends signals to subsequent layers. The outside layer interprets signals from the previous layer to produce a result that is transmitted to the outside world as the network's understanding of the input data.

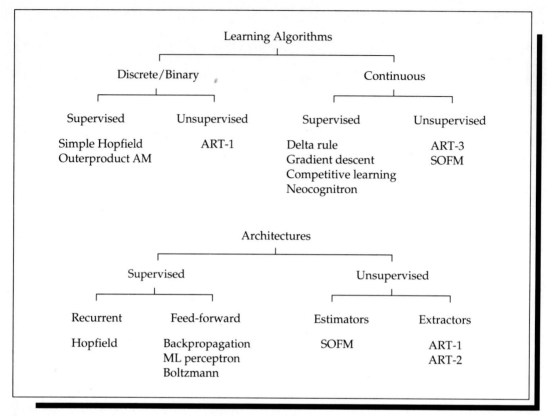

FIGURE 11.3   Taxonomy of ANN architectures and learning algorithms.

Input

Each input corresponds to a single attribute of a pattern or other data in the external world. The network can be designed to accept sets of input values that are either binary-valued or continuously valued. For example, if the problem is to decide whether or not to approve a loan, an attribute can be income level, age, and so on. Note that in neurocomputing, we can only process numbers. Therefore, if a problem involves qualitative attributes or graphics, the information must be preprocessed to a numerical equivalent before it can be interpreted by the ANN.

Examples of inputs to neural networks are pixel values of characters and other graphics, digitized images and voice patterns, digitized signals from monitoring equipment, and coded data from loan applications. In all cases, an important initial step is to design a suitable coding system so that the data can be presented to the neural network, commonly as sets of 1s and 0s. For example, a 6 × 8-pixel character would be a 48-bit vector input to the network.

Output

The output of the network is the solution to the problem. For example, in the loan application case it may be yes or no. The ANN, again, will assign numerical values (e.g., + 1 means yes; zero means no). The purpose of the network is to compute the value of the output. In the supervised type of ANN, the initial output of the network is usually incorrect and the network must be adjusted or tuned until it gives the proper output.

Hidden Layers

In multilayered architectures, the inner (hidden) layers do not directly interact with the outside world, but rather add a degree of complexity to allow the ANN to operate on more interesting problems. The hidden layer adds an internal representation of the problem that gives the network the ability to deal robustly with inherently nonlinear and complex problems.

Weights

The weights in an ANN express the *relative strengths* (or mathematical values) of the various connections that transfer data from layer to layer. In other words, the weights express the *relative importance* of each input to a PE. Weights are crucial to ANN because they are the means by which we repeatedly adjust the network to produce desired outputs and thereby allow the network to learn. The objective in training a neural network is to find a set of weights that will correctly interpret all the sets of input values that are of interest for a particular problem. Such a set of weights is possible if the number of neurodes, the architecture, and the corresponding number of weights form a sufficiently complex system to provide just enough parameters to adjust (or "tune") to produce all the desired outputs.

Summation Function

The summation function finds the weighted average of all the input elements. A simple summation function will multiply each input value (X_j) by its weight (W_{ij}) and total them for a weighted sum, S_i. The formula for N input elements is

$$S_i = \sum_{j=i}^{N} W_{ij} * X_j$$

The neurodes in a neural network thus have very simple processing requirements. Mainly, they need to monitor the incoming signals from other neurodes, compute the weighted sums, and determine a corresponding signal to send to other neurodes.

Transformation Function

The summation function computes the internal stimulation or activation level of the neuron. Based on this level, the neuron may or may not produce an output. The relationship between the internal activation levels may be either linear or nonlinear. Such relationships are expressed by a *transformation function*. The sigmoid function, which is commonly and effectively used, is discussed here. The selection of the specific function, as well as of the transformation function, is one of the variables considered in choosing a network architecture and learning paradigm. Although many different functions are possible, a very useful and popular nonlinear transfer function is the *sigmoid* (or logical activation) function. Its formula is

$$Y_T = \frac{1}{1 + e^{-s}}$$ where S is the weighted sum of the inputs to the neurode.

The collective action of a neural network is like that of a committee or other group making a decision. Individuals interact and affect each other in the process of arriving at a group decision. The global average or consensus of the group is more significant than an individual opinion and can remain the same even if some individuals drop out. Also, a group can have different mechanisms for arriving at the collective decision.

Learning

The sets of weight values for a given neural network represent different states of its memory or understanding of the possible inputs. In supervised networks, training involves adjustment of the weights to produce the correct outputs. Thus, the network learns how to respond to patterns of data presented to it. In other types of ANN, the networks self-organize and learn categories of input data (Figure 11.3)

An important function of the artificial neuron is the evaluation of its inputs and the production of an output response. A weighted sum of the inputs from the simulated dendrites is evaluated to determine the level of the output on the simulated axon. Most artificial systems use threshold values, and a common activation function is the sigmoid function, f, that can squash the total input summation to a bounded output value, as shown in Figure 11.2.

This model of the neuron, or basic perceptron, requires a learning algorithm for deriving the weights that correctly represent the knowledge to be stored. A fundamental concept in that regard is Hebbian learning, based on Donald Hebb's work[1] in 1949 on biological systems, which postulates that active connections should be reinforced. This means that the strengths (weights) of the interconnections increase if the prior node repeatedly stimulates the subsequent node to generate an output signal. In some algorithms, the weights of connections may also be decreased if they are not involved in stimulating a node, and negative weights can also be used to represent inhibiting actions.

For more complex neural computing applications, neurodes are combined together in various architectures useful for information processing (Figure 11.4).

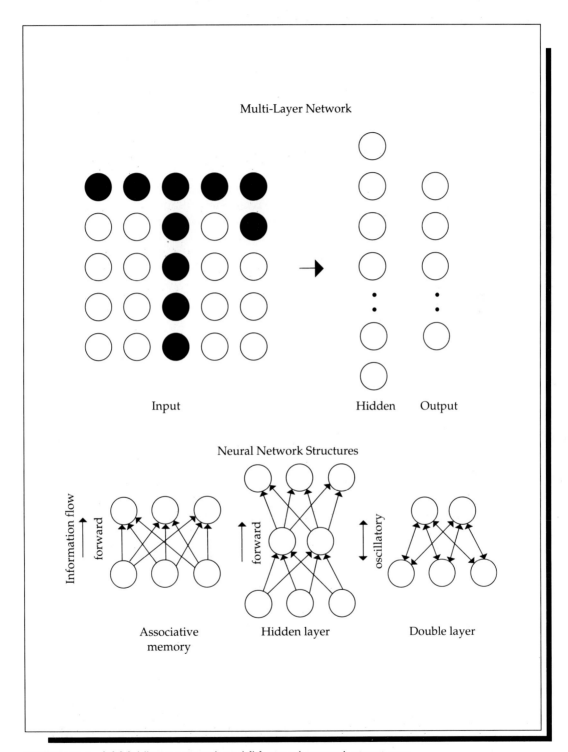

FIGURE 11.4   (a) Multilayer network and (b) neural network structures.

A common arrangement has layers of neurodes with forward connections to every neurode except those in the same or the prior layer. Useful applications require multiple (hidden) layers between the input and output neurodes and a correspondingly large number of connections.

Information processing with neural computers consists of analyzing patterns of data, with learned information stored as neurode connection weights. A common characteristic is the ability of the system to classify streams of input data without the explicit knowledge of rules and to use arbitrary patterns of weights to represent the memory of categories. During the learning stages, the interconnection weights change in response to training data presented to the system. In contrast, during recall, the weights are fixed at the trained values.

Although most applications use software simulations, neural computing will eventually use parallel networks of simple processors that use the strengths of the interconnections to represent memory. Each processor will compute node outputs from the weights and input signals from other processors. Together the network of neurons can store information that can be recalled to interpret and classify future inputs to the network.

11.4 Neural Network Architectures

Many different neural network models and implementations are being developed and studied. Three representative architectures (with appropriate learning paradigms) are shown in Figure 11.4 and are discussed next.

1. *Associative memory systems.* These systems correlate input data with information stored in memory. Information can be recalled from incomplete or noisy input, and the performance degrades slowly as neurons fail. Associative memory systems can detect similarities between new input and stored patterns. Most neural network architectures can be used as associative memories; and a prime example is the Hopfield network[12].

2. *Multiple-layer systems.* Associative memory systems can have one or more intermediate (hidden) layers. An example of a simple network is shown in Figure 11.4. The most common learning algorithm for this architecture is back propagation, which is a kind of credit-blame approach to correcting and reinforcing the network as it adjusts to the training data presented to it. Another type of supervised learning, competitive filter associative memory, can learn by changing its weights in recognition of categories of input data without being provided examples by an external trainer. A leading example of such a self-organizing system for a fixed number of classes in the inputs is the Kohonen network[7,8].

3. *Double-layer structures.* A double layer structure, exemplified by the adaptive resonance theory (ART) approach[5], does not require the knowledge of a precise number of classes in the training data but uses feed-forward and feedback to adjust parameters as data is analyzed to establish arbitrary numbers of categories that represent the data presented to the system.

Parameters can be adjusted to tune the sensitivity of the system and produce meaningful categories.

11.5 Learning Paradigms

An important consideration in ANN is the appropriate use of algorithms for learning. ANN's have been designed for different type of learning:

- Heteroassociation—mapping one set of data to another. This produces output that generally is different in form from the input pattern. It is used, for example, in stock market prediction applications.
- Autoassociation—storing patterns for error tolerance. It reproduces an output pattern similar to or exactly the same as the input pattern. It is used in optical character recognition systems.
- Regularity detection—looking for useful features in data (feature extraction). It is used in sonar signal identification systems.
- Reinforcement learning—acting on feedback. This is a supervised form of learning in which the teacher is more of a critic than an instructor. It is used in controllers in ultrasonic spaceplanes.

Two basic approaches to learning in an ANN exist: supervised and unsupervised. These approaches will now be discussed.

Supervised Learning

In the supervised learning approach, we use a set of inputs for which the appropriate outputs are known. In one type, the difference between the desired and actual outputs is used to calculate corrections to the weights of the neural network (learning with a teacher). A variation on that approach simply acknowledges for each input trial whether or not the output is correct as the network adjusts weights in an attempt to achieve correct results (reinforcement learning).

Unsupervised Learning

In unsupervised learning, the neural network self-organizes to produce categories into which a series of inputs fall. No knowledge is supplied about what classifications are correct, and those that the network derives may or may not be meaningful to the person using the network. However, the number of categories into which the network classifies the inputs can be controlled by varying certain parameters in the model. In any case, a human must examine the final categories to assign meaning and determine the usefulness of the results. Examples of this type of learning are the ART and the Kohonen self-organizing feature maps.

Perceptron Learning

As a simple example of learning, consider that a single neuron learns the inclusive OR operation. The neuron must be trained to recognize the input patterns and classify them to give the corresponding outputs. The procedure is to present to the neuron the sequence of input patterns and adjust the weights after each one. This step is repeated until the weights converge to one set of values that allow the neuron to classify correctly each of the four inputs. The results shown in the following example were produced using Excel spreadsheet calculations.

In this simple case of perceptron learning, the following example uses a step function to evaluate the summation of input values. After outputs are calculated, a measure of the error between the output and the desired values is used to update the weights, subsequently reinforcing correct results. At any step in the process,

$$delta = Z - Y$$

where Z and Y are the desired and actual outputs, respectively. Then the updated weights are $w_i = w_i + alpha * delta * x_i$, where alpha is a parameter that controls how rapidly the learning takes place.

As shown in Table 11.1, each calculation uses one of the x_1 and x_2 pairs and the corresponding value for the OR operation, along with initial values, w_1 and w_2, of the neurode weights. In this example, the weights are assigned random values at the beginning and a learning rate, alpha, is set to be relatively low. The value Y is the result of calculation using the equation just described, and delta is the difference between Y and the desired result, Z. Delta is used to derive the final weights, which then become the initial weights in the next row.

The initial values of weights for each input are transformed, using the previous equation, to values that are used with the next input. The threshold value causes the Y value to be 1 if the weighted sum of inputs is greater than 0.5; otherwise, the output is set to 0. In this example, after the first step, two of the four outputs are incorrect and no consistent set of weights has been found. In the subsequent steps, the learning algorithm produces a set of weights that can give the correct results. Once determined, a neuron with those weight values can quickly perform the OR operation.

Back Propagation

Although many supervised learning examples exist, other important cases, such as the exclusive OR, cannot be handled with a simple neural network. Patterns must be linearly separable—that is, in the x–y plot of pattern space, it must be possible to draw a straight line that divides the clusters of input-output points that belong to the desired categories. In the previous example, the input-output pairs (0,1), (1,0), and (1,1) are linearly separable from (0,0). Although the requirement of a linearly separable input pattern space caused initial disillusionment with neural networks, recent models such as back propagation in multilayer networks have greatly broadened the range of problems that can be addressed.

Back propagation[9], a popular technique that is relatively easy to implement, requires training data to provide the network with experience before using it for processing other data. Externally provided correct patterns are compared with

TABLE 11.1 Example of Supervised Learning

Alpha = 0.2
Threshold = 0.5

ITERATION	INPUT X_1	X_2	DESIRED OUTPUT Z	W_1	INITIAL W_2	ACTUAL OUTPUT Y	DELTA	FINAL W_1	W_2
1	0	0	0	0.1	0.3	0	0.0	0.1	0.3
	0	1	1	0.1	0.3	0	1.0	0.1	0.5
	1	0	1	0.1	0.5	0	1.0	0.3	0.5
	1	1	1	0.3	0.5	1	0.0	0.3	0.5
2	0	0	0	0.3	0.5	0	0.0	0.3	0.5
	0	1	1	0.3	0.5	0	1.0	0.3	0.7
	1	0	1	0.3	0.7	0	1.0	0.5	0.7
	1	1	1	0.5	0.7	1	0.0	0.5	0.7
3	0	0	0	0.5	0.7	0	0.0	0.5	0.7
	0	1	1	0.5	0.7	1	0.0	0.5	0.7
	1	0	1	0.5	0.7	0	1.0	0.7	0.7
	1	1	1	0.7	0.7	1	0.0	0.7	0.7
4	0	0	0	0.7	0.7	0	0.0	0.7	0.7
	0	1	1	0.7	0.7	1	0.0	0.7	0.7
	1	0	1	0.7	0.7	1	0.0	0.7	0.7
	1	1	1	0.7	0.7	1	0.0	0.7	0.7

the neural network output during training, and feedback is used to adjust the weights until all training patterns are correctly categorized by the network. In some cases, a disadvantage of this approach is prohibitively large training times.

For any output neuron, j, the error delta $= (Z_j - Y_j) * f'$, where Z and Y are the desired and actual outputs, respectively, and f' is the slope of a sigmoid function evaluated at the jth neuron. If f is chosen to be the logistic function, then $f' = df/dx = f(1 - f)$, where $f(x) = [1 + \exp(-x)]^{-1}$ and x is proportional to the sum of the weighted inputs of the jth neuron. A more complicated expression can be derived to work backward from the output neurons through the inner layers to calculate the corrections to their associated weights.

The procedure for executing the learning algorithm is as follows: Initialize weights and other parameters to random values, read in the input vector and desired output, calculate actual output via the calculations forward through the layers, and change the weights by calculating errors backward from the output layer through the hidden layers. This procedure is repeated for all the input vectors until the desired and actual outputs agree within some predetermined tolerance.

11.6   Advantages and Limitations of Neural Networks

Although ANNs offer exciting possibilities[10,11,12], they also have certain limitations. Traditional AI approaches have in their favor the more transparent mechanisms, often expressed in terms such as logic operations and rule-based representations, that are meaningful to us in our everyday lives. By comparison, ANNs do not use structured knowledge with symbols used by humans to express reasoning processes. Furthermore, ANNs have so far been used for classification problems and, although quite effective in that task, need to be expanded to other types of intelligent activites.

An ANN's weights, even though quite effective, are just a set of numbers that in most cases have no obvious meaning to humans. Thus, an ANN is a black box solution to problems, and an explanation system cannot be constructed to justify a given result. As noted before, another limitation can be excessive training times, for example, in ANNs using back propagation[13,14].

Neurocomputing is a relatively new field, and continued research and development will surely minimize the limitations and find the further strengths of this approach[15]. The fault tolerance aspects of ANNs will be improved, allowing them to be effective as indivdual neurodes fail or have incorrect input. The exciting prospects of self-organizing networks will be exploited to produce systems that learn on their own how to categorize input data. Future systems will improve in the areas of generalization and abstraction, with the ability to go beyond the training data to interpret patterns not explicitly seen before. Finally, the collaboration between scientists in neurocomputing and neurobiology should lead to advances in each field as computers mimic what we understand about human thinking and as neuroscientists learn from computer simulations of the theories of human cognition.

References

1. D. O. Hebb, *The Organization of Behavior,* New York: Wiley, 1949.
2. F. Rosenblatt, *Principles of Neurodynamics,* New York: Spartan, 1962.
3. M. Minsky and S. A. Papert, *Perceptrons,* MIT Press, Cambridge, MA, 1969.
4. J. Hopfield, "Neural Networks and Physical Systems with Emergent Collective Computational Abilities," *Proceedings of the National Academy of Sciences of the United States of America,* Vol. 79 (1985).
5. G. Carpenter and S. Grossberg, "A Massively Parallel Architecture for a Self-organizing Neural Pattern Recognition Machine," *Computer Vision, Graphics and Image Processing,* Vol. 37 (1987), pp 54–115.
6. B. Widrow, "Generalization and Information Storage in Networks of Adaline 'Neurons,'" *Self-Organizing Systems,* ed. M. C. Yovitz, G. T. Jacobi, and G. Goldstein, Washington, DC: Spartan, 1962.
7. T. Kohonen, *Self Organization and Associative Memory,* Berlin: Springer-Verlag, 1984.
8. T. Kohonen, "An Introduction to Neural Computing," *Neural Networks,* Vol. 1, No. 1 (1988).

9. P. Werbos, "Back-Propagation and Neuro-Control: A Review and Prospectus," *Proceedings, Joint Conference on Neural Networks*, Washington, DC, June 1989.

10. W. Allman, *Apprentices of Wonder*, New York: Bantam Books, 1989.

11. R. Beale and T. Jackson, *Neural Computing*, Bristol, England: Adam Hilger, 1990.

12. P. Wasserman, *Neural Computing: Theory and Practice*, New York: Van Nostrand Reinhold, 1989.

13. M. Caudill, "Using Neural Nets: Hybrid Expert Networks," *AI Expert*, Vol. 5, No. 11 (November 1990).

14. M. Caudill, "Using Neural Nets (Six Parts)," *AI Expert* (December 1989, April 1990, June 1990, July 1990, September 1990, December 1990).

15. M. Caudill and C. Butler, *Naturally Intelligent Systems*, Cambridge, MA: MIT Press, 1990.

Chapter 12

Applications of Neural Networks

In several application areas, neural networks can be effective substitutes for traditional AI systems. In other cases, neural network and AI system components can work synergistically. This chapter presents a brief survey of current neural network application areas that have traditionally been addressed mainly with AI techniques. Further details and more examples can be found in the references[1–8].

12.1 Overview of Application Areas

Recent developments in theory and practice are creating great interest in ANN technology as a component of hybrid systems for effective real-world problem solving. Existing systems involving neural networks have large segments of conventional software, and the combination with AI components is a natural step. Certain types of symbolic as well as traditional numerical processing are still best done by traditional software systems; however, the natural synergism of the two technologies suggests a promising approach to solving real-world problems that involve information processing and decision making.

In neurocomputing, appropriate applications would generally be ones in which a nonprogrammed solution is desirable or is the only possible solution. This can occur when the application is so complex that closed mathematical expressions or manageable algorithms are not known. Just as computer simulations are more desirable in other types of quantitative problem solving, neural networks may be able to analyze and solve complex problems that would be difficult or impossible to solve conveniently with traditional techniques.

One natural area for neural network applications is pattern recognition. The applications areas traditionally addressed with AI or other techniques include vision systems and speech understanding and synthesis. In these cases, digitized speech and visual signals are analyzed by neural networks, first to identify and learn training patterns. Subsequently, the trained neural network system can routinely interpret patterns. A natural application area for neural computing is problems in which the system needs to learn classifications. In these cases, the neural network is best used for rapid processing of large volumes of data to place items in categories.

In all these types of applications, a general advantage of the neural network is its ability to work with incomplete or noisy data. Also, the neural network may sometimes be able to operate on data beyond that for which it was explicitly trained. In those cases the network is able to interpolate to find the closest matches with the learned patterns, thus extending the range of useful input data that can be interpreted.

The following existing or in-progress projects are examples of the uses of neural computing. They are organized by (1) physical or geometric feature classification, (2) classification of patterns in data, and (3) optimization problems.

1. One area involves applications that pick out previously learned features in data and systems that learn new features in data not previously seen by the system.

- Data transmission—fast matching of patterns of data used in compression techniques for transmission of voice, image, and text.
- Motion detection for military applications—aircraft identification, terrain analysis, recognition of underwater targets from sonar signals.
- Bomb detection—neural networks trained to recognize the shapes of bombs in displays from spectrograph signals that indicate high nitrogen compound content in luggage.
- Speech generation—system that learns phonemes in order to pronounce English text.
- Voice recognition systems—voice-activated control of devices and voice typewriters.

- Robot learning—hand-eye coordination, through training, for grasping objects; possible use with space station assembly systems.
- Automation of operations in hazardous environments such as earth observatories, power plants, and undersea vehicles.
- Character recognition, both typewritten and handwritten, even if distorted; verification of signatures on checks; recognition of zip codes.
- Diagnosis of defective equipment—analysis, based on training cases, of monitor data to identify malfunctions in electrical circuits, and so on.

2. Another application area involves the interpretation of other types of data where analytical tools are needed to make generalizations or draw conclusions from large amounts of data from different sources or sensors.

- Financial services—identification of patterns in stock market data and assistance in bond trading strategies.
- Loan application evaluation—judge the worthiness of loan applications based on patterns in previous application information.
- Jet and rocket engine diagnostics—train neural network with sensor data to identify faults.
- Medical diagnosis—training of neural networks using previous cases.
- Credit card information—fast detection of fraud from purchasing patterns.
- DNA sequencing—analysis of patterns in DNA structures and rapid comparison of patterns in new sequences.
- Airline forecasting—prediction of seat demand after training with historical data; rapid modification by retraining with new data as it becomes available.
- Evaluation of personnel and job candidates—matching personnel data to job requirements and performance criteria; allows flexibility and tolerance of incomplete information.

3. Another application area for neural networks involves optimization. A classic example is the traveling salesman problem (TSP), in which we seek the order of locations that should be visited to minimize the distance traveled. Optimization problems include telephone network traffic routing, circuit wiring layout design, project management and other resource allocation problems in which finite resources are to be used efficiently or configured to meet a specific need. Examples of neural network models for optimization are the Boltzmann and Cauchy machines. These cases borrow from physics the concept of energy levels to describe different states of the neural network. The problem becomes how to adjust the weights to find a small enough energy level of the network to give a satisfactory solution. For TSP, this corresponds to identifying the paths (connections with nonzero weights) that minimize the distance traveled.

Another type of problem uses neural networks to represent a function that maps input to output. The training of the network establishes the functional relationship, and subsequent operation is aimed at rapid and accurate translation of input data, including situations where the input is incomplete or noisy. Examples of application types are translation of codes and languages and mapping of tables of engineering data from one form to another.

Examples of Neural Network Applications Involving Pattern Recognition

- Credit Card Fraud Detection (Chase Manhattan Bank): This system is used to determine zip code areas in which the risk of credit card abuse is high. The system is trained with previous data to analyze patterns of fraudulent use of credit cards.
- NestorWriter (Nestor, Inc.): This system can recognize handwritten characters entered via a light pen on a pad.
- Airline Marketing Tactician (BehavHeuristics): This system solves airline yield management problems involving the proper number of seats on a given flight in different fare categories. The neural network forecasts the demand for seats given information such as time, day, and origin/destination.
- Mortgage Risk Evaluator (Nestor, Inc.): This system appraises mortgage applications to identify people who are likely to default on payments. The neural network learns from past examples accepted or rejected by human evaluators. The system can be retrained as newer, more accurate data becomes available.

12.2   Natural Language Processing and Speech Understanding

Goals of research and development in this area include the ability to find correct interpretations of words in surrounding text from written text or from spoken words and the translation of one language into another. For speech recognition (Figure 12.1), neural networks store, via training, information on speech parts for later rapid matching to input patterns[9]. A system developed by Teuvo Kohonen has the highest accuracy and largest vocabulary. A front-end neural network recognizes short, phoneme-like fragments of speech, and another neural network

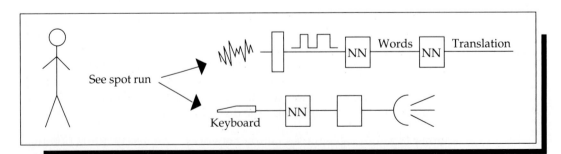

FIGURE 12.1   Architecture for a neural network system for speech recognition.

constructs works from combinations of the fragments. Finally, another component clarifies ambiguities involving words with similar sounds.

A system called NETtalk (developed by Sejnowski and Rosenberg[10]) is a three-layer network that synthesizes speech from text. The system has no programmed rules and pronounces an unrestricted range of English text. The steps of the training phase mimic the developmental phases of children learning to speak.

An important requirement for language processing systems is to discriminate the meanings of words, depending on the context. Neural networks can be used to establish associations between words commonly used together. During operation, the neural network checks these linkages for words in the sentence being analyzed to choose the best interpretation.

12.3   Neural Networks in Robotics and Vision Systems

Autonomous machines have long been a goal of AI research and development[11]. This area includes processing and understanding of sensor data, coordination between visual perception and mechanical actions, sensing the context of the local environment, and the ability to learn and adapt to a changing environment. Clearly, neural computing can play an important role. The availability of chips for parallel processing of ANN will allow easy integration with robotics hardware.

In the vision component of robotic systems, neural networks can use the associative memory feature to learn to interpret visual data such as partially obscured faces or objects and choose a close match with an image in memory. The systems take incoming visual data and extract features as subtasks of larger systems that use the feature extraction information.

Much of the work in robotic learning is in the simulation stage; however, the research results are encouraging. Recent work aims to produce systems that can interpolate learned data to create smoother motions and vary speeds as needed in specific situations. In the area of robot control, two aspects under intense study are path and trajectory planning and nonlinear control of motors and gears. ANN systems are being developed for obstacle detection and adaptive response and for coordination of robot arms with input from cameras.

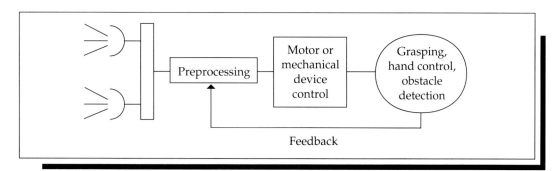

FIGURE 12.2   Architecture for a sensor processing system.

An example of the integration of neural computing into robotics systems is the work on autonomous learning machines by Handelman *et al.*[12]. Their work takes advantage of the complementary features of AI and ANNs to build subsystems appropriate to the task. The system combines the reflexive knowledge typical of motor skills with a declarative mode that modifies the system when the robotic arm starts to deviate from the desired motion.

A rule-based module monitors other tasks and invokes rule-based or neural computing components, depending on whether steady-state operations are appropriate or adjustments need to be made. Initially, the rule-based module supervises the training of the neural network, which generalizes the data about arm movement. Subsequently, in operational mode, the neural network can associate given inputs with similar outputs and therefore can be more sensitive to small changes in motion.

12.4 Character Recognition

Another use of neural networks is in the recognition of characters. The range of characters that can be analyzed includes graphics symbols and Japanese and Chinese characters. Some systems read words directly from paper documents so that the user does not have to type.

The recognition of handwritten characters has several important applications. For example, automatic verification of signatures on checks and other documents could save processing costs and reduce losses due to unauthorized transactions. Machine reading of forms filled out in handwriting is advantageous because people do not always have convenient access to typewriters, and they tend to make fewer mistakes if forms are entered by handwriting. The post office can save billions of dollars if machines can read handwritten addresses.

One system, developed by Fukushima and Miyaki[3], uses an ANN model they call the *neocognitron.* That system achieved 95 percent accuracy in recognizing hand-printed characters. Because ANNs are tolerant of variations in input, the system is successful even with a certain amount of variation in the characters' positions, scale, and clarity.

Another example is the Intelligent Character Recognition System developed by NYNEX Corporation to process business checks. The system can determine if the amounts written on checks are within predetermined limits. Applications being developed by other groups include systems to read zip codes from letters and packages, process insurance forms, and read numbers from credit card slips.

Neural computing systems have great potential for increasing the efficiency of the many organizations involved in processing forms. Furthermore, accurate verification systems could allow more control over fraudulent authorizations. The burden of data entry tasks could be greatly alleviated by the development of light pen systems and other electronic entry systems using ANN components.

12.5   Automatic Theorem Proving

Many AI research projects have focused on reasoning systems that mimic cognitive processes based on formal logic systems. The issues studied range from theorem proving to commonsense reasoning.

Work in theorem proving has recently included the study of possible roles for neural networks. For example, the SEquential THEoremprover (SETHEO) uses a neural network component to enhance a conventional symbolic theorem prover[13]. The goal in this case is to improve the overall performance of the system.

A statement in propositional logic is presented in symbolic form and is translated into a binary vector suitable for input to a neural network as well as a symbolic theorem prover. The function of the neural network is to provide the theorem prover with heuristic clues about the most efficient proof strategy to pursue. These clues are learned by the neural network in prior training sessions in which selected proofs are input so that the network can extract the salient features for later use.

12.6   Decision Support Systems

An important area of information systems deals with tools and techniques that aid decision makers, especially at the middle and top levels of management. The objective of DSS is to provide computerized support to decision makers, especially at these levels, as well as to support staff analysts.

Because of their complementary nature, neural networks provide capabilities not available in DSS or expert systems—some of the human qualities that allow decision makers to perform much better than computer systems. Specifically, neural networks provide the ability to adapt to new situations. This is important for open systems, which are typical of real-world situations confronted by human decision makers. Neural networks provide the ability to generalize from experience and interpolate from learned facts in recognizing situations similar to ones previously enountered. Thus, ANN components reduce the need for systems to provide a complete set of solutions that anticipate all possible problems a manager may encounter.

A basic model of the behavior of decision makers (H. Simon[14]) starts with an *intelligence* phase in which information is gathered and structured in order to identify problems and opportunities that require decisions. Subsequently, the decision maker *designs* alternate solutions and *sets criteria* for testing and evaluating the alternatives. Finally the best (or a good enough) alternative is *chosen*. A natural application of neural networks is the processing of large data sets to identify patterns and features that require further analysis and that may reveal the need for decisions (the intelligence phase). Also, in the design phase, proposed solutions may be evaluated by matching results with solution criteria. Finally, neural networks can help in the choice phase by analyzing historical cases for their solutions.

A natural application of neural networks is the processing of large data sets to

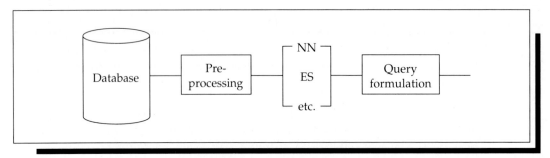

FIGURE 12.3   Architecture for an intelligent database system.

identify patterns and features that require further attention and that may reveal the need for decisions. Neural networks could be components of database mining systems that run in the background or overnight to look for problems or interesting correlations in a database that may be of interest to a managerial decision maker. A goal of intelligent database systems[15] is to handle information and decision making in a way more similar to human methods. The neural network components may be crucial for finding patterns in data, finding approximate matches and best-guess estimates, and facilitating inexact queries.

Examples of Applications Supporting DSS

Financial analysis—preprocess information from large databases to look for patterns and trends. Results can be used in investment decisions.

Structured models—used in statistics and operations research/management science. ANNs can be used to solve very difficult optimization and allocation problems that are not amenable to standard models.

Optimization—use of neural network models such as Hopfield nets to find optimal solutions to problems involving many parameters. For example ANN was used to solve the TSP[16].

Resource allocation—based on historical, experiential data.

Hybrid systems—systems that perform standard statistical analyses on data sets selected by the neural network.

Intelligent databases—in connection with the database aspect of decision support, future systems will increasingly need flexible and convenient access to heterogeneous distributed databases (Figure 12.3). The intelligent features of these systems will be provided by a variety of technologies including expert systems, object orientation, and neural networks.

12.7   Future Research and Development

In this chapter, we have seen that most of the application areas traditionally addressed with AI techniques also provide excellent opportunities for neurocomputing solutions. Furthermore, some AI applications are proving to be very difficult to implement efficiently, if at all. Often those problems are areas of human intelligence such as pattern recognition and learning that are appropriate for ANN. Much research and development is and will be devoted to these areas, and the potential for very useful systems is great.

In the last few years, many practical applications of neural networks have started to appear. This is due, to a large extent, to the introduction of neural network shells and other development tools, which are greatly expanding the potential for practical development of useful systems. This is similar to the history of expert system popularity. With expert systems, applications became widespread soon after the development capability became available to software groups and end users who did not need to be proficient in specialized AI languages.

Some research and development areas of future interest include the study of alternative architectures and learning techniques for neural networks and the development of guidelines based on experience of what systems are best for each possible application. Another issue is the translation of real-world problems into appropriate neural network solutions. This includes work on how best to represent information for input in neural networks and how to verify and validate the performance of the network. Because neural networks are most powerful when embedded in other systems, the interface issues, including how to communicate between symbolic and neural systems, are very important.

Another big technological improvement will occur with the cost-effective availability of neural networks on chips. One important advantage will be the parallel implementation of neural networks in hardware to improve the performance and minimize some of the existing drawbacks of training times and operating speeds. Another opportunity will be the ability to embed neural networks in all kinds of larger systems, ranging from robots to appliances, to give them more characteristics of human intelligence.

High-payoff areas for the future include the automation of systems with human intelligence capabilities for use in hazardous environments such as undersea vehicles, nuclear power plants, and space observatories. An important role for neural networks will be neurocontrol systems that monitor and direct processes in larger systems. Other areas with good potential are code and language translation in telecommunications systems, especially with the arrival of Integrated Systems Digital Networks (ISDN) and full voice, image, and text transmission. Other areas mentioned earlier in the chapter will expand in the number and type of applications in the areas of information retrieval and pattern recognition in data.

12.8 Summary

Neural network applications are rapidly appearing as convenient development systems become available and theoretical advances in neurocomputing are made. Neural networks address many of the typical areas of AI and in some cases are proving to be better alternatives. In other applications, AI and neural network techniques complement each other to provide better solutions than can be achieved with either type of solution alone. As successful neural network systems are publicized, interest will continue to grow and neural network applications will become a standard alternative in the design of computing and information systems.

References

1. W. Allman, *Apprentices of Wonder*, New York: Bantam Books, 1989.
2. C. W. Engel and M. Cran, "Pattern Classifications: A Neural Network Competes with Humans," *PC AI*, (May-June 1991).
3. K. Fukushima and S. Miyaki, "Neocognition: A New Algorithm for Pattern Recognition Tolerant of Deformation and Shifts in Position," *Pattern Recognition*, Vol. 15 (June 1982).
4. C. T. Harston, "Applications of Neural Networks to Robotics," in A. Maren, C. Harston, and R. Pap (eds.), *Handbook of Neural Computing*, Academic Press, San Diego, CA, 1990, pp. 381–385.
5. R. Hecht-Nielsen, *NeuroComputing*, Reading, MA: Addison-Wesley, 1990.
6. C. C. Klimasauskas, "Applying Neural Networks—Part 2," *PC AI*, (March-April 1991).
7. P. K. Simpson, *Neural Networks: Research and Applications Series*, Pergamon Press, New York, 1990.
8. R. Trippi and E. Turban, *Neural Network Applications in Investment and Financial Services*, Chicago: Probus Publishers, 1992.
9. R. P. Lippman, "Review of Neural Networks for Speech Recognition," *Neural Computation*, Vol. 1, No. 1 (1989).
10. T. Sejnowski and C. Rosenberg, "Parallel Networks That Learn to Pronounce English Text," *Complex Systems*, Vol. 1 (1987), pp. 145–168.
11. G. Josin, "Integrating Neural Networks with Robotics," *AI Expert* (August 1988).
12. D. Handelman, S. Lane, and J. Gelfand, "Integrating Neural Networks and Knowledge-Based Systems for Intelligent Robotic Control," *IEEE Control Systems Magazine*, (April, 1990).
13. J. Schumann, W. Ertel, and C. Suttner, "Learning Heuristics for a Theorem Prover Using Back Propagation," Report FKI–100–89, Technische Universität München, January, 1989.
14. H. A. Simon, *The New Science of Management Decision*, New York: Harper & Row, 1960.
15. K. Parsave, M. Chignell, S. Khoshafian, and H. Wong, *Intelligent Databases*, New York: Wiley, 1989.
16. H. Szu and R. Hartley, "Fast Simulated Annealing," *Physics Letters*, Vol. 122, Nos. 3 and 4 (1987).

Chapter 13

Building a Neural Network Application

The processes for developing expert systems and neural networks have important parallels, as shown in Figure 13.1. An inspection of the two processes for their similarities and differences is instructive for understanding the neural network development process.

Knowledge engineers and neural network builders each have to acquire and represent a body of knowledge as facts and rules or as data sets, respectively. For supervised neural networks, data sets must be chosen accurately to represent examples of input data and their corresponding results. With unsupervised networks, a domain expert must examine and interpret the categories and perhaps recommend running the network again to obtain a different number of categories. For expert systems or neural networks, domain experts need to be involved to ensure the accuracy of the rules or data sets.

The knowledge engineer spends a great deal of time and effort formulating and testing rules. Neural network builders have to put data sets into the proper representations and formats for presentation to the network for training. This is

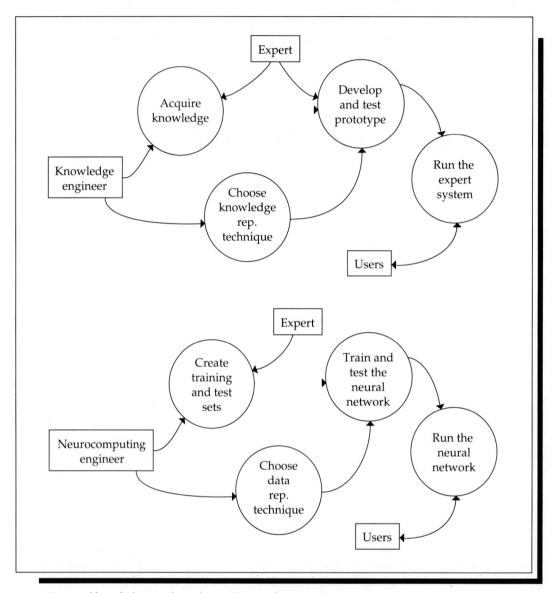

FIGURE 13.1   Knowledge engineering and neural computing processes.

not only a data processing problem; the particular format may also affect the quality and efficiency of the training task.

Knowledge engineers next develop the knowledge base and test the design, usually via prototyping with feedback from the expert. Neural network builders train the network to an acceptable level of accuracy and then run it on test cases with known results. In each case, complete V&V of the system is an important but very difficult task.

13.1   Development Strategy

Thousands of neural network tools are in use today for research and commercial applications[1,2]. Large systems require a methodology that will lead to efficient development of correct systems. The development process of any advanced computing application contains an inherent risk. One means of reducing this risk is to adopt a development methodology.

Development Process

The development of neural network applications can be described in a way that is similar to structured design methodologies for information processing; however, some steps are unique to neural network application development or have additional considerations. A straightforward methodology[3] for developing either neural networks or expert systems consists of four phases (Figure 13.2): concept, design, implementation, and maintenance. The process described here assumes that other phases of systems development, such as information requirements and feasibility analysis for the project, have been successfully completed.

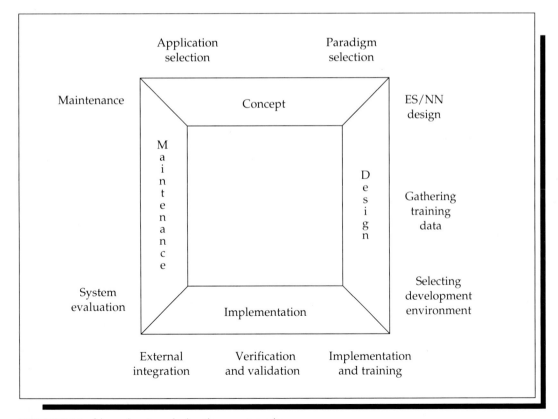

FIGURE 13.2 Neural network development cycle.

In the *concept phase*, the application is selected, the problem is bounded and scoped, and the basic functionality of the system is determined. The requirements for a neural network to be integrated into a larger system should include distinct tasks to be performed and the level and points of required integration. The point here is to focus on the applicability of neurocomputing as an appropriate technology to solve the problem at hand. As noted earlier, standard procedures of systems analysis and design should also be followed to determine specific characteristics of the overall system and to specify clearly the users' requirements.

The concept phase also involves choosing the appropriate neural network paradigm for the problem. In principle, the properties of the problem should be matched to paradigms such as those shown in Chapter 11 (see Figure 11.3). Existing successful applications can be studied to confirm the choice for your application. For example, if training data are readily available in sufficient quantity, supervised training can be used; however, if the features and categories of the data are not clear, an unsupervised paradigm may be needed to reveal potential categories. When several alternatives are adequate, the decision may be made on the basis of available software and the experience level of the developer. For example, back propagation systems are readily available and may have been used by the developer in previous projects.

The *design phase* builds on the requirements formulated in the concept phase, and begins to create general and detailed designs of the individual systems as well as the integration utilities. In addition, the development environment is identified, and preliminary knowledge and data are gathered.

In the *implementation phase*, the neural network environment is established and the neural network is created and trained. Unit testing is performed, and the units are integrated and tested. V&V procedures are also performed in this phase, and the units are integrated with any existing external systems.

More specifically, the following steps take place:

- *Data transformation*—The purpose here is to transform the application data into the type and format required by the neural network. This may mean writing software for preprocessing the data. Data storage and manipulation techniques and processes need to be designed for retraining the neural network, when needed, conveniently and efficiently. Also, the way the application data is represented and ordered often determines the efficiency and possibly the accuracy of the neural network's results.
- *Training*—This step is an iterative process of presenting input and desired output data to the network so that the weights can be determined. The previously derived test data should be used to measure to what extent the network matches the ideal performance. In order to avoid long training times, the choice of the number of nodes and layers, as well as the initial conditions (such as transfer function, learning rule, and momentum) of the network, are important and require careful consideration at the outset of the process.
- *Unit implementation*—At this point in the process, a set of weights has been obtained that allows the network to reproduce the desired outputs given inputs like those in the training set. The network is ready for use as a stand-

alone system or as part of another software system, which could include expert system components.

The purpose of the *maintenance phase* is to evaluate periodically the system's performance and to modify it as the need arises. Given the adaptive nature of some of the components, care must be taken to keep the entire system consistent and validated if incremental training is permitted.

Development Issues

Other issues arise when developing a neural network. For example, when should the network be trained? Depending on the situation, training can occur prior to operation, incrementally, or periodically. If the input data is stable, the initial training produces a system that can be used from then on. An example is the routine categorizing of speech signals where all patterns of interest are known. In other applications, the characteristics of the data may change over time, and retraining may be required at certain points. For example, searches for patterns in business data may have changing requirements over time, so that new historical data needs to be used to retrain the network.

In addition, the role and form of the explanation facility need to be determined. If the neural network is combined with an expert system, the explanation facility of the expert system can deal with the higher-level reasoning. However, at the neural network level, explanations based on weight values are not always possible, and additional software is needed to provide the logic to explain the result of the neural network.

13.2 Concept Phase

We now take a more detailed look at the concept phase of the development strategy. This phase needs to focus on understanding the problem to be addressed to see if a neural network solution is appropriate. Then the development process is planned and certain decisions are made.

Guidelines for Choosing Appropriate Applications

Guidelines from experience with neural network techniques are starting to emerge based on the characteristics of working applications. Important considerations are the following:

- *Inadequate knowledge bases*—An expert may not be available or affordable. Even when the expert is available, rules may be very difficult to formulate. The rule-based approach may not be the appropriate form of knowledge representation for a particular domain, and alternative expert system techniques may be too expensive or difficult to develop. If an abundance of historical data is available, the neural network is feasible.
- *Volatile knowledge bases*—These are situations where rules and facts need to

be modified frequently. The knowledge in the rules may be evolutionary, depending on human experience in a new domain, and therefore may need to be changed over time. This is one sense in which expert systems learn; however, human intervention is required to keep changing the rule base. If an equivalent neural network application can be constructed, retraining via data sets can be much easier than modifying, and subsequently debugging, a rule base.

- *Data-intensive systems*—These applications involve high rates of data input, requiring rapid processing. Once trained, neural networks can efficiently process the data. Examples are control systems using feedback data. Data-intensive systems may also have ambiguous, noisy, or error-prone inputs requiring interpolation. Neural networks are strong in this area. Interactions involving vision and speech subsystems are examples.
- *Regression analysis*—The types of problems that have been solved using regression analysis can also be solved using neural networks. In these applications, statistical or business data is analyzed for patterns or trends. In a neural network solution, the network is trained on different examples of line shapes. The network can then classify future input data.
- *Parallel hardware*—The coming economical availability of parallel implementations of neural networks will give additional advantages to the neural computing approach. Compact networks capable of fast parallel processing will allow fast training and retraining and rapid processing in operation. Hardware implementations of neural networks will allow improved applications in areas such as robotics and smart appliances.

The neural network approach is particularly good for certain classes of applications. These include character recognition, signal processing, robotics and vision systems, and forecasting. Other types of applications should be avoided: traditional business applications such as accounts receivable that are done well with algorithmic techniques and applications that require deduction and sequential logic.

Current successful neural network applications have cited the following analysis of the situations faced by conventional techniques:

- Standard technology is inadequate, ineffective, or too difficult to implement.
- Qualitative or complex quantitative reasoning is required.
- Many highly interdependent parameters are involved, so that a clear understanding of the analysis and solution of a problem is difficult.
- Data are intrinsically noisy or error-prone.
- Project development time is short, and the training time for the network is reasonable.

The concept phase includes the traditional steps of gathering requirements for the problem to be solved and assessing resource needs and project risks. Constraints on the project include time and equipment resources; type, cost, accuracy, and timing of data; and project development, training, and operation times.

A careful analysis of these aspects will ensure that, if proved to be feasible and desirable, the project will have a good chance of success.

Paradigm Selection

In this step, a network architecture (structure) and a learning method are chosen. The characteristics of the application need to be analyzed and compared with the capabilities of different paradigms. Although ideally all possible alternatives would be considered, the availability of a particular development shell or the capabilities of development personnel may strongly influence the choice of the type of neural network to be used.

Areas of concern in paradigm selection include network size, nature of the inputs and outputs, memory mechanism, type of training employed, and time constraints for routine operations of the working system. Examples of neural network capabilities are show in Table 3.1.

An important consideration is the number of neurons and the number of layers to be used. The application problem needs to be analyzed carefully to see if the number of nodes required to represent the input and produce useful output is feasible for the available technologies. Of the current techniques, some are intended for smaller networks (a few hundred nodes) and others for larger networks (approximately 1,000 nodes). For example, the Boltzmann machine is a smaller network, and back propagation can be used for larger ones.

Neural network models vary in the type of output they can produce:

- *Classification*—These applications generally require discrete outputs that specify to which of several categories a given input corresponds. Two or more output nodes may be required with only one active at a time, depending on the input to the network. For example, an application for forecasting product demand may have output nodes that correspond to high, medium, and low.
- *Pattern recognition*—This widespread use of neural networks requires several nodes, some or all of which can be active. The active output nodes represent the pattern that has been identified. For example, a system that identifies characters might operate on the output shown in Figure 13.3,

TABLE 13.1 Capabilities of Neural Networks

PARADIGM	TRAINING METHOD	TRAINING TIME	EXECUTION TIME
Back propagation	Supervised	Slow	Fast
ART2	Unsupervised	Fast	Fast
Kohonen	Unsupervised	Medium	Fast
Hopfield	Supervised	Fast	Medium
Boltzmann	Supervised	Slow	Slow

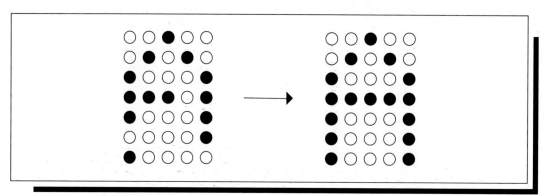

FIGURE 13.3 Output of a system identifying characters.

where an input with errors is identified as the pattern for the character "A". (Of course, these patterns would be input and output as vectors that represent the positions of the pixels in the pattern.)

- Real numbers—This output represents values such as machine settings, dollars, and degrees. Application areas include financial planning and robotics.
- *Optimization*—Applications such as those found in operations research use matrices of numbers to represent things such as resources to be allocated. Neural network implementations use the weights to calculate objective functions that are minimized to find the best solution to a problem. Examples are the traveling salesman problem and scheduling.

The memory mechanism influences how the network will recall things from partial information. For example, humans are excellent at reconstructing information so that, for example, another person can be identified from only a few clues about parts of the face.

One type of memory in neural networks, called *associative*, is represented by single-layer, highly connected neural networks. With associative memory, input patterns are correlated with corresponding outputs and, as with biological vision systems, visual space can be mapped onto memory storage areas in organized patterns. Applications range from target classification to trend analysis of financial data.

Autoassociative memory networks take partial information and reconstruct previously memorized patterns. Each pattern is associated with itself; that is, a clean version of itself is stored, so that the exact pattern can be recalled even though future inputs may be incomplete or garbled. The Hopfield network, brain-state-in-a-box, and adaptive resonance theory (ART) are examples of neural network models using autoassociative memory. Heteroassociative memory translates one set of patterns into a possibly different set, as in lookup tables or translation systems (e.g., tables of ASCII code with the corresponding symbols). Examples of specific neural network models are BAM and Kohonen feature maps.

The training method depends on the type of data available and the time constraints. The nature of the data may indicate *supervised learning*, that is, the outputs associated with given inputs are well known. In that case, the application may need the neural network for the rapid production of desired outputs from future inputs. A set of inputs with corresponding correct outputs known from past experience is required to teach the network how to respond.

In cases where classifications of inputs are uncertain, *unsupervised learning* may be needed to discover correlations in the data. With these techniques, the network creates its own classifications of input sets that are presented to the network. Certain parameters can be adjusted to make the network vary the number of categories it creates. The resulting outputs must then be inspected by humans to provide interpretations of their meanings.

Timing constraints are important for the successful use of a working neural network. The two factors are training time and operation time. Training time is the time needed to adjust the weights by repeatedly presenting the training set until accurate results are produced. Training time is different for different types of neural network models, and varies with the size of the network and the quality of the data. On the latter point, if the training data is inconsistent or does not cover all of the possible cases evenly, the network can waste time trying to focus on the proper information to learn.

13.3 Application Design

During the concept phase, the application is analyzed for suitability for a neural network solution and an appropriate paradigm is selected. As more experience is gained with neural network development, more formal methods of risk analysis can be created to assist project leaders in identifying and managing potential problems. If the prospects for the project are still favorable, we enter the design phase in order to plan specific steps and add detail to the development process.

System Design

The neural network is a system that needs to be designed at different levels: node, network, and training. We must determine the types of processing elements, the size and connectivity of the network layers, and the learning algorithm. The options among the various paradigms are different.

Neural networks are usually described in terms of a *layer,* a set of nodes whose weights are modified as a unit. That is, during the training process, different groups of weights are affected at different times, so each group would be associated with the same layer. Although some people refer to the input and output nodes as a layer, we restrict this definition to the nodes between them. Within a given layer, groups of nodes may have specialized purposes (e.g., representing a certain feature of the memory); in this case, they are referred to as *slabs.*

At the node level, the designer needs to address the types of inputs, the means of combining inputs, and the transfer function to be used. As discussed in Chapter 10, combining usually involves a simple summation over all the inputs of each weight times the corresponding activation level on that input line. Most neural networks use a transfer function to decide if the node is to be activated and to determine the value of the output that goes on to another node.

The choice of transfer function, such as linear or sigmoid, is based on the types of inputs and outputs desired and on the learning algorithm to be used. With development shells, these choices would be predetermined or presented to the developer for making a decision. For example, the back propagation technique uses the sigmoid transfer function because of the intrinsic nature of the training algorithm.

At the network level, the designer must choose the number of layers, the size of each layer, the nature of the inputs and outputs, and the way each layer is to be connected. Network paradigms such as Hopfield, ART, and Kohonen SOFM, by their nature, require either one or two layers. Back propagation, on the other hand, can have multiple (hidden) layers, which abstract features from the inputs.

Increasing the number of inner-layer nodes makes the network more powerful; however, the training time is greatly increased, both because of the number of calculations that must be done and the necessity of providing more examples in the training set. The hidden layers also make the network more difficult to understand in terms of explaining the reasons behind its results. A good procedure is to start with one layer and experiment with the performance characteristics by adding additional layers. An important point is that if an operational network later is determined to require a different number of nodes, the modification will require essentially a complete redesign of the network and the input data.

In each layer, the number of nodes must be selected. The input nodes are chosen to represent the data sources adequately. This step should follow a thorough analysis of the data relevant to the application. Insufficient information in the data will lead to an inaccurate network, and the presence of unnecessary data will add to the training time and may give inferior results.

In analyzing all the possible data sources relevant to the application, remove unnecessary and unreliable data and rule out data that is impractical or uneconomical to collect. Look for ways to preprocess data into efficient forms that will lead to desirable training times. For example, ratios of numbers are often more useful than raw data because information has been added that would otherwise have to be discovered by the network.

Next, the data must be put into the appropriate format for input to the type of neural network model being used. For example, data with continuous values are sampled at certain time intervals and input to the network. One node would be used for each source of continuous-valued data in the set.

If the network being used accepts only binary input, the data must be arranged as a set of numbers (a vector), with each element assigned to a particular input node. The order in which the elements are arranged in the vector can strongly influence the accuracy of the network and the training time. For example, certain elements grouped together in the vector may represent a certain aspect or feature of the data, and arranging them together will make it easier for the network to recognize that aspect or feature. Conversely, randomly arranging the elements will require more work and training time for the network to recognize features.

Some data is natural to represent as binary inputs. A series of attributes, such as symptoms of a disease, could use a 1/0 value to represent the presence or absence of those symptoms. In other cases, where continuous values are involved, they can be broken into ranges such as 0–3, 4–7, 8–11, and so on, so that a node or a combination of nodes, with inputs 0/1, represent the continuous value. Patterns can be represented by a series of binary nodes. As shown in Figure 13.3, characters can be represented as a vector whose elements stand for the different pixels that make up the character.

As mentioned earlier, the number of nodes affects the training time and the performance of the network. The presence of too many nodes leads to a table lookup effect in which the network rigidly maps the training set inputs to outputs. In this case, the network loses the ability of generalization, which gives neural network technology one of its attractive advantages. With too many nodes, the network memorizes data rather than learning features of the data or gleaning basic principles for later use.

During the training process, statistics should be generated to gauge the progress of the training. At first, the percentage of correct responses to input data will be too low, but the performance will improve as training goes on. In practice, the trained network may not be perfect, especially for large problems. In this case, a predetermined tolerance should have been set and used to decide when to stop the training. During the design phase of a new system, the number of nodes and layers will usually be varied to come up with the best architecture before accepting the neural network for routine use in an application.

The system designer must determine how the results at the output nodes will be used. Categorization applications will have a single node active to indicate to which of several categories an input corresponds. For pattern outputs, enough nodes are needed to represent the pattern, and various nodes will be active for any given case. For example, the number of nodes must be sufficient to represent each pixel and give the needed detail. In either case, postprocessing must be done to convey the neural network's result to another system or to provide a user interface.

Various parameters are associated with each neural network paradigm, providing opportunities for refining the system design. The number and types of parameters are peculiar to the paradigm. A development shell makes it easy for the user to experiment with the settings and optimize the design.

Data Collection

The process starts with the collection of data to be used for training and testing. As described earlier, the problem must be amenable to neural network solution, and adequate data must exist and be obtained. Training data must be identified, and network performance must be planned.

The first two steps in the process involve collecting data and separating it into a training set and a test set. These tasks are based on a thorough analysis of the application, so that the problem is well bounded and the functionality of the system and the neural network's context are well understood.

In conjunction with a domain expert, the developer must identify and clarify data relevant to the problem. This means formulating and conceptualizing the task in a data-oriented way that will be amenable to a neural network solution. Textual descriptions need to be reformulated to allow the knowledge base to be described numerically as vectors. The developer needs to check for biases due to the particular way the data is represented and normalized. Another consideration is the stability of the input and the extent to which environmental conditions may require changes in the number of input nodes to the neural network or frequent changes in the training data. At this point, difficulty in expressing the data in the form needed for a neural network may lead to cancellation of the project.

In collecting and preparing the data, the anticipated structure of the neural network determines the data type, such as binary or continuous. High-quality data collection requires care to minimize ambiguity, errors, and randomness in the data. The data should be collected to cover the widest range of the problem domain and should cover not only routine operations, but also exceptions and conditions at the boundaries of the problem domain.

Another task is to confirm reliability by using multiple sources of data; however, ambiguities will have to be resolved. In general, the more data we use, the better as long as quality is not sacrificed. Larger data sets will increase processing time during training, but better data will improve the accuracy of the training and could lead to faster convergence to a good set of weights.

Current neural network models have various parameters for tuning the network to the desired performance level. This process includes initialization of the network weights and parameters, followed by modification of the parameters as performance feedback is received. In many cases, the initial values are important for determining the efficiency and duration of the training.

Development Environment Selection

The last part of the design phase involves matching the application's description and design to an appropriate development environment. Ideally, all possible tools and techniques would be considered, so that a thorough analysis of the application would indicate the best approach to use. In reality, various constraints will limit the possibilities, but to the extent possible, this step should be done with objectivity to avoid using the wrong tool for the job.

In the design phase, selection of the development environment should include a systematic analysis, with an accurate appraisal of the costs and time for various alternatives. At this stage, a poorly chosen project could still be modified or canceled before the investment is made in a particular development tool.

One of the constraints in choosing the development environment is obviously the cost. The size of the project and its importance to the organization will be decision factors that could justify the cost. Another consideration is the familiarity of the developers with tools used in previous projects. The cost in time and money of retraining personnel is important.

13.4   Example: Bankruptcy Prediction

To illustrate some of the points discussed in this chapter, we will look at an application for predicting bankruptcy[4]. This study shows that neural network solutions can be an alternative to the multivariate discriminate analysis that might traditionally be used.

Concept Phase

The use of neural networks for this problem follows from the known ability of neural networks to analyze and model business data. The ability to generalize from training data enables the network to make forecasts for new data subsequently presented to the system. This bankruptcy application is appropriate, too, because of the lack of understanding of principles of and rules for bankruptcy prediction. Other neural networks have been developed for predicting ratings of corporate bonds and evaluating mortgage underwriting decisions, so this application was judged to be appropriate for neural network solutions.

Much work had previously been done on bankruptcy prediction using financial ratios and discriminant analysis. Because certain restrictions are necessary for that approach to be used, operations researchers are currently looking for improved methods. Neural networks have the potential for less strict constraints and therefore could be a more robust approach.

The paradigm chosen for this problem was a three-layer network using back propagation. The data for training the network consists of a small set of numbers of well-known financial ratios, and data is available on the bankruptcy outcomes corresponding to the known data sets. Thus a supervised network is appropriate, and training time is not anticipated to be a problem for the amount of data involved. The ready availability of back propagation networks makes this paradigm a reasonable choice.

Application Design

The input to the network was designed to have five nodes, corresponding to five financial ratios for which data is available:

$X1$: Working capital/total assets
$X2$: Retained earnings/total assets
$X3$: Earnings before interest and taxes/total assets
$X4$: Market value of equity/total debt
$X5$: Sales/total assets

Five hidden layers were chosen and proved adequate for obtaining useful results. A single output node gave the final classification showing whether the input data for a given firm indicated bankruptcy or nonbankruptcy.

The data source for this problem consists of various financial ratios for firms that went bankrupt between 1975 and 1982, as given in Moody's industrial manuals. The training sample included 38 firms that went bankrupt and 36 that did not. Financial ratios were calculated for each of the five aspects shown in the preceding list, and each number became the input for one of the five nodes. For each set of data, the known result, whether or not bankruptcy occurred, could be compared to the neural network's output to measure the performance of the network and monitor the training.

The development environment, Neuroshell, release 1.1, was chosen. This commercial neural network simulator package was used on a PC-XT. The implementation of the network for the bankruptcy application will be discussed in the next chapter.

References

1. Efraim Turban, *Expert Systems and Applied Artificial Intelligence*, New York: Macmillan, 1992.
2. Marilyn McCord Nelson and W. T. Illingsworth, *A Practical Guide to Neural Nets*, Reading, MA: Addison-Wesley, 1991.
3. D. Bailey and D. Thompson, "How to Develop Neural-Network Applications," *AI Expert*, Vol. 5 (June 1990).
4. Marcus Odom and Ramesh Shardo, "A Neural Network Model for Bankruptcy Prediction," *Decision Support Systems*, 1993.

Chapter 14

Development Methods and Systems

The previous two chapters have taken us through the neural network application development process to the implementation phase. At this point, an application has been developed and trained. The remaining activities in the implementation phase are testing, V&V, and integration of the application unit with external systems. In this chapter, we will learn about these topics, along with maintenance and management considerations.

In the previous chapter, we learned about a development strategy that consists of four phases: concept, design, implementation, and maintenance[1,2]. In this chapter, we assume that in previous steps a network architecture (structure) and a learning method were chosen. A neural network shell or development method was also chosen, possibly based on the availability of a particular development shell or the capabilities of development personnel.

In this chapter, we concentrate on implementation and maintenance (see

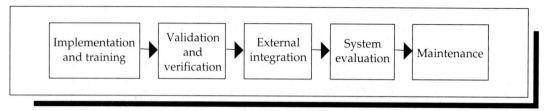

FIGURE 14.1   The second half of the neural network development strategy.

Figure 14.1). Implementation involves neural network development, training, V&V, and external integration. The objective of these phases is to obtain an accurate and consistent working system that exploits the advantages of neural computing. After examining the steps in these phases, we look at an example of a neural network application for bankruptcy prediction.

14.1   Implementation

The implementation phase involves the actual construction of the neural network and makes use of the data gathered for training and testing. In addition to the need for a sufficient quantity, the data must cover a wide range of the problem domain in order to produce a system that can interpolate and generalize beyond the training. As mentioned earlier, ideally the network learns features of the data for handling novel input.

Current neural network models have various parameters for tuning the network to the desired performance level. This process includes initialization of the network's weights and parameters, followed by modification of the parameters as performance feedback is received. In many cases, the initial values are important for determining the efficiency and length of the training.

The next step is to transform the application data into the type and format required by the neural network[3]. This may mean writing software for preprocessing the data. Data storage and manipulation techniques and processes need to be designed for retraining the neural network when needed, and must be convenient and efficient. Also, the way the application data is represented and ordered often determines the efficiency and possibly the accuracy of the neural network's results.

Preparation of the data includes calculating ratios, converting to the needed data type (e.g., binary), and filtering out unnecessary detail. The data may also need to be put into vector form or normalized to a common scale. The data then needs to be separated into training and test data. The test data will be used after the training is finished as input for verifying the effectiveness of the network.

The actual development of the neural network will, in some cases, involve programming (e.g., in C) modules to implement known neural computing algorithms and to manipulate the input/output data. Neural network development systems are becoming available for popular paradigms, so that less programming is required[4].

Many development systems allow a choice of neural paradigms. Once the paradigm is chosen, the number of nodes and layers is decided and learning algorithm parameters are set. Then the training set is loaded and the network is initialized. Training proceeds until the preset criteria for stopping are achieved. The problems that may occur include getting stuck in a local minimum of the error space or overtraining. These problems may be corrected by retraining with different values for the parameters. In some cases, the input vector format may have to be changed or the sequence of the training set vectors varied. Retraining may also have to be done with different numbers of nodes and/or layers.

14.2 Training

The training step is an iterative process of presenting input and desired output data to the network so that the weights can be determined[5]. The previously derived test data should be used to measure to what extent the network matches the ideal performance.

At this point in the process, a set of weights has been obtained that allows the network to reproduce the desired outputs given inputs such as those in the training set. The network is ready for use as a stand-alone system or as part of another software system, which could include expert system components.

In any case, the training needs to be monitored by comparing the network's output with the observed outputs known to correspond to the training data. For example, a running calculation of the percentage of correct outputs will show how good the training is.

In order to give specific examples of training considerations, we now focus on back propagation systems, which are most commonly used today. To review, in this type of network, the difference between the actual output and the desired value is calculated and used to determine corrections to the weights of the connections from the middle layer. In order to do this, errors are also propagated back to the input layer.

Thus, the overall task is to minimize the mean square error for the whole system by making small changes, as prescribed by the back propagation algorithm, to the weights until acceptable performance is achieved. For useful systems, the necessary complexity leads to various scenarios for changing the weights, many of which have dead ends and pitfalls that need to be avoided or overcome. The inherent complexity of neural networks also leads to many different sets of weights that will give acceptable performance. The model has different parameters and initialization points that give the trainer a great deal of freedom in achieving the best set of weights. The following methods can be used to improve the training process when problems occur (see [5] for further details):

- *Limit the design*—Back propagation becomes increasingly difficult as the size of the system increases, so minimizing complexity is recommended. Keeping the network to three layers is important, as well as restricting it to a moderate size of less than 300 nodes (assuming software simulation). More complex systems should be reserved for necessary applications. In choosing the num-

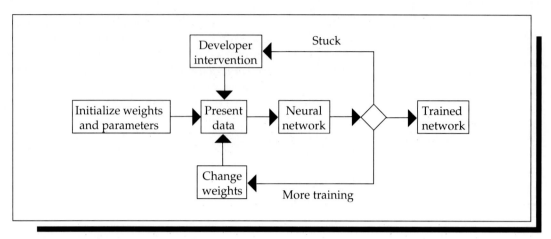

FIGURE 14.2   Procedure for training a neural network.

ber of middle layer nodes, however, keep in mind that it needs to be smaller than the number of patterns to be learned from the input data. Otherwise, the network associates a node with each pattern and does not learn or extract features for generalization.

- *Expand the middle layer*—Within the limitations just mentioned, excessive training times can be reduced by increasing the number of nodes in the middle layer. A relatively small increase can have a dramatic effect.
- *Use momentum*—Most development systems for back propagation provide a momentum parameter that keeps the training going when snags occur. This is accomplished by adding a fraction of the last weight change to the next change to encourage change in the same direction as in the previous step.
- *Raise the tolerance*—The acceptable difference between desired and actual output values can be increased. This protects weights that are correctly predicting some of the data and allows the training to focus on other weights that are contributing to poor results.
- *Nudge the network*—When a training obstacle is encountered, the weights can be modified by some random amount, although this may have to be tried several times to produce the desired results (see Figure 14.2). No guidelines are yet known for choosing how much or in what direction to make the correct nudge.
- *Add noise*—The random addition of a small amount of noise to the input data can improve the training efficiency. This technique can also give better results by training the network to produce the desired result even when the input is somewhat corrupted. It encourages generalization and generation of the important features in the input data.
- *Start over*—Try a new initial state, using a different set of random values for the initial weights. This will start a new path that may have fewer problems; however, you may have to throw away a set of weights that was almost good enough to find that the new starting point does not work either.

Eventually, starting over may finally work, but training times may become excessive.

14.3 Testing

Testing is part of the larger process of V&V, which we will discuss further on in this section. For neural network development, testing is a specific activity closely associated with training and will be discussed first.

Procedures and Considerations

In the first steps of the development process, the data is divided into training and testing categories. Now that training has been performed, it is necessary to test the network. The testing phase examines the performance of the network using the derived weights, measuring the ability of the network to classify the test data correctly. The weights are usually difficult or impossible to interpret, so black-box testing is the primary approach, verifying that inputs produce the appropriate outputs[6].

Some aspects of debugging a neural network are similar to those of other software systems. The user interface involves the same problems as do the areas of data structures and the monitoring and control of the network. Thus, availability of the source code is essential for making improvements. The training aspect of neural networks causes different problems than those encountered in traditional software debugging. For training, the developer needs to have numerical and graphical output to show how weights and activation levels change during training and testing.

In many cases, the network is not expected to perform perfectly, but a certain level of quality is required. Usually the neural network application is an alternative to some other computer method that can be used as a standard. For example, a statistical technique or another quantitative method may be known to classify inputs correctly 70 percent of the time. The neural network implementation often increases that level. If the network is replacing manual operations, performance levels of human processing may be the standard for deciding if the testing phase is successful.

The test plan should include routine cases and other potentially problematic situations (e.g., at the boundaries of the problem domain). If testing reveals problems, the training set needs to be reexamined and the training process possibly modified. Predetermined thresholds for acceptable performance are important for evaluating the network.

In some cases, other methods can supplement the straightforward testing described previously. For example, the weights can be analyzed to look for large values that indicate overtraining and very small weights indicating unnecessary nodes. Also, certain weights that represent major factors in the input vector can be selectively activated to make sure that corresponding outputs respond properly.

Another way of testing the network is to input special cases to study its response. For example, the relationship between inputs and outputs can be examined by strongly activating individual input nodes. Positive activation of the asset-liability ratio input node in a loan underwriting application should have a positive effect on approving the loan. Sometimes activation patterns in hidden layers make sense, indicating abstraction of information from the input nodes. If problems are revealed in testing, various factors may be examined, including the quality or format of the training data, sampling method, model parameter values, and the structure of the network.

Even at a performance level comparable to that using a traditional method, the neural network may have other advantages. For example, the neural network is more easily modified by retraining with new data. Other techniques may require extensive reprogramming when changes are needed.

Verification and Validation

The commercialization of AI and neural network systems requires developers to give more attention to producing correct systems. From the standpoint of both professional ethics and legal issues, systems that endanger human life or financial well-being require considerations that go beyond the need to prove the results of research systems.

Although much has been learned about V&V from software engineering of conventional systems, intelligent systems development has only recently turned more attention and funding to this important problem. Much more work needs to be done to make sure that correct systems are reliably deployed.

First, let us consider the meanings of the two terms. *Validation* refers to a process of demonstrating that the correct system has been built. This means checking the final system against the stated requirements identified in the earlier stages of the project. A system can work from a mechanical standpoint but may not be solving the intended problem. *Verification* involves proving that the system was constructed properly from the mechanical standpoint—for example, whether a specific input gives the expected result and whether the user interface allows data to be entered with fidelity.

Although considerable research has focused on V&V for neural networks, the most common approach currently is trial-and-error testing. Test sets need to check the ability of the network to generalize to novel inputs, including boundary cases such as the hardest or most unusual cases likely to be encountered.

14.4   External Integration

Incorporation of the neural network into routine operations requires proper interfaces and training for users. Ongoing monitoring and feedback to the developers are required for system improvements and long-term success. It is important to gain the confidence of users and management early in development so that the system is accepted and used properly.

As part of a larger system, the neural network will need convenient interfaces to other information systems, input/output devices, and manual operations of the users. The system may need input/output manipulation subsystems such as signal digitizers and file conversion modules. Good documentation and user training are necessary to ensure successful integration into the organization's operations. A convenient procedure must be planned for updating the training sets and initiating periodic retraining of the network. This includes the ability to recognize and include new cases that become known as the system is routinely used.

Ongoing monitoring and feedback to the developers are necessary for maintaining the neural network system. Periodic evaluation of system performance may reveal environmental changes or previously missed bugs that require changes in the network. Enhancements may be suggested as users become more familiar with the system, and feedback may be useful in the design of future versions or new products.

14.5 Example

Now we return to the bankruptcy prediction application introduced in Chapter 13 to look at the implementation phase. We will examine the development, training, and testing steps.

Development

A three-layer network using back propagation was chosen in the design phase, and NeuroShell was selected as the development system (see Figure 14.3). As described earlier, the input data consisted of five financial ratios, along with the corresponding bankruptcy or nonbankruptcy condition. As continuous values, the set of ratios for various cases were stored in a file that could be specified to the neural network simulator program produced via NeuroShell.

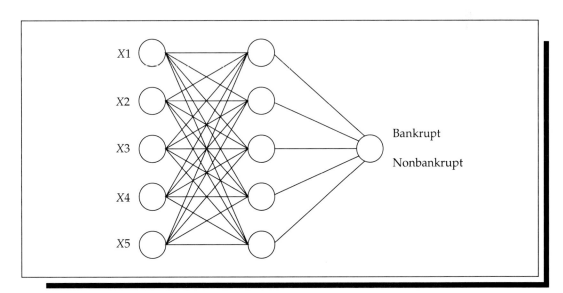

FIGURE 14.3 Architecture of the neural network used for bankruptcy prediction.

The single output node was set up to give a value of 0 for bankruptcy and 1 for nonbankruptcy.

Training

The data set, which covered 129 firms, was divided into a training set and a test set. The training set of 74 firms consisted of 38 that went bankrupt and 36 that did not. The needed ratios were computed and stored in the input file to the neural network and in a conventional discriminant analysis program for comparison of the two techniques.

Three parameters were available in the Neuroshell implementation: learning threshold, learning rate, and momentum. The learning threshold allows the developer to vary the acceptable overall error for the training case. The learning rate and momentum allow the developer to control the step sizes the network uses to adjust the weights as the errors (i.e., discrepancies) between actual and desired outputs are fed back.

An inherent problem with back propagation is the lengthy training times that may be required. In this case, with 5 input nodes and 74 training vectors, the network converged to a good set of weights after 191,400 iterations. This took 24 hours on a PC-XT. However, the network's final set of weights was adequate to predict correctly all 74 cases.

Testing

The neural network was tested in two ways: by using the test data set and by comparison with discriminant analysis. The test data set consisted of 27 bankrupt and 28 nonbankrupt firms. The neural network was able to predict correctly 81.5 percent of the bankrupt cases and 82.1 percent of the nonbankrupt cases (see Figure 14.4). An analysis of the errors showed that five of the bankrupt firms that were classified as nonbankrupt were also misclassified by the discriminant analysis method. A similar situation occurred for the nonbankrupt cases. Although not done in this example, retraining could have been redone with different numbers of hidden layers and nodes. The parameters could also have been varied to see if the performance could be improved.

The result of the testing showed that the neural network implementation is at least as good as the conventional approach. Accuracy of about 80 percent is usually acceptable for neural network applications. At that level, a system is useful because it automatically identifies problem situations for further analysis by a human expert.

Even when, as in this case, the neural network does not perform significantly better than a conventional technique, other factors may make the neural network the preferred method. For example, the ability to adjust the system via retraining from data files could be an advantage over alternative methods.

For further details on the development process, see the Appendix for an additional example. That case shows how to use NeuroShell to classify employees according to their job skills.

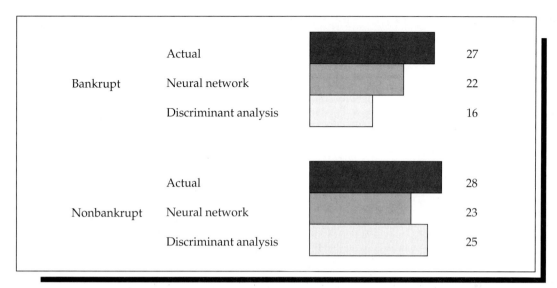

FIGURE 14.4   Results for the bankruptcy prediction problem.

14.6 Development Systems

Most development tools can support many network paradigms (up to several dozen). In addition to the standard products, there are many special products. For example, several products are spreadsheet based (e.g., the neural network Sheet, from Inductive Solutions, Inc.). Several other products are designed to work with expert systems as hybrid development products (e.g., KnowledgeNet from HNC and NeuroSMARTS from Cognition Technology). For a list of neural network tools, see *Intelligent Software Strategies,* Vol. 7 No. 6 (June 1991), pages 8–12. See also Tables 14.1–14.3.

As with any other development tool, the use of neural networks is constrained by their configurations. Therefore, builders may prefer to use programming languages such as C or spreadsheets to program the model and execute the calculations.

Neural network shells are starting to appear for commercial use. As with expert systems, the advantage of the shell is that extensive programming experience is not required to produce useful systems. Of the systems listed in Table 14.1, we will take a closer look at two.

NeuralWorks Professional

NeuralWorks Professional is a comprehensive, high-end, and relatively expensive neural network prototyping and development system. Over 20 network types can be generalized as well as custom designed. Over 30 network types can be generated automatically by supplying information via the graphic interface.

TABLE 14.1 Neural network development systems (includes information from [7]).

NAME	AUDIENCE	NOTABLE FEATURES	DEFICIENCY	PLATFORM	PRICE	NEURAL OR PARALLEL HARDWARE	LANGUAGE SUPPORT	VENDOR
@Brain	Introductory	•Lotus 1-2-3 add-on		PC	$495	-	Lotus 1-2-3 macros	Talon Development
Advanced Application NN Simulator	Programmer	•Source available		Any C compiler	>$495	Possible with source	C library or C source	Logical Design Consulting
AIM	General	•Statistical •Carving factor •Auto data import	•Test and train file must be the same	Mac, DOS	$1495	-	Generate C	Abtech
AutoNet	General	•Automated architecture selection		DOS	$395	-	API	Peak Software
BLINK	Introductory Business			DOS	$125-$500	-	C API	Marlstream Inc.
BrainCel	Introductory Finance	•backperc •runtime module •Sheet add-on		Windows 3.0, Excel, Lotus1-2-3	$249	-	Excel, 1-2-3 macros	Promised Land
BrainMaker Professional	General	•Explain feature •Data interface		Mac, DOS DOS	$195-$13,000	Transputer, DSP	None	California Scientific
DynaMind	General	•Truetime net •Incremental removal of data		DOS	$145-$495	Intel 80170NX	C library	NeuroDynam X
ExplainNet	Introductory	•Generate nets in C (ANSI or K&R)		DOS, OS/2, UNIX	$450	-	Generate nets in C	Vleermuis Software

TABLE 14.1 Neural network development systems. *(continued)*

NAME	AUDIENCE	NOTABLE FEATURES	DEFICIENCY	PLATFORM	PRICE	NEURAL OR PARALLEL HARDWARE	LANGUAGE SUPPORT	VENDOR
ExploreNet 3000	General	• Iconic language • Explain feature		Windows 3.1	$750+$500 for Explain	Balboa	Custom	HNC
Genesis	General			DOS, other	$1995	Possible	-	Neural Systems
HNet	General	• Data Interface • DDL support • Holographic Net		Windows 3.0	$1995-$40,000	Transputer	-	AND America
MacBrain	Introductory Intermediate	• Iconic language • Genetic weights	• Slow	Mac	$1495+ $495 for genetics	-	HyperTalk, SuperCard API	Neurix
ModelWare	Intermediate	• Statistical	• Proprietary theory	DOS	$495	-	-	TeraNet
N-Net	General	• Network delivery		DOS, SPARC, Mac	$1995-$2995	-	N/A	AIWare
NeuralCASE	General		• Limited paradigms	Contact vendor	$199	-	-	NeuroSym
NeuralDesk	Introductory			Windows 3.0	$1750	-	-	Neural Computer Sciences
NeuralWorks Explorer	Introductory	• Historical nets • Assortment • Instanet	• Limited input formatting	Mac, DOS	$99	-	-	NeuralWare

TABLE 14.1 Neural network development systems. *[continued]*

NAME	AUDIENCE	NOTABLE FEATURES	DEFICIENCY	PLATFORM	PRICE	NEURAL OR PARALLEL HARDWARE	LANGUAGE SUPPORT	VENDOR
NeuralWorks Prof. II+	Advanced	•SaveBest •Genetic Reinforcement •Projection net	•Difficult to create new paradigms	Mac, DOS, VMS, UNIX	$1500-$5000	-	Generate C only for feedforward nets	NeuralWare
Neuralyst	Intermediate Business	•Excel add-on		Mac, DOS	$165-$495	-	Excel Macros	EPIC
Neuro Windows	Introductory-Intermediate	•DLL •Large # PEs	•Slow	Windows, Visual BASIC	$369	NeuroBoard	Visual BASIC	Ward Systems
Neuro-Solutions	Signal Processing Advanced	•Iconic language •Modular design •Realtime data capability •Recurrent nets		NeXT	Contact Vendor	-	C, C++, Objective C	Neuro-Dimension
Neuro-Computing Library	Programmer	•DLL or C++		•Windows •All C++	$179-$399	Possible with C++	DLL, C++	NeuroSym
NeuroForecaster	Intermediate Finance Time-Series	•Training set selection from graph •NeuroFuzzy, and FastProp nets	•Sometimes confusing user interface	Mac, Windows 3.0, SPARC	$600-$995	-	-	NIBS Pte

TABLE 14.1 Neural network development systems. *(continued)*

				Platform	Price		Generate nets in C, Fortran, Pascal, Basic	Vendor
NeuroShell	Intermediate	•Generate nets in C, Fortran, Pascal, Basic •Neurosheet option		DOS	$195	–	Generate nets in C, Fortran, Pascal, Basic	Ward Systems
NeuX	Introductory	•Hybrid system	•Limited paradigms	Mac, HyperCard	$295	–	HyperTalk	Charles River Analytics
NN Toolkit	General	•MATLAB add-on •Flexible	•Slow	Mac, DOS, UNIX, VMS	Contact vendor	–	MatLab Language	MathWorks Inc
NN Utility	Programmer	•Iconic language		OS/2, OS/400, Windows 3.0	$1550-$12,700	–	C API	IBM
NNSheet NNSheet-C	Introductory-Intermediate Business	•Excel add-on	•Limited network size	Mac, Windows 3.0	$99-$495	–	Excel Macros C library	Inductive Solutions
OWL NN Library	Programmer			Mac, DOS, others	$499-$3000	–	C library	HyperLogic
Plexi	General	•Graphic Interface		Sun 3, SPARC	$4750	–	–	Lucid
QNSpec	Programmer			Mac, DOS, Windows 3.0	$250	–	–	Odin Corp
Syspro	Programmer	•Klopf Drive Reinforcement		DOS	$595	Possible	Fortran, C	Martingale Research
WinBrain	Introductory			Windows 3.0	$89	–	None	Applied Cognetics

TABLE 14.2 Neural network vertical applications.

NAME	AUDIENCE	NOTABLE FEATURES	DEFICIENCY	PLATFORM	PRICE	NEURAL OR PARALLEL HARDWARE	LANGUAGE SUPPORT	VENDOR
CAD/Chem	Chemists			UNIX, VAX	$28,000-$30,000	N/A	N/A	AIWare
NestorReader NestorWriter	OCR of text and writing			RS/6000, SPARC	>$15,000	Transputer	N/A	Nestor
NetTools	Endusers Gambling Finance	•Pre-trained	•Cannot be retrained	Windows 3.0	$349-$895	N/A	N/A	RaceCom
Neural$	Finance	•Hybrid system •Market turning point forecaster		DOS	>$895	N/A	N/A	TeraNet
NeuroVision	Image Analysis	•Menu based		Contact Vendor	$3495-$9995	Intel 1860	C API	Vision Harvest
StockSight	Finance	•Pre-trained	•Cannot be retrained	DOS, OS/2, SPARC	$495-$1275	N/A	N/A	GriffinNets

TABLE 14.3 Public Domain Neural Network Simulators

NAME	SPECIAL FEATURES	SOURCE (S) EXECUTABLE (E)	PLATFORM	PRICE	LOCATION OR CONTACT
Asprin/Migraines		S,E	UNIX	-	ftp.cognet.ucla.edu
ATree	Adaptive Logic Networks	S,E	UNIX, Windows 3	-	menaik.cs.ualberta.ca
CasCor1 Simulator	Cascade Corelation	S	Any C-able machine	-	pt.cs.cmu.edu
DartNet	Extensible using XCMDs	E	Mac	-	dartvax.dartmouth.edu
GENESIS	Neuron as well as Network modelling	S,E	UNIX, X11	Must register	genesis.cns.caltech.edu
Mactivation		E	Mac	-	bruno.cs.colorado.edu
MUME	Modular	S	UNIX		marwan@sedal.su.oz.au
Neocognitron	Neocognitron	S	Any C-able machine	Cost	tamsun.tamu.edu
NeuralShell		S,E	UNIX	-	quanta.eng.ohio-state.edu
NeurDS		E	DEC	-	gatekeeper.dec.com
PDP	PDP vol 3	S	UNIX, PC	-	nic.funet.fi
PlaNet 5.x		S,E	UNIX, X11	-	tutserver.tut.ac.jp
Pygmalion		S	UNIX, X11	-	bells.cs.ucl.ac.uk
QuickProp	Quick Porpagation	S	Any C-able machine	-	pt.cs.cmu.edu
Rochester Connectionist Simulator		S,E	UNIX, X11	-	cs.rochester.edu
SNNS	Substantial Interface	S,E	UNIX, X11	-	ifi.informatik.uni-stuttgart.de
SOMX	Self Org. Map	E	NeXTSTEP	-	cader@chopin.cas.american.edu
UCLA-SFINX		S,E	UNIX	-	retina.cs.ucla.edu
Xerion	Recurrent	S,E	UNIX, X11	-	ftp.cs.toronto.edu

For building custom networks from scratch, C code must be written. Versions of this system are available on DOS, Macintosh, VAX, Sun Systems, and other systems.

NeuralWorks allows developers to modify networks to experiment with their own summation, transfer, learning rules, and so on. Trained neural network modules can be translated or "flashed" into C-code modules and used by other software systems.

Network diagnostic tools are also included for monitoring and displaying data, and probes can be used to collect information about the network. An Explain command allows the user to check which input nodes affect specific output nodes.

Ward Systems Products

NeuroShell is a relatively inexpensive neural network development environment based on back propogation and is best for stand-alone systems. NeuroShell is especially good for pattern recognition and works with companion products to give a wide range of capabilities.

The designer answers on-screen questions, filling out forms and entering the names of data input and output fields. The data can be entered via keyboard or from a variety of standard file formats, including those for Lotus, ASCII, and dBase III. Minimum/maximum values for each field can be specified or can be automatically set, and a utility is provided to split data files into training and test data. During training, NeuroShell lets you select the number of hidden nodes, learning rate, and momentum values; alternatively, you can use default values.

The packages in the Ward Systems collection include the following:

- NeuroSheet—An interface to Lotus files, this product reads a spreadsheet and creates NeuroShell data files. It can write results back to the spreadsheet, including those to a specific cell.
- NeuroBoard—This product plugs into any computer with an AT bus and runs at 100 times the speed of an 80386 20-MHz computer. It implements NeuroShell in machine language.

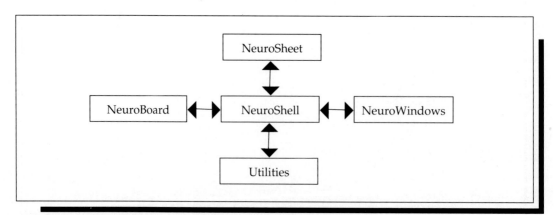

FIGURE 14.5 NeuroShell and related products.

- NeuroWindows—The newest product is a dynamic link library designed for use with MicroSoft's Visual Basic Programming Language. NeuroWindows allows reading of data from Excel, Word, and so on via dynamic data exchange (DDE). A series of neural network functions, it allows you to create up to 128 interconnected neural networks. Thus, you can produce several neural networks to process data for other neural networks or to decide which other neural networks to call. Thus, Visual Basic becomes the vehicle for building applications with neural networks embedded in the Windows environment.

Graphics capabilities allow the display of important data, assisting the examination of the quality of the data. For example, one can create scatterplots of one data field versus another and line charts of one data field for all records in a file. NeuroShell checks the performance of the test data periodically to see how well the neural network is doing; it can also detect overtraining. That is, as training goes on, the neural network performs better and better on both training and test data. At some point, the neural network starts memorizing details of the training file and the performance on the test data deteriorates.

Some of the screens in NeuroShell are shown in the series of figures in this section. In the initial screen (Figure 14.6), the developer is presented with the

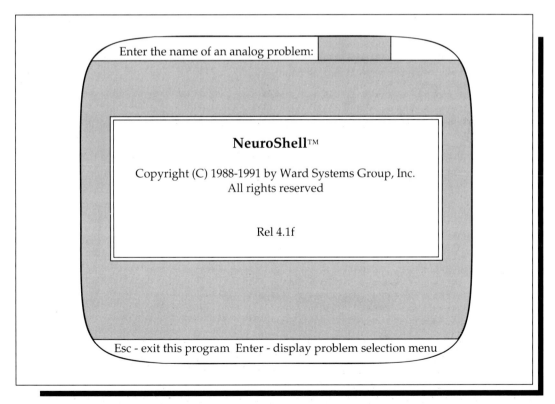

FIGURE 14.6   NeuroShell logo screen.

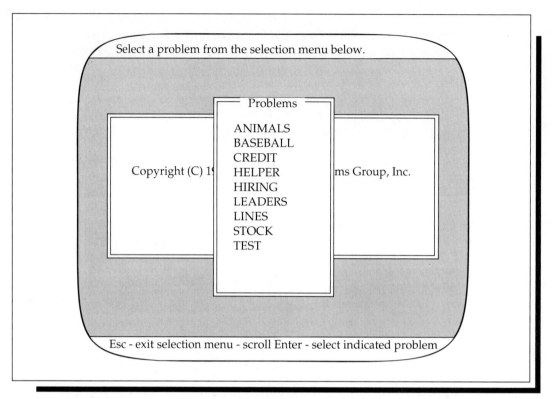

Select a problem from the selection menu below.

Problems

ANIMALS
BASEBALL
CREDIT
Copyright (C) 1   HELPER   ms Group, Inc.
HIRING
LEADERS
LINES
STOCK
TEST

Esc - exit selection menu - scroll Enter - select indicated problem

FIGURE 14.7   NeuroShell problem selection menu.

option of analog or binary input applications. As shown in Figure 14.7, a previous system can be selected or a new system constructed. A new implementation of the XOR problem is shown in the next figures. As shown in Figure 14.8, the developer can select from a menu of steps. Defining the characteristics involves entering the names of input nodes (called *characteristics* in NeuroShell) above the line and the names of output nodes (called *classifications*) below the line (see Figure 14.9). The numbers to the left of the variable names are examples of input values that go with the output values.

After enough cases have been entered, the system is ready to start the learning process. For the monitor screen shown in Figure 14.10, NeuroShell default values were used for the back propagation parameters; however, the developer can choose different values. Figure 14.11 shows a test case, which in this example produces an answer close to the correct answer. Figure 14.12 is an example of a display giving the parameter values and other data related to the learning that took place. Other menus allow the developer to call other utilities and make changes to the network. Weights can be displayed and various values such as the input can be viewed graphically.

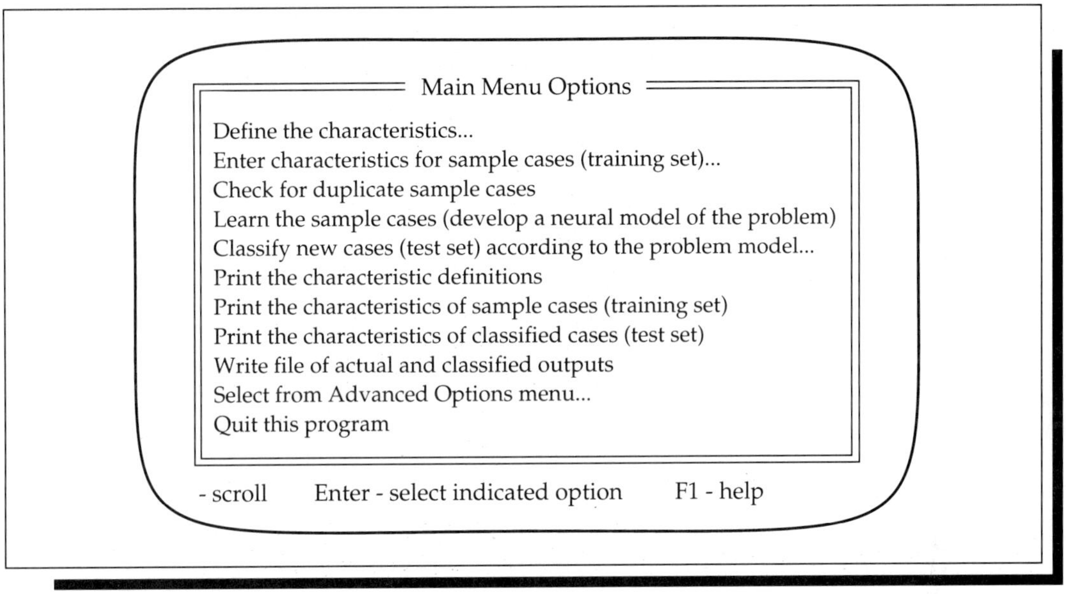

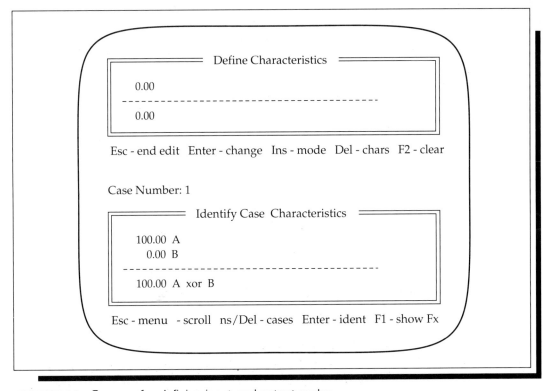

FIGURE 14.8   NeuroShell main menu options.

FIGURE 14.9   Screens for defining input and output nodes.

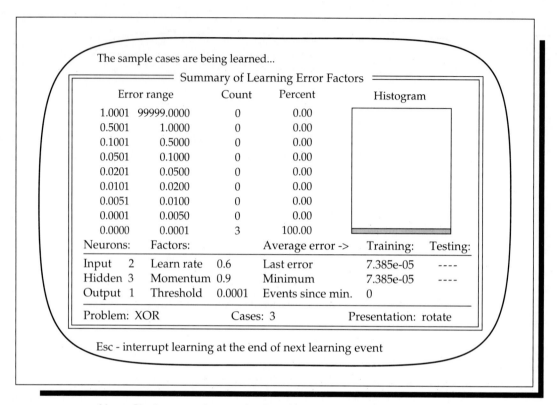

FIGURE 14.10   NeuroShell screen for monitoring the training process.

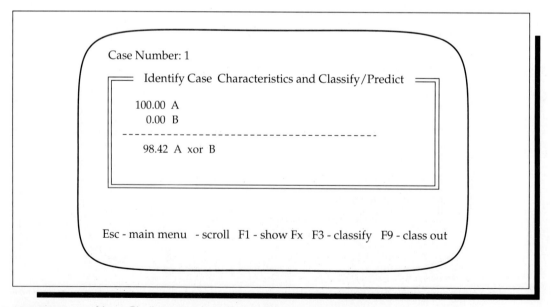

FIGURE 14.11   NeuroShell screen for testing the trained system.

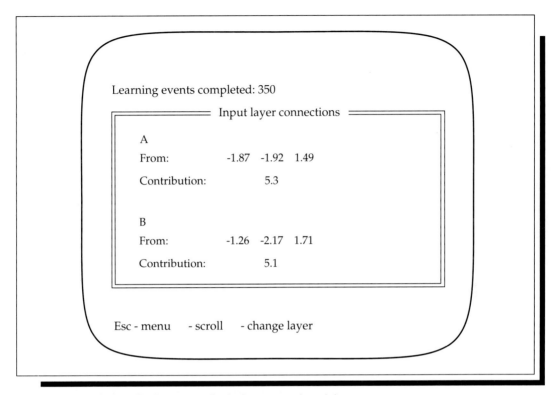

Learning events completed: 350

Input layer connections

A
From: -1.87   -1.92   1.49
Contribution: 5.3

B
From: -1.26   -2.17   1.71
Contribution: 5.1

Esc - menu   - scroll   - change layer

FIGURE 14.12   NeuroShell screen displaying network weights.

14.7 Neural Network Hardware

Most current neural network implementations involve simulations on conventional sequential computers. However, advances in hardware technology will greatly enhance the performance of future neural network systems by exploiting the inherent advantage of massively parallel processing. Hardware improvements will meet higher requirements for memory and processing speed for shorter training times of larger networks.

Simulating a neural network means mathematically defining the nodes and weights assigned to it. So, instead of using one central processing unit (CPU) for each neuron, we use one CPU for all of the neurons. This simulation may require extended processing time.

Each processing element computes node outputs from the weights and input signals from other processors. Together the network of neurons can store information that may be recalled in order to interpret and classify future inputs to the network.

Traditional Hardware Solutions

In order to reduce the computational work of a neural network (which can involve hundreds of thousands of manipulations) when the work is done on regular computers, one can use one of three approaches:

1. *Faster machines.* For example, a machine with an Intel 80486 processor supplemented by a math coprocessor can expedite work (e.g., 2 to 10 times faster).

2. *Neural chips.* Most chips can execute computations very rapidly, but they do not allow training. Thus, it is necessary to train off the chip. This problem is expected to be corrected soon. In the interim, it is practical to use acceleration boards. The idea is to implement neural network data structures on a chip[8,9]. These chips can be analog (e.g., the Intel 80170 electronically trainable neural network) or digital or even optical. (See Caudill[7] for details.) Most neural chips are still in the development stage.

3. *Acceleration boards.* These are dedicated processors that can be added to regular computers, similar to a math coprocessor, but because they are specially designed for neural networks, they can work very rapidly (e.g., 10 to 100 times faster than a 20 MHZ 30386/387 processor). Acceleration boards are currently the best approach to speeding up computations. Examples include the Brainmaker Accelerator Board (from California Scientific Software), Balboa/860 boards (from HNC), and NeuroBoard (from the Ward Systems Group). NeuroBoard is at least 100 times faster than the 30386/387 processor. Acceleration boards are extremely useful because training may take a long time. For example, one independent test with NeuroBoard reduced the training time from 7 minutes to 1 second.

Optical Computing

Optical computers are being developed that use light beams instead of electrical currents. For neural network applications, optical multiplication is performed using lenses and mirrors, and the optical multiplication of a matrix and a vector can be done extremely rapidly. The matrix represents the neural network weights, and the vector values represent the strengths of the inputs.

With optical computers, the strength of an input signal is encoded as the intensity of a laser beam. Neural networks require a laser for each input node, and the intensities correspond to the strength of the input signal. The first lens spreads the beam so that it covers a rectangular area. This light then passes through a spectral light modulator (SLM), which selectively absorbs light in different parts of the rectangular area. This represents the different neural network weights. With the light from all the input lasers treated this way, the final intensity at the photoreceptors represents the matrix multiplication of the weights and the input vector. Fortunately, the SLM device can change its transparency pattern in response to an applied voltage. This corresponds to the adjustment of the weights in response to the feedback required for the neural network to learn.

Optical computing has several problems. For one, the physical size of the current devices, with their lasers and bases, needs to be reduced. On-chip lasers may eventually solve this problem. Also, the systems are fragile and sensitive to alignment problems. In addition, better SLMs are needed with properties for representing the weight matrix more effectively. Good progress in developing optical neurocomputers is being made; however, commercial use is years away.

14.8 Maintenance Issues

In operational systems, maintenance is required when accuracy decreases or new requirements arise. Routine use of the network may eventually encounter changes in the data due to environmental factors that affect decision making.

If modifications in the input data are significant, the training set must be changed and the network must be retrained and evaluated, as was done initially. In some applications, periodic retraining as better historical data is obtained is an advantage of the neural network approach. Other systems require time-consuming and error-prone changes in the software or rule bases. However, a problem occurs when the changes require redesigning or reformatting the input vector. In this case, using the original data along with new data requires inconvenient reprocessing of training data and changing the number of nodes in the network.

Another significant change in the maintenance phase is software modification to change the neural network interfaces to users or other parts of the overall system. This change can involve redoing the design phase of the developmental process.

References

1. D. Bailey and D. Thompson, "How to Develop Neural-Network Applications," *AI Expert*, Vol. 5 (June 1990).
2. D. Bailey and D. Thompson, "Developing Neural-Network Applications," *AI Expert*, Vol. 5 (September 1990).
3. Jeanette Lawrence, "Data Preparation for Neural Networks," *AI Expert*, Vol. 6 (November 1991).
4. Dan Jones and Stanley P. Franklin, "Choosing a Network: Matching the Architecture to the Application," *Handbook of Neural Computing Applications*, ed. by A. Maren, C. Harston, and R. Pap, San Diego: Academic Press, 1990, pp. 219–231.
5. Maureen Caudill, "Neural Network Training Tips and Techniques," *AI Expert*, Vol. 6 (January 1991).

6. G. David Garson, "Interpreting Neural-Network Connection Weights," *AI Expert*, Vol. 6 (April 1991).

7. K. Reid and A. Zeichick, "Neural Network Resource Guide," *AI Expert*, Vol. 7 (June, 1992).

8. Maureen Caudill, "Embedded Neural Networks," *AI Expert*, Vol. 6 (April 1991).

9. Jessica Keyes, "AI on a Chip," *AI Expert*, Vol. 6 (April 1991).

Chapter 15

Integration of Expert Systems and Neural Networks

Expert system and neural network technologies have developed to the point where the advantages of each can be combined into more powerful systems. In some cases, neural computing systems are replacing expert systems and other AI solutions. In others, neural networks provide features not possible with conventional AI systems, and they may provide aspects of intelligent behavior that have thus far eluded the AI symbolic/logical approach[1–4].

Recent advances in neural network technology now allow the development of hybrid intelligent systems that can address new problems. As these systems grow in number and importance, developers need frameworks to understand the combination of neural networks and expert systems, as well as models and guidelines for effective implementation. This chapter describes such a framework and presents examples of current hybrid systems to illustrate the models.

15.1   Expert Systems and Neural Computing

Expert systems perform reasoning using previously established rules for a well-defined, narrow domain. They combine knowledge bases of rules and domain-specific facts with information from clients or users about specific instances of problems in the knowledge domains of the expert systems. Ideally, reasoning can be explained and the knowledge bases easily modified, independent of the inference engine, as new rules become known.

Expert systems are especially good for closed-system applications for which inputs are literal and precise, leading to logical outputs. They are particularly useful for interacting with the user to define a specific problem and bring in facts peculiar to the problem being solved. A limitation of the expert system approach arises from the fact that experts do not always think in terms of rules. In these cases, an expert system does not mimic the actual reasoning process of human experts. For stable applications with well-defined rules, expert systems can be easily developed to provide good performance. Furthermore, most development systems allow the creation of explanation systems to help the user understand questions being asked or conclusions and reasoning processes.

The state of the art in neural computing is inspired by our current understanding of biological neural networks; however, even after all the research in biology and psychology, important questions remain about how the brain and the mind work. Advances in computer technology have allowed the construction of interesting and useful ANNs that borrow some features from the biological systems. Information processing with neural computers consists of analyzing patterns of activity, with learned information stored as weights between neurode connections. A common characteristic of these systems is their ability to classify streams of input data without the explicit knowledge of rules and to use arbitrary patterns of weights to represent the memory of categories. The network of neurons can store information that can be recalled in order to interpret and classify future inputs to the network. Because knowledge is represented as numeric weights, the rules and the reasoning process in neural networks are not readily explainable.

Neural networks have the potential to provide some of the human characteristics of problem solving that are difficult to simulate using the logical, analytical techniques of expert system and standard software technologies. For example, neural networks can analyze large quantities of data to establish patterns and characteristics in situations where rules are not known and can often make sense of incomplete or noisy data. These capabilities have thus far proven too difficult for the traditional symbolic/logic approach.

The immediate practical implication of neural computing is its emergence as an alternative or supplement to conventional computing systems and AI techniques. As an alternative, neural computing offers the advantage of rapid execution speed once the network has been trained. The ability to learn from cases and train the system with data sets, rather than having to write programs, may be more cost effective, as well as more convenient when changes become necessary. In applications where rules cannot be known, neural computers may be able to represent rules, in effect, as stored connection weights.

15.2   Comparisons and Synergistic Nature

Beyond its role as an alternative, neural computing can be combined with conventional software to produce more powerful hybrid systems. Such integrated systems could use databases, expert systems, neural networks, and other technologies to produce the best solutions to complex problems. Thus, intelligent systems could eventually mimic human decision making under uncertainty and in situations where information is incomplete or contains mistakes. A goal is to produce systems including components that exhibit mind-like behavior in order to handle information as flexibly and powerfully as humans do.

Expert systems and ANNs have unique and sometimes complementary features. From functional and applications standpoints, each approach can be equally feasible, although in some cases one may have an advantage over the other. In principle, expert systems represent a logical, symbolic approach, while neural networks use numeric and associative processing to mimic models of biological systems. The features of each approach are summarized in Table 15.1.

Neural networks rely on training data to program the system. Thus, neural network components can be useful for hybrid systems by using an appropriate training set that allows the system to learn and generalize for operation on future input data. Inputs exactly like training data are recognized and identified, while new data (or incomplete and noisy versions of the training data) can be matched most closely to patterns learned by the system.

Neural network components can be useful when rules are not known, either because the topic is too complex or because no human expert is available. If training data can be generated, the system may be able to learn enough information to function as well as or better than an expert system. This approach also has the benefit of easy system modification by retraining with an updated data set, thus eliminating programming changes and rule reconstruction. The data-driven aspect of neural networks allows adjustment in response to changing environments and events. Another advantage of neural network components is the high speed of operation after the network is trained, which will be enhanced dramatically as neural chips become readily available. NN chip development also focuses on making training faster.

The two technologies in many ways represent complementary approaches. Neural network components can be the best solutions for some of the problems

TABLE 15.1   Features of Expert Systems and Neural Networks

EXPERT SYSTEMS	NEURAL NETWORKS
Symbolic	Numeric
Logical	Associative
Mechanical	Biological
Sequential	Parallel
Closed	Self-organizing

that have proven difficult for expert system developers, and hybrid systems may allow developers to address problems not amenable to either approach alone. The integration of these and other intelligent system components with conventional technologies promises to be an important area for research and development in the 1990s. Developers need models and guidelines to make good use of the new opportunities presented by the synergism of neural networks and expert systems. They need to know when to choose each technology and how to implement systems that combine the two effectively.

15.3   Models of Integration

Several techniques for integrating expert systems and neural networks have emerged over the past two years, ranging from primarily independent to highly interactive. While there are different approaches to categorizing these integration techniques, this section classifies them according to their software architecture.

Five different integration strategies have been identified (Figure 15.1): stand-alone models, transformations, loose coupling, tight coupling, and full integration[4]. The following sections discuss each of these strategies, providing basic concepts and descriptions, an application example, variations on and expected uses of the model, and benefits and limitations of the approach. Application examples are representative of but do not describe actual integrated systems.

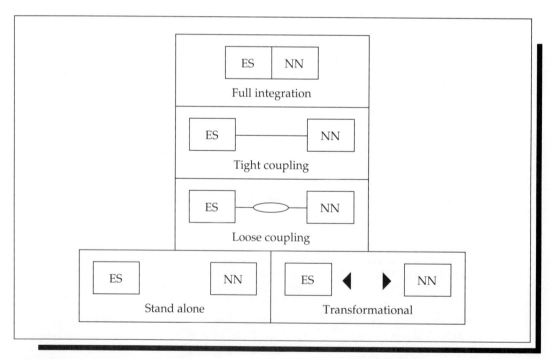

FIGURE 15.1   Models for integrating expert systems and neural networks.

Stand-alone Models

Stand-alone models of combined expert system and neural network applications consist of independent software components. These components do not interact in any way. While stand-alone models are a degenerate case for integration purposes, they are an alternative worth discussing.

There are several reasons for developing stand-alone expert systems and neural networks. First, they provide a direct means of comparing the problem-solving capabilities of the two techniques for a specific application. Second, used in parallel, they provide redundancy in processing. Third, developing one technique after finishing a model of the other facilitates validation of the prior development process. Finally, running two models in parallel permits a loose approximation of integration.

An example of a stand-alone expert system/neural network model involves the diagnostic classification of symptoms in computer repair. Two distinct components, an expert system and a neural network, are developed to solve the same classification problem. When a computer malfunctions, symptoms are presented to both the expert system and the neural network, and both return a solution. The independent solutions are compared, and if there is disagreement, the user decides which solution to implement. The expert system can also be queried for justification of its result.

Stand-alone models serve three primary purposes. First, as parallel systems, they offer two sets of capabilities: the generalization and adaptability of neural networks and the stepwise deduction and explanation facilities of expert systems.

Second, stand-alone models provide verification of previous applications. Often developers will build a neural network to solve the same problem handled by an existing expert system. This permits the developers both to compare the capabilities of expert systems to those of neural networks and to ensure that the initial system performs properly.

Third, stand-alone models are used to develop an initial prototype quickly while a more time-consuming application is being designed. For example, a neural network might be trained to solve a problem temporarily while a more complete expert system solution is being developed. A rapid prototype of either a neural network or an expert system provides two benefits. First, it provides a quick problem-solving tool that can satisfy short-term needs while the full-scale system is being developed. Second, the initial development process often provides important guidance for the full-scale system by highlighting requirements and pointing out pitfalls.

Stand-alone models have two principal benefits compared to other expert system/neural network models. First, because they do not attempt to interface with each other, the model is straightforward to develop. Second, there are no impediments to the use of commercially available software packages.

However, stand-alone models have several limitations. Other than conceptual issues, there is no effective means of leveraging the development of one technique when developing the other. Neither the neural network nor the expert system can support the weaknesses of the other. The systems are completely independent, and their benefits are simply those derived from their separate technologies. Finally, developing separate systems effectively doubles the maintenance requirements for the model. Both must be updated simultaneously to avoid confusion, and updates to one cannot help the other.

Transformational Models

Transformational models are similar to stand-alone models in that the end result of development is an independent model that does not interact with another. What distinguishes the two types of models is that transformational systems begin as one type of system (e.g., a neural network) and end up as another (e.g., an expert system).

There are two forms of transformational models: expert systems that are transformed into neural networks and neural nets that are transformed into expert systems. Determining which technique is used for development and which is used for delivery is based on the desirable features that the technique offers.

An application example of a transformational model is a marketing decision aid. Initially, a neural network is developed to identify trends and relationships within sales data. Then the network is used as the basis for an expert system that assists marketing researchers in allocating advertising resources. In this example, the neural network is used to adapt quickly to a complex, data-intensive problem, to provide generalization, and to filter errors in the data. An expert system was targeted as the delivery system because of the desire to document and verify the knowledge used to make decisions and because the users required justification capabilities.

Neural networks that are transformed into expert systems are often used for many of the same purposes described in the previous example. Data analysis and preliminary knowledge engineering are principal applications for this type of transformational model. Neural networks are transformed into expert systems for reasons such as knowledge documentation and verification, the desire for step-wise reasoning, and the need for explanation facilities.

While less common, the transformation from expert system to neural network is also useful. Expert systems are usually converted for one of two reasons. Either the expert system was incapable of solving the problem adequately, or the speed, adaptability, and robustness of neural networks were required. Knowledge from the expert system is used to set the initial conditions and training set for the neural network, and the neural network evolves from there.

Transformational models offer several benefits to developers. They are often quick to develop and ultimately require maintenance on only one system. Development occurs in the most appropriate environment. Similarly, the delivery technique offers operational benefits suitable to its environment.

The limitations of transformational models are significant. First, there is no fully automated means of transforming an expert system into a neural network or vice versa. In fact, there is no known method for accurately and completely performing the transformation. However, the fact that transformational models are relatively common demonstrates that adequate transformations are possible with reasonable resources.

Another limitation is that significant modifications to the system may require a new development effort, which leads to another transformation. In addition to maintenance issues, the finished transformational system is limited operationally to the capabilities of the target technique. Thus, the benefits of integrated systems are not truly enjoyed.

Loosely Coupled Models

Loosely coupled models are the first true form of integrated expert systems and neural networks. The application is decomposed into separate neural network and expert system components that communicate via data files. Among the variations on loosely coupled models are preprocessors, postprocessors, coprocessors, and user interfaces. In this discussion, we will consider the neural network component of the model to be the pre- or postprocessor.

As an application example, consider a model forecasting the utilization of a work force. Data is fed into a neural network that predicts the workload for a given time period. The forecast is placed into a data file and passed to an expert system that uses the workload to determine the utilization of the work force.

In preprocessing loosely coupled models, the neural network serves as a front end that conditions data prior to passing it on to the expert system. Expected uses for this type of model include using the neural network to perform data fusion, to remove errors, to identify objects, and to recognize patterns. The expert system component can then use this information to solve problems in classification, identification, scene analysis, and problem solving.

Postprocessing models are the converse of preprocessing models. In postprocessing, the expert system produces output that is passed via a data file to the neural network. In this type of architecture, the expert system performs data preparation and manipulation, classify inputs, and make decisions. The neural network component then performs functions such as forecasting, data analysis, monitoring, and error trapping.

The coprocessing model involves data passing in both directions, which allows interactive and cooperative behavior between the neural network and the expert system. While very few coprocessing applications are available, they have the potential to solve difficult problems. Possible applications include incremental data refinement, iterative problem solving, and dual decision making.

User interfaces are turning to neural networks as a pattern recognition technology capable of increasing the flexibility of user interactions with expert systems. Initial research often takes the form of loosely coupled models, which allow projects to focus on pattern recognition rather than integration issues. Speech processing and handwritten character recognition are perhaps the most common forms of user interfaces, but image processing and user modeling are also being studied.

Compared to the more integrated expert system and neural network applications, loosely coupled models are easy to develop. They can use commercially available expert system and neural network software, which reduces the programming burden. The system design and implementation processes are simplified with loosely coupled models. Finally, maintenance time is reduced because of the simplicity of the data file interface mechanism.

Loosely coupled models have four limitations. First, because of the interface, operating time is longer. Second, there is often a great deal of redundancy in developing the separate neural network and expert system components. Both must be capable of solving subproblems in order to perform their unique computations, but because they lack direct access to each other's internal processing, they must develop independent capabilities. This also leads to overlap in the data input requirements and internal processing. Finally, there is a high communications cost for loose coupling.

Tightly Coupled Models

The categories of loose and tight coupling have significant overlap. Both utilize independent expert system and neural network components. Tight coupling, however, passes information via memory-resident data structures rather than external data files. This improves the interactive capabilities of tightly coupled models in addition to enhancing their performance.

Tightly coupled models can function under the same variations as loosely coupled models, except that the tightly coupled versions of pre-, post-, and co-processors are typically faster. Variations unique to tight coupling include blackboards, cooperative systems, and embedded systems.

Another forecasting application provides an example of tight coupling. In this instance, stock option data is presented to a neural network. The network uses financial and stock option data to predict the options strike price over a three-day period. This information is then passed to the expert system, which determines the appropriate unwind (action) strategy for the option.

One of the most interesting expected uses of tightly coupled models is in the area of blackboard architectures. *Blackboards* are shared data structures that facilitate interactive problem solving via independent agents. Typically the agents are knowledge-based systems. It is both technically feasible and operationally important to consider the potential of adding neural networks to the blackboard paradigm. Applications for integrated blackboard systems include complex pattern recognition, fault isolation and repair, and advanced decision support.

Cooperating systems are one of the most common variations of tightly coupled expert system/neural network models. Cooperating systems are similar to coprocessing loosely coupled models but tend to be highly interactive due to the ease of data passing. Applications of cooperating systems occur in monitoring and control, decision making, and several problem-solving domains.

Embedded systems are a third variation of tightly coupled models that use modules from one technique to help control the functioning of the other. For example, neural networks can be embedded in expert systems to control the inferencing process. Embedded neural network components are used to focus inferencing, guide searches, and perform pattern matching. Expert system components are used to interpret the results of the neural network, to provide internetwork connectivity, and to provide explanation facilities. Applications of embedded systems exist in the areas of robotics, education, and classification.

Tight coupling has the benefits of reduced communications overhead and improved runtime performance compared to loose coupling. By maintaining the modularity of the expert system and neural network components, several commercial packages are suitable for developing tightly coupled models. Overall, tight coupling offers design flexibility and robust integration.

Tightly coupled systems have three principal limitations. First, the complexity of development and maintenance increases due to the internal data interface. Second, tight coupling, like loose coupling, suffers from redundant data gathering and processing. Once again, this is due to the independence of the expert system and neural network components. Finally, V&V is more difficult, particularly for embedded applications.

Fully Integrated Models

In this configuration, the expert system and the neural network are two components of the same system. The neural network component represents the knowledge base implicitly as connection weights. The system can be designed with the weights representing branches in the logic of the rule base so that the lines of reasoning can be explained. Alternatively, the neural network's associative memory just stores relationships between patterns of inputs and corresponding conclusions.

Fully integrated expert system/neural network models share data structures and knowledge representations; thus, components of the system communicate as a natural consequence of the integration. Several variations of fully integrated systems are under investigation by researchers and developers. Connectionist expert systems represent relationships between pieces of knowledge, with weighted links between symbolic nodes. Applications of connectionist expert systems exist in medical diagnosis, information retrieval and analysis, and pattern classification. For example, Gallant[5] has designed connectionist networks for use as expert systems.

An often discussed example of a connectionist expert system is Gallant's model, which has been applied to diagnosis problems. As shown in Figure 15.2, the the nodes of the neural network represent specific facts or aspects of the knowledge domain. The input nodes represent different symptoms, and input values of +1, −1, or 0 indicate whether that symptom is present, absent, or not checked, respectively. Training data, consisting of symptoms with known diagnoses, is used to find the weights among the nodes that give the desired performance. Additional intermediate nodes allow the system to be more accurate and rubust, suggesting treatments for the diagnosed diseases.

The connectionist expert system in effect represents the knowledge base by the weights of the neural network. In Gallant's model, an inference engine is used for further interpretation of the results. It is also used to direct questions from the user to minimize the amount of input while still allowing conclusions to be drawn. The expert system aspect of this system also provides explanations of

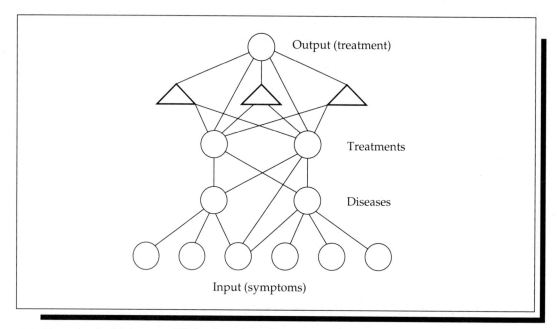

Input (symptoms)

FIGURE 15.2   Architecture of Gallant's connectionist expert system.

results. An advantage of this model is the ability to use files of training data to change the system's behavior without knowing or rewriting the rules in the knowledge base.

The benefits of full integration include robustness, improved performance, and increased problem-solving capabilities. Robustness and performance improvements stem from the dual nature of the knowledge representations and data structures. In addition, there is little or no redundancy in the development process because the systems can leverage off of each other. Finally, it has been demonstrated that fully integrated models can provide a full range of capabilities—such as adaptation, generalization, noise tolerance, justification, and logical deduction—not found in nonintegrated models.

Full integration has limitations caused by the increased complexity of the intermodule interactions. First, there is the complexity of specifying, designing, and building fully integrated models. Second, there is a lack of tools to facilitate full integration. Finally, there are important questions in verifying, validating, and maintaining fully integrated systems.

15.4   Hybrid System Applications

Interesting applications are starting to appear using a combination of expert system and neural network technologies[2]. The complementary nature of the two approaches allows novel applications and solutions to more complex problems. The following sections give examples of applications in some of the categories

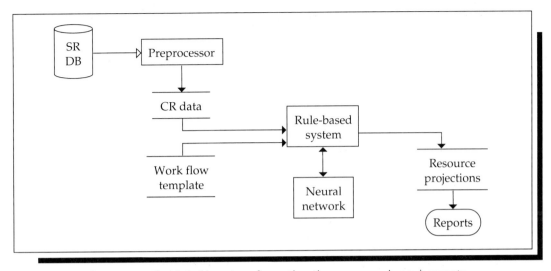

FIGURE 15.3   Loose-coupling hybrid system for estimating personnel requirements.

previously described. These examples are good applications of hybrid systems because they involve data sets that can be modified as external conditions change and then used to modify the system's behavior without reprogramming or revising the knowledge base.

Personnel Requirements

A tight-coupling hybrid system has been developed by Hanson and Brekke[6] for projecting personnel requirements for maintaining networks of workstations at NASA (Figure 15.3). A rule-based system estimates the final resource requirements for individual service requests, but a neural network provides projections on completion times for services requested. The neural network uses historical data as training sets. The input vector is the list of activities required, and the output is a gaussian curve whose center is the actual completion time for the service requested. In routine operation, the neural network gives the expert system an estimate of the completion time corresponding to a given activity list. The neural network is easily retrained via new data sets on completion times for recent services.

This PC-based system uses OPS83 as the expert system language and is linkable to C modules. Output of the system is in the form of spreadsheet files. Service request data is first processed to produce data files needed by the hybrid expert system and neural network. The rule-based knowledge comes from interviews with managers about activity assignments and with technicians about issues such as allotment of time to different tasks. The neural network is implemented in a callable C module, and the weight file is selected from a menu.

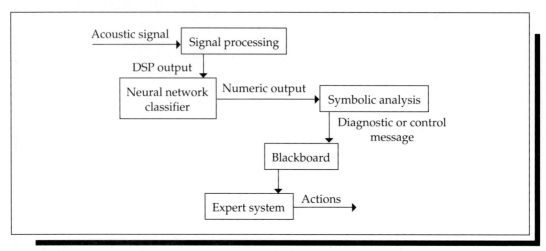

FIGURE 15.4   Tight-coupling hybrid system for analyzing acoustic signals.

Underwater Welding Robot Temperature Controller

The SCRuFFy system by Hendler[7] uses a tight-coupling model for integrating expert systems and neural networks. The system includes a temporal pattern matcher that mediates between the two and provides mapping from acoustic signals to symbols for reasoning about changes in signals over time. SCRuFFy uses a back propagation neural network and an OPS5-based expert system that communicate via a blackboard architecture, which allows for future expansion to include sensors of other types of processing modules in addition to expert systems and neural networks.

One application of this technique is in temperature control of an underwater welding robot. As shown in Figure 15.4, signals from acoustic measurements of the welder are inputs to a digital signal processor that creates input to the neural network. The network is pretrained to give four numbers indicating the relative classification of either normal welding or three error conditions. The symbolic analysis module tracks the changes over time in the signal classifications by the neural network and produces symbolic information describing the time course of the acoustic signal. This information can be used by the reasoning module to recommend corrective actions early before more extreme, expensive measures are required.

Case-based Hybrid Systems

Gutknecht, Pfeifer, and Stolze developed tight-coupling systems[8] that can use several different components for problem solving (Figure 15.5). The system learns how to focus on problems, and it narrows down to likely hypotheses and questions in a way that is similar to the way experts operate. The neural network component is trained to recognize possible hypotheses or tests to do, given cer-

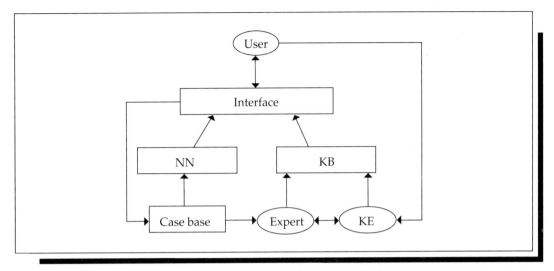

FIGURE 15.5 Tight-coupling hybrid system for case-based applications.

tain conditions. The system finds and rates different hypotheses and possible tests, and then focuses on the best course of action.

The system uses a case base to store information from observations of human experts' choices of hypotheses and tests. The case base is also updated as the system is used and new instances of expert performance are observed. It is also updated where the hybrid system is shown to be deficient.

This hybrid system is coupled tightly via the architecture that uses calls to neural network and expert system modules as needed. The system also provides for extensive interaction with the user in order to collect information on system performance and to update the case base. The neural network accesses the case base during initial training and for retraining as needed.

Neural Networks in Knowledge Acquisition

ANN can support the knowledge acquisition task for expert system cases where historical data are available. In principle the approach is similar to rule induction or case-based reasoning. However, as discussed earlier, rule induction requires an initial set of *attributes*. These may not be available if experts are not available to produce them or if the experts cannot identify all the relevant attributes.

In situations where rules cannot be directly determined or when it may take too long to elicit them, ANN can be useful for fast identification of implicit knowledge by automatically analyzing cases of historical data. The ANN analyzes these data sets to identify *patterns* and relationships that may subsequently lead to rules for expert systems. ANN may be the sole technique for knowledge acquisition or it may supplement explicit rules derived by other techniques (such as interviews).

Another possible contribution of ANN to knowledge acquisition is when the interface with an expert may best be accomplished with an expert system module that asks questions and directs the data gathering from the expert efficiently and comprehensively. A trained neural network can then rapidly process information to produce associated facts and consequences. Finally, an expert system module can perform further analysis and report results. Thus, fewer explicit rules may be necessary since the neural network contains general knowledge embedded in its connection weights and produces specific knowledge relevant to the user's problem.

Thus, to the extent possible, neural networks make an important contribution to knowledge engineering by replacing knowledge bases with associative memory that encodes knowledge implicitly as connection weights. The analysis of data for patterns and relationships that lead to rule (or other knowledge representation) creation can be a useful tool for knowledge engineers.

Database Resource Requirements Advisor

One type of hybrid system uses pre- and postprocessing with standard or expert system software to interface with neural network components. This configuration uses an expert system to collect data from a user and for the reasoning required to present final conclusions. The neural network analyzes data to supply information needed by the expert system for a complete analysis. An advantage of this model is its ability to use files of training data to change the system's behavior without knowing or changing rules in the knowledge base.

An example of this type of application is a prototype system[9] using the expert system shell AUBREY and the neural network tool NeuroShell. The system was designed to advise users on the resource requirements for developing database systems (Figure 15.6). The neural network analyzes experiential data on the

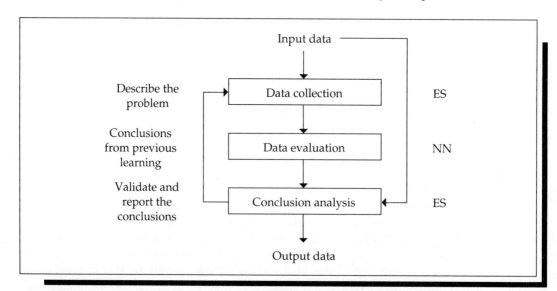

FIGURE 15.6   Hybrid system for estimating database resource requirements.

time and effort required to finish previous database projects. Thus, the system provides the flexibility of presenting new data files to supply information to the system without having to enter new rules or information extracted from separate data analyses.

15.5 Hybrid System Development Tools

Several development systems have recently become commercially available for building expert systems or neural networks. Many of these systems can be used to create loosely coupled hybrid systems, usually requiring file transfers. The data manipulation becomes a major task for the developer; however, useful systems can be produced. Table 15.2 shows several popular systems and their manufacturers. Some vendors are addressing the interface problem specifically to facilitate the linkage between expert systems and neural networks. NueX is the first commercial system for developing hybrid neural network and expert systems. Examples of the use of NueX, and of NeuroShell in conjunction with Level5, are included in the next section of this chapter and in the Appendix.

NueX Example: The Light Switch Problem

A small example of the use of NueX is provided with the demonstration disk and is discussed here. Although this example is very simple, it shows the fundamental components and development steps of NueX. The problem is to diagnose whether or not a light bulb is broken. The XOR neural network is trained to recognize the characteristics of light switches (up or down) and the associated output (whether the circuit is open or closed). The expert system component reasons

TABLE 15.2 Examples of Hybrid System Development Tools

PRODUCT	MANUFACTURER
NueX	Charles River Analytics
Nexpert Object	Neuron Data
Net-Link+	Norrad
NeuralWorks Professional II /Plus	NeuralWare
NeuroShell, NeuroBoard	Ward Systems Group
ExploreNet, KnowledgeNet, NeuroSoft	HNC
DynaMind, NeuroLink	NeuroDynamix
NeuroSmarts	Cognition Technology
BrainMaker Professional	California Scientific Software
Neural Inference System (NIS)	Integrated Inference Machines
Level5 Object	Information Builders
C, OPS5, LISP	

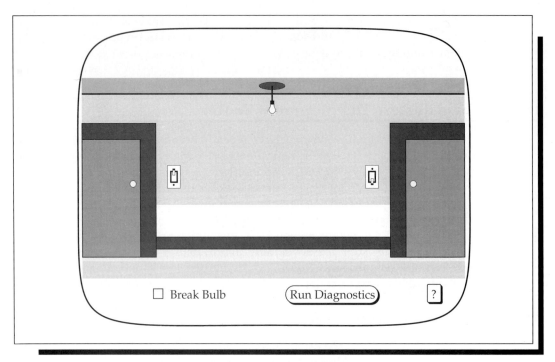

FIGURE 15.7   NueX Hypercard screen for displaying results.

from the neural network output to determine if the bulb is broken (if the circuit is closed but no light is detected).

Figures 15.7–15.16 show some of the features of NueX that are useful in developing this light switch application. First, because NueX uses hypercard, the output interface can be more elaborate than simply printed results. In this case, a room can be portrayed, and the light switches can be changed by clicking them on. The system changes if light is or is not produced.

Figure 15.8 shows the initial screen presented to the developer. The application stack and its associated knowledge base and neural network can be selected, if already created, or a new application can be started. Figures 15.9 and 15.10 are examples of rules, with distinct sections for the IF and THEN parts. Library commands can be invoked to produce links to the neural network and to specify hypertext interface instructions. Figure 15.11 shows the ability to summarize rules in the knowledge base and associated parameters.

On the neural network side of NueX, the architecture is specified graphically, as shown in Figure 15.12. Via pull-down menus and sidebars, nodes and layers can be designed in the configuration desired. Figures 15.13 and 15.14 show the windows that display node and path information, which can be modified by the developer. As an example of other facilities, the weights can be randomized, as shown in Figure 15.15. The training of the neural network can be monitored, as shown in Figure 15.16, to check progress and look for changes to be made in the parameters in subsequent retraining attempts.

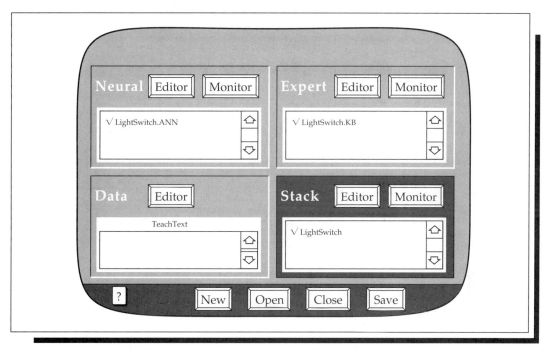

FIGURE 15.8   Initial screen in the NueX development system.

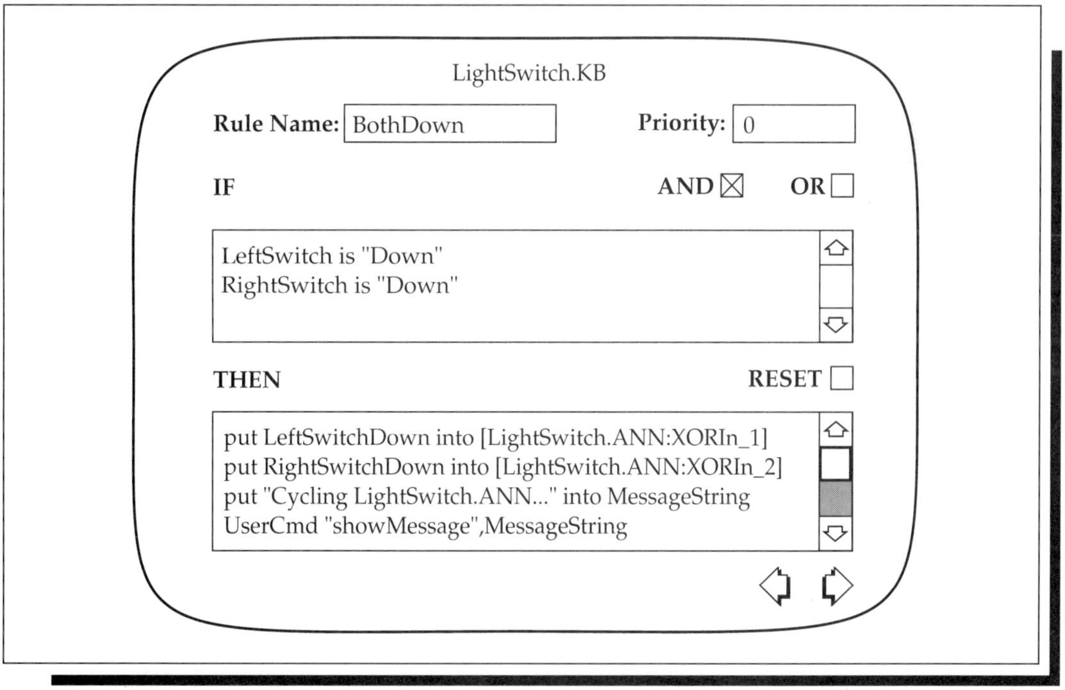

FIGURE 15.9   Sample screen for entering rules.

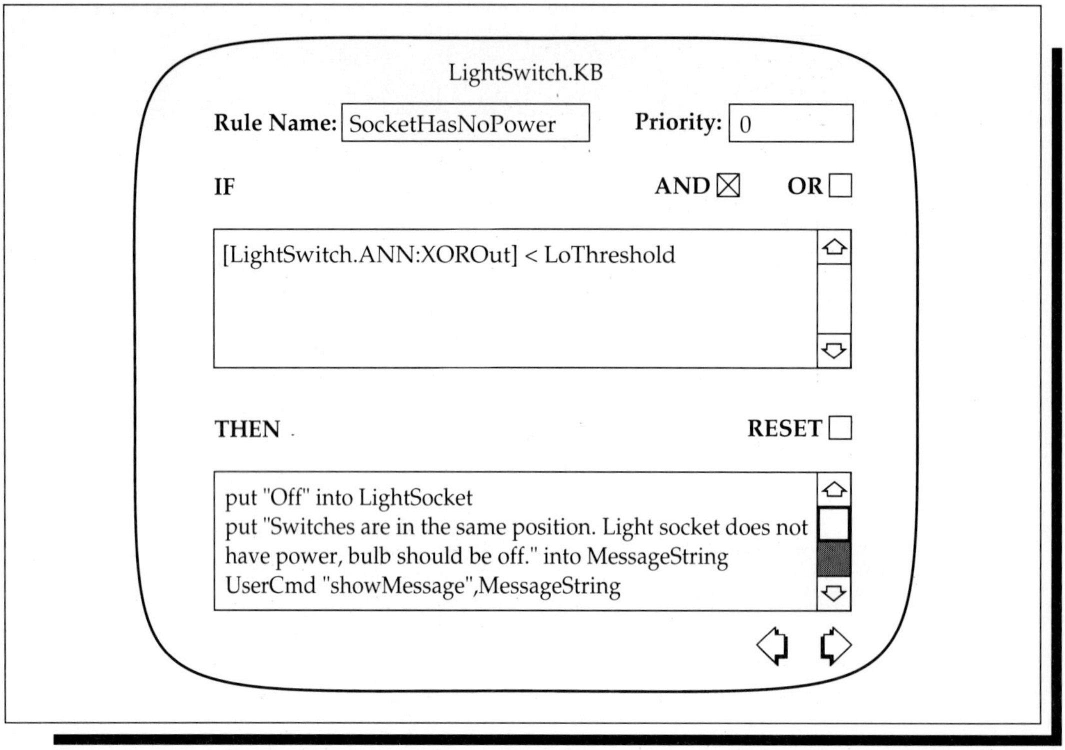

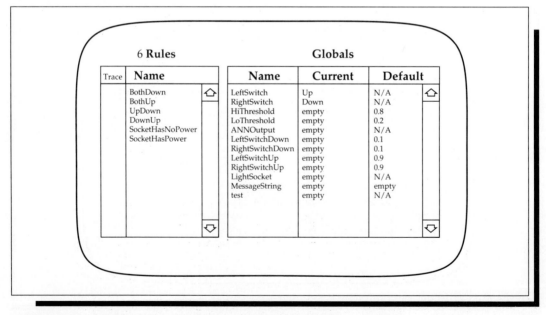

FIGURE 15.10   Sample screen for entering rules.

FIGURE 15.11   NueX screen showing a summary of variables and rules.

NueX
LightSwitch.ANN
1
1

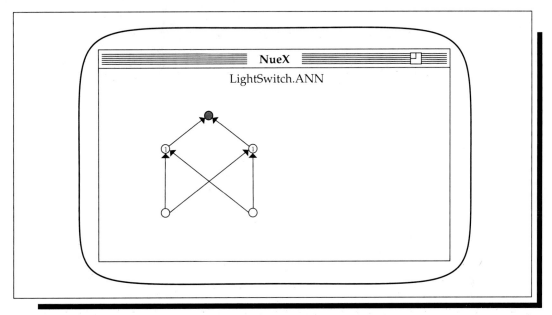

FIGURE 15.12 NueX screen for entering the architecture of the neural network.

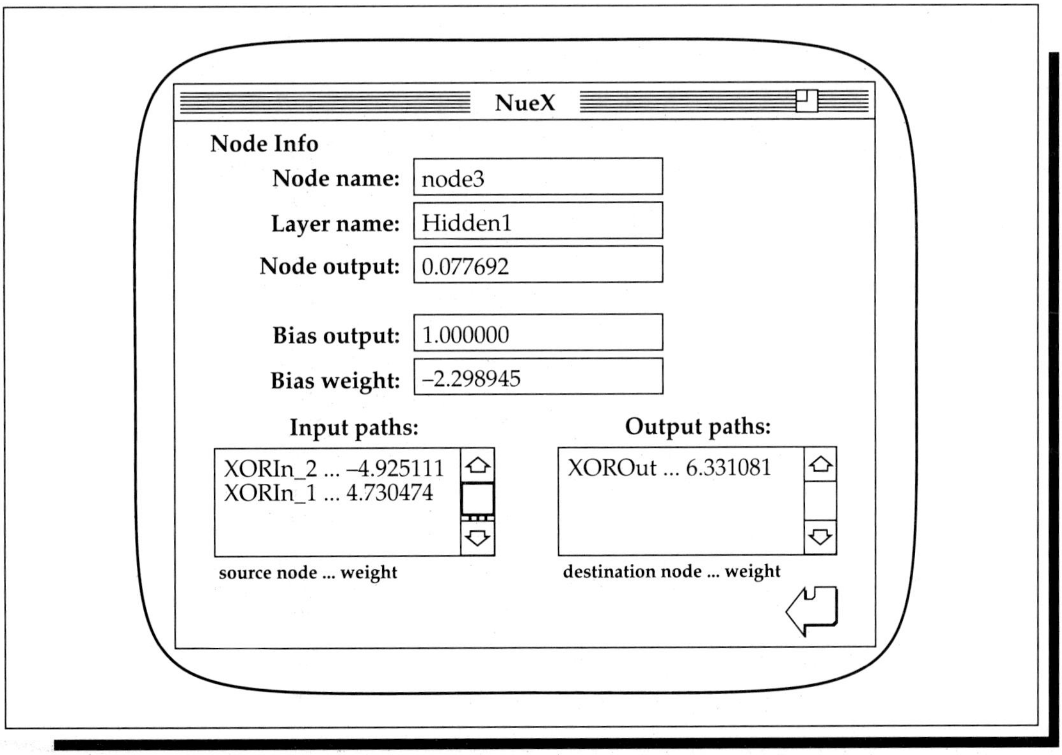

NueX
Node Info
Node name: node3
Layer name: Hidden1
Node output: 0.077692
Bias output: 1.000000
Bias weight: –2.298945
Input paths:
XORIn_2 ... –4.925111
XORIn_1 ... 4.730474
source node ... weight
Output paths:
XOROut ... 6.331081
destination node ... weight

FIGURE 15.13 NueX screen displaying information about neural network nodes.

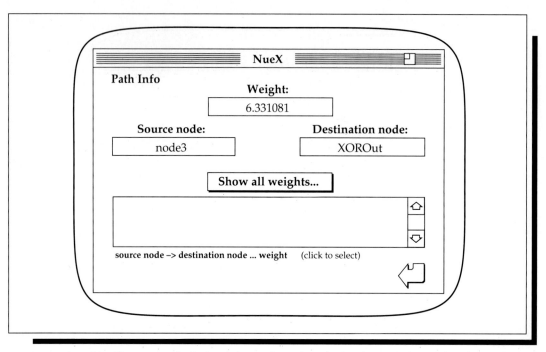

FIGURE 15.14   NueX screen displaying information about neural network weights for individual nodes.

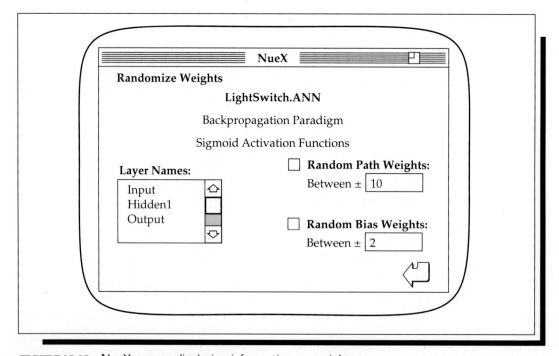

FIGURE 15.15   NueX screen displaying information on weights.

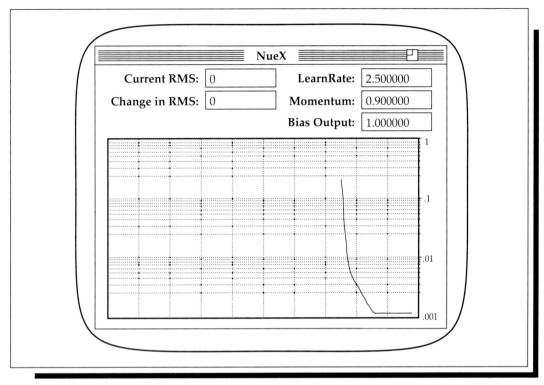

FIGURE 15.16   NueX screen showing the progress of a training session.

15.6 Summary

ANNs have been revived in recent years and labeled by some as sixth-generation computing. This label gives the erroneous impression that fifth-generation computing, of which expert systems is a major field, is going to be replaced by the new generation of computing, the ANN. In fact, while in some cases ANN can perform tasks better (or faster) than expert systems, in most instances the two technologies are not in competition. Furthermore, their characteristics are so different that they *complement* each other rather nicely in some case.

Review of Expert System and Neural Network Differences

A major limitation of the expert system approach is that experts do not always think in terms of rules. Thus, in such cases, an expert system does not mimic the reasoning process of human experts. For example, credit application evaluation involves aspects such as human factors and organizational issues; these are difficult to capture in rules, but they appear as text in the application processing approval.

For stable applications with well-defined rules, expert systems can be easily developed to provide good performance. Furthermore, most development software packages allow the creation of explanations to help the user understand questions being asked or conclusions and reasoning processes. In contrast, in ANN, knowledge is represented as numeric weights; therefore, the rules and the reasoning process are not readily explainable.

Neural networks may be preferable to expert systems when rules are not known, either because the topic is too complex or because no human expert is available. If training data can be generated, the system may be able to learn enough information to function as well as or better than an expert system. This approach also has the benefit of easy maintenance. That is, modifications are made by retraining with an updated data set, thus eliminating programming changes and rule reconstruction. The data-driven property of neural networks allows adjustment in response to changing environments and events. Expert systems are knowledge driven, so changes can be made only if the knowledge is being changed. Another advantage of the neural network is the speed of operation after the network is trained; the natural use of parallel systems and neural chips enhances this aspect dramatically.

Guidelines

Guidelines for choosing appropriate applications for hybrid expert systems and ANN are starting to emerge. Some important situations in which neural networks may be useful are as follows:

- **Inadequate knowledge bases**—An expert may not be available or affordable; rules may be very difficult to formulate; the rule-based approach may not be an appropriate representation for the domain. Adding an ANN as a front end may be helpful.
- **Volatile knowledge bases**—Rules and facts may be frequently modified; the knowledge captured in rules may change, depending on human experience in a new domain. ANN, if feasible, handles such changes better.
- **Data-intensive systems**—Applications involving high rates of data input, requiring rapid processing; feedback data for control systems; ambiguous, noisy, or error-prone inputs requiring interpolation; and interactions involving vision and speech subsystems are all candidates for ANN support.
- **Parallel hardware**—Availability of parallel implementations provides additional advantages to neural computing.

The similarities between expert system and neural network development, and their complementary nature, make hybrid systems a very promising area for research and development. The integration of these and possibly other intelligent components with conventional computer-based information systems promises to be an important area both for research and development and for implementation in the 1990s.

References

1. M. Caudill, "Using Neural Nets: Hybrid Expert Networks," *AI Expert,* Vol. 5, No. 11 (November, 1990).
2. L. R. Medsker (ed.), Special issue of *Expert Systems with Applications: An International Journal,* Vol. 2, No. 1 (1991).
3. D. L. Bailey, D. M. Thompson, and J. L. Feinstein, "The Practical Side of Neural Networks," *PC AI,* (November-December 1988).
4. D. L. Bailey and D. M. Thompson, "How to Develop Neural-Network Applications," *AI Expert,* Vol. 5, No. 9 (1990).
5. S. I. Gallant, "Connectionist Expert Systems," *Communications of the ACM,* Vol. 31 (1988).
6. M. A. Hanson and R. L. Brekke, "Workload Management Expert System— Combining Neural Networks and Rule-Based Programming in an Operational Application," *Proceedings of the Instrument Society of America,* Vol. 24, 1988, pp. 1721–1726.
7. J. Hendler and L. Dickens, "Integrating Neural Network and Expert Reasoning: An Example," *Proceedings of the AISB Conference on Developments of Biological Standardization.* 1991, Leeds, U.K.
8. M. Gutknecht, R. Pfeifer, and M. Stolze, "Cooperative Hybrid Systems," *Institut fur Informatik Technical Report,* University of Zurich, 1991.
9. D. Hillman, "Integrating Neural Networks and Expert Systems," *AI Expert,* Vol. 5, No. 6 (June, 1990).

Chapter 16

The Future:
Integration of
Intelligent Systems

The concepts and examples presented here represent a range of areas in which neural computing can replace or supplement AI technologies. Applications involving stand-alone neural networks are rapidly emerging, and the combination with expert systems and conventional software is a natural step.

Although neural computing may be an alternative in many cases, many more problems are still best solved with AI or conventional data processing tools. Expert system techniques are best when hard and fast, reasonably sized, stable sets of rules can be derived. In some cases, though, the expert may not be available or the knowledge acquisition process may be too expensive and time-consuming.

Neural computing can, in appropriate applications, address the knowledge acquisition bottleneck by gleaning knowledge from training data and storing the information as connection weights. Having learned from experiential data and sample cases, neural networks can rapidly process information presented to them in the future and recognize patterns, classify data, and diagnose problems. Neural computing is best for changing and uncertain data when human-like perceptual reasoning is needed.

The two technologies can represent different characteristics of intelligent behavior and thus can be combined to solve more complex and useful problems. The use of neural computing is growing rapidly, and convenient shells and development systems are emerging that permit widespread commercialization. The availability of parallel implementations and neural chips greatly enhance the benefits of neural computing. Many research and development opportunities are available to exploit the potential synergism between neural computing and AI.

16.1   A Look Ahead at the Expert Systems Market

In expert systems over the next 10 years, integration will continue to be a major trend. Expert systems are already integrated with existing databases, management information systems, neural networks, spreadsheets, CAD/CAM packages, CASE tools, simulation and optimization packages, DSS, multimedia, and other technologies. This integration trend, as well as embedded expert systems, will continue. In the next generation, expert systems will probably become more model based and will capture the underlying functional processes of such generic tasks as classification, interpretation, diagnosis, scheduling, and others. They will have improved user interfaces through such technologies as hypermedia, multimedia, and virtual reality, and they will possess better ways of automating the knowledge acquisition process and handling learning. Expert system shells will become more specialized, evolving into, for example, expert scheduling system shells, expert classification system shells, and expert system shells solely for real-time applications.

In terms of their market worldwide, applications of expert systems will abound. Expert systems are already being used in many diverse areas, and this trend will continue. Expert systems used for help desk applications and for policy and regulatory compliance applications will flourish. According to ServiceWare, 87 percent of the service industry will be using expert systems within the next 3 years. According to the Market Intelligence Research Company, the U.S. expert systems market is currently valued at $820 million per year (in 1991) and will climb to at least $6 billion per year in total revenues by 1995. Over the next few years, competition will intensify. Several AI companies have already closed their doors, and others will merge to gain further power and diversity. By the year 2000, the term *expert systems* will be common worldwide, and knowledge of expert systems development will be necessary for systems analysts.

16.2 Capabilities and Limitations of Neural Networks

Like expert systems, neural networks have both strengths and limitations. An analysis of both will help identify areas of research and the need for alternative technologies.

Capabilities

Neural computing is significant from the standpoint of both theory and applications. The neural network approach represents a new paradigm for computing and joins a renewed interdisciplinary interest in understanding how the brain and the mind work. Researchers from fields such as neuroscience, physics, computer science, psychology, and philosophy are collaborating to develop new models explaining how we think. Computer implementation and testing of models may be crucial in verifying theoretical models of the brain and mind. In 1990, the U.S. government declared the 1990s to be the decade of the brain, in recognition of the unprecedented opportunity to build on previous research and find cures for neurological disorders.

While our theoretical understanding is increasing, new computing techniques inspired by biological concepts are producing a wide range of interesting applications. As an indication of the potential of neural computing, corporations and government agencies in the United States and other countries have begun generously funding research and development (e.g., the Sixth Generation Project in Japan). Opportunities for the use of neural computing are appearing in various programs, such as those for intelligent manufacturing and space exploration.

Neural network technology is useful for pattern recognition, learning, classification, generalization and abstraction, and the interpretation of incomplete and noisy inputs. Natural overlap with traditional AI applications occurs in the area of pattern recognition for character, speech, and visual recognition. Systems that learn are more natural interfaces to the real world than systems that must be programmed, and speed considerations point to the need to take advantage of parallel implementations.

Neural networks have the potential to provide certain human characteristics of problem solving that are difficult to simulate using the logical, analytical techniques of expert system and standard software technologies. For example, neural networks can analyze large quantities of data to establish patterns and characteristics in situations where rules are not known. Neural networks may be useful for financial/business applications like measuring stock fluctuations for determining an appropriate portfolio mix. They can also provide the human characteristic of making sense of incomplete or noisy data. Neural networks may eventually be able to mimic the commonsense way humans function in day-to-day situations and to gain insights from experience. Thus far, these features have proved too difficult for the symbolic/logical approach of traditional AI.

Thus, the immediate practical implications of neural computing are its emergence as an alternative or supplement to conventional computing systems and AI techniques. As an alternative, neural computing offers the advantage of increased execution speed once the network has been trained. The ability to learn from cases and train the system with data sets, rather than having to write programs, may be more cost effective, as well as more convenient when changes become necessary. In applications where rules cannot be known, neural computers may be able to represent rules as stored connection weights. Beyond its role as an alternative, neural computing can be combined with conventional software to produce more powerful hybrid systems. Such integrated systems can use database, expert system, neural network, and other technologies to produce the best solutions to complex problems. Thus, intelligent systems could eventually mimic human decision making under uncertainty, as well as in situations where information is incomplete or contains mistakes. A goal is to produce systems that include components exhibiting mind-like behavior in order to handle information as flexibly and powerfully as humans do.

Limitations

The current applicability of ANN is limited by the present state of research and development and possibly by some inherent characteristics. In general, ANN does not do well at tasks not done well by people. For example, arithmetic and data processing tasks are not suitable for ANN and are best accomplished by conventional computers. Current applications of ANN excel in the areas of classification and pattern recognition.

Most neural network systems lack explanation facilities. Justifications for results are difficult to obtain because the connection weights do not usually have obvious interpretations. The limitations and expense of current parallel hardware technology restrict most applications to uniprocessor software simulations. Research and development is still underway to find better learning algorithms, architectures, and development methodologies.

In the area of knowledge acquisition, technical applications still require a domain expert to obtain and verify the training and testing of input data and the corresponding outputs. With current technologies, training times can be excessive and tedious; thus, the need for frequent retraining may make a particular application impractical. The best way to represent input data, and the choice of architecture and the number of nodes and layers, are still subject to trial and error. Methods for handling temporal aspects of data are still in the research stage.

Most of these problems are the subjects of current research and development. Current applications focus on the areas that are easily done well with neural networks, and further uses await the many technological advances on the horizon.

16.3   Integrated Systems

As described earlier, expert systems and neural networks are each, and together, more powerful and effective as subsystems embedded in larger systems. A common situation is to have these intelligent technologies embedded in conventional systems such as standard software and database systems. The future promises a continuation of this trend as traditional software needs to become more intelligent[1]. Furthermore, future hardware developments in parallel processing and chip technology will benefit the conventional and intelligent components alike.

The coupling of expert systems with neural networks and other technologies has already become quite prevalent. Neuron Data and NeuralWare are developing an expert systems–neural network shell; American Cimflex-Teknowledge has coupled expert systems with CAD/CAM; Aion Corporation and KnowledgeWare are developing intelligent CASE tools; Intellicorp and James Martin & Company are developing intelligent CASE tools; and the list continues. Today the stand-alone expert system is becoming rare. Real-world operational expert systems need to be integrated with existing databases, management information systems, and other support systems.

Expert system integration with interactive multimedia will also grow. NASA's Kennedy Space Center, for example, is using expert systems technology with multimedia to help scientists, engineers, journalists, and others search intelligently for particular photographs of a shuttle launch/mission. About 100,000 pictures are taken during a typical launch. These pictures are now being digitized onto a PC and can be intelligently searched, via an expert system, by the user. An IBM–Apple joint venture is aimed at developing platforms and software to accommodate interactive multimedia applications, possibly with the coupling of knowledge-based systems technology.

Knowledge-based simulation applications will continue to grow in engineering, scientific, military, and medical applications. Expert systems coupled with simulation are already being used to integrate qualitative and quantitative system knowledge for the operation of a mill and are helping chemists better understand their analyses. In the future, knowledge-based simulation may be an important engineering component.

In order for the synergy between expert systems and other technologies to become more common, more research is needed to facilitate and enhance this coupling. Research into distributed AI, knowledge representation, knowledge acquisition, machine learning, V&V, productivity, technology transfer and organizational issues, and other areas is greatly needed to ensure successful development and deployment of integrated intelligent systems.

16.4   Other Intelligent Technologies of the Future

Research and development is currently underway to increase the mix of technologies that can be integrated into ever more intelligent systems. This section provides an overview of some of the most promising areas. The technologies that will have important roles are shown in Figure 16.1.

Advances in Neural Network Technology

Back propagation will continue to dominate the commercial applications market for some time. This is due to the relative ease of use and the availability of low-cost development tools. In addition, supervised training allows the developer to engineer the system to a desired performance level in an efficient and predictable way. During routine operation, back propagation networks are feed-forward systems that produce outputs rapidly in response to inputs.

Applications advances will include a wider range of areas. For example, in DSS, success in areas such as stock market trading and analysis of real estate options will increase the visibility of neural networks and their role in corporate intelligence. The wealth of experience will produce better guidelines for choosing

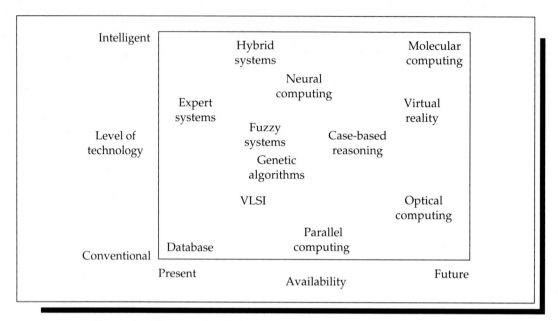

FIGURE 16.1   Future intelligent technologies.

applications and more useful development strategies. Combinations of neural networks will allow increasingly complex applications, enhancing interest in and acceptability of neural networks.

Progress in hardware technology will strongly affect neural network use as follows:

1. Hardware for software implementation—improved hardware for software simulation of neural computing, currently the most prevalent method. Supercomputers provide fast, efficient performance, usually using vector processing. Massively parallel computers use many individual processors and require the simulation to be written in a special language.
2. Electronic implementations—circuits designed specifically for neural computing. This category includes VLSI chips and processors that are attached to conventional computers. In the latter case, processing speeds can be significantly increased.
3. Optical or electro-optical implementations—systems involving the use of optical components. While currently in the research phase, these systems have the potential to perform at the speed of light and achieve dense connectivity in a three-dimensional implementation.

The areas not handled well with conventional computers will be appropriate for neural networks on massively parallel processors. These areas include speech, vision, signal processing, and real-time control of systems. VLSI neural networks will provide general-purpose, trainable neural network chips that are small enough to fit in all kinds of devices, including mobile robots. Although much is still to be done in this area, Synaptics, Inc., has already announced a neural network chip about one-fifth of an inch long with 20,000 components.

A likely development in back propagation is the addition of recurrent features. These properties of other networks, such as Hopfield and ART, were mentioned in earlier chapters. The main concept is that activity flows around the network, rather in one direction, until some equilibrium in the weights is achieved. This stable state of the network corresponds to a concept or fact that the network "knows." In back propagation networks, certain extra nodes might be added to represent information from a pattern previously presented to the network. This would allow the network to learn differences in sequences of patterns.

Another advance in neural networks could be models that more closely resemble the human brain. Currently, the neurode is an analogy to the biological neuron that gives useful computational results. Actual neural cells are more complex than our simple nodes with sigmoid activation functions and a relatively small number of connections between the nodes. Biological neural networks have many more connections and are not fully and symmetrically connected.

Neural computing research will involve neuroscientists, physiologists, and psychologists. The disciplines will benefit from each other, producing new knowledge about the brain and about neural network architectures. One important area is the development of a model mimicking the control mechanisms with feedback that are involved in human thinking and that allow us to make choices and reason. Neural network developments can be expected in areas in which biological systems are superior to conventional computing systems. Research in those areas may lead to unique approaches to long-standing problems as we learn more about how the brain functions. As neural networks are used to model ideas in neuroscience and psychology, new understandings could have an impact on medical applications and lead to new treatments for disorders.

Another problem area is the application of chaos theory, which addresses complex system stability and systems change. Chaos research studies how complex systems, such as weather conditions and clouds, are organized, and how small changes in input can sometimes produce dramatic changes in the system, resulting in chaotic behavior. Recurrent neural networks have been able to represent such systems.

Human–computer Interface

The behavior of intelligent systems will seem more human-like as research and development in interface technologies progresses. Natural interfaces may someday allow users to converse with computers to seek expert advice or provide input for neural processing.

In robotics, the use of VLSI chips for expert systems and neural networks will allow compact embedded AI that will make robots more like humans. This includes advanced vision, speech, and touch capabilities allowed by the use of neural networks. For example, robots will be able to learn from the demonstration of movements, rather than by means of detailed algorithms for all possible motions.

Again, because of VLSI capabilities, intelligent features such as speech recognition will be embedded in all kinds of appliances to allow speech input from users. Intelligent features will be available in a wide variety of everyday systems such as televisions, telephones, and voice typewriters.

A recent surge of interest in human–computer interactions is seen in the research on virtual reality[2]. New means of interacting with computers, such as gloves and eye movements, promise to lead to many new, creative applications that enhance the intelligent appearance of expert systems and neural networks. Real-world applications will allow virtual-world simulations and visualization of situations.

16.5 Summary

Expert system and neural network fields are very young by scientific standards. Although they are based on research dating to the 1940s, the technical feasibility and commercial availability of these two techniques have grown dramatically only in the last decade. Expert systems and neural networks have done very well in their complementary areas of classification and pattern recognition. In the future, each technique should have a wider range of capabilities and application areas, and they should be increasingly involved in hybrid systems and embedded in conventional systems.

The advances will come more rapidly because of national and international organizations and projects that are being created to address the vast opportunities presented by these two technologies. The DARPA Strategic Computing Project has been a source of research and development support for U.S. work in expert systems and neural networks, as has been the Fifth Generation Project for Japan. The Sixth Generation Project will emphasize neural networks, and the Seventh Generation Project will focus on molecular computing. MCC has been another U.S. AI effort involving cooperation among high-technology companies. Since, the 1990s has been declared the decade of the brain in the United States, funding for neural networks may be increased. The Foundation for Brain Research has recently been formed to encourage interdisciplinary work among researchers from areas including neurocomputing scientists and neuroscientists to enhance each other's progress.

The rapid developments in expert systems and neural networks in the 1980s have created both immediate opportunities for useful practical applications and a solid basis for research and development in the 1990s. The future looks bright for many important developments in software capabilities for intelligent systems. Anticipated developments in hardware technology will also create dramatic changes in performance and architecture. In all of these advances, the integration of many different complementary techniques will lead to computing systems that display remarkable degrees of human intelligence. Whether or not these systems become exactly like humans, they will provide vast opportunities for useful and profitable applications.

References

1. Maureen Caudill, "The View from Now," *AI Expert,* Vol. 7 (June 1992).
2. Linda Jacobson, "Virtual Reality: A Status Report," *AI Expert,* Vol. 6 (August 1991).

Appendix

Hybrid System Example: Job Skills Analyzer

This detailed example was developed by Fran Labate, a graduate student at The American University. The authors wish to thank Fran for this careful and thoughtful project, which illustrates the practical considerations important for building expert systems and neural networks. In this case, a hybrid system was constructed by linking systems built with Level5 and NeuroShell.

In this case study, enough details and data are given so that advanced students can implement this hybrid system using the software provided with this textbook. By building their own systems, students can experiment with aspects of development such as different parameters and training sets. We hope that this practical learn-by-doing approach will give a deeper understanding of the design and development of neural network and expert systems.

A.1   Introduction

Locating the appropriate personnel to staff a project often needs to be done in a more structured and thorough manner. In large companies with sizable professional and support staffs, assessing the capabilities of the entire staff when selecting the team can be difficult. Even with smaller companies, an individual is often

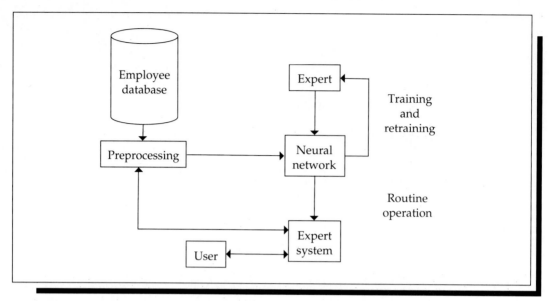

FIGURE A.1   Analysis of an employee database with a hybrid system.

selected without giving adequate consideration to other qualified candidates. Also, new hires or interviewees for a project are often relative unknowns compared with longer-term employees.

The Skills Analyzer tool described here is part of an investigation of the potential of hybrid intelligent system technologies for solving management problems—in this case, improving the staff selection process. The tool combines the pattern-matching abilities of a neural network with the logical, goal-driven approach of a knowledge-based or expert system.

The fundamental problem addressed by this project (Figure A.1) is to support decision making in an organization by analyzing an employee database. As shown, the data is preprocessed and used in two ways. First, when training the neural network, human intervention is required to select the appropriate training data subset and to monitor the training to ensure valid performance. Intervention is also required when retraining becomes necessary. The second use of the data is in the routine operation, using the trained neural network and the expert system as a hybrid system. Again, human intervention is needed to specify problem details and requirements. The expert system calls upon the neural network to select employees who fall into desired categories. For the selected employees, additional information is analyzed in terms of the rules in the knowledge base so that a recommendation can be made. The expert system also serves as the intelligent interface to the user and as a means of explaining the recommendations.

This hybrid system approach provides several advantages that help justify this design decision. Among the features of this type of system are the following:

- Large databases are processed efficiently.
- Detailed queries or rules are not required; historical data and empirical observations are adequate.

- The system is readily updated via retraining with fresh data.
- The system can extrapolate beyond the explicit training data to produce correct results for cases not previously seen.

A.2 Hybrid System Architecture

This case study investigates a fundamental aspect of the generic problem previously described. As a particular application of the analysis of an employee database, a hybrid system has been designed and implemented to investigate the feasibility of hybrid systems in this area.

The hybrid implementation, which runs on a PC using DOS, utilizes the NeuroShell neural network tool from Ward Systems and the Level5 expert system shell from Information Builders, Inc. Two main processes compose this hybrid architecture. The first step is a neural network that accepts a set of skills values describing a job candidate and categorizes the individual according to his or her job type (e.g., Senior System Engineer or Programmer). The expert system then takes the data from the neural network and compares the candidate to a set of job requirements provided by the user.

The raw data used to build the Skills Analyzer system used up to 323 different skill codes collected for each of 51 individuals currently employed by a small company. The data was originally formatted for an office database system and is essentially Boolean in nature. Each entry in the database consists of an employee name and a skill code, such as "Experience Doing Trade-Off Analyses." The individual either does or does not have the particular skill. A preprocessor compresses the raw data into a dataset that is appropriate for the neural network. This compressed format consists of a set of counts of the number of skills possessed by each employee in each major area, such as Management or Software Engineering. Forty-five training cases were randomly selected from the full set of 51, and the remaining 6 were set aside for testing the network. An example of how the data was provided to the neural network is shown in Figure A.2.

Number of training cases: 45

Input1:   0 7 2 10 24 6 8 15 3 12 13 2 1 3 55 8 4 3
Output1:   0 0 0 1 0 0 0 0

Input2:   7 27 1 7 30 5 10 3 6 11 7 4 3 4 66 12 10 3
Output2:   0 0 0 0 0 0 1 0
•
•
Input45:   0 7 1 4 11 1 6 0 3 7 5 0 0 2 40 6 2 3
Output45:   0 1 0 0 0 0 0 0

FIGURE A.2 Partial listing of the training file for the Skills Analyzer.

For this application, the neural network consists of 18 input nodes, 10 hidden nodes, and 8 output nodes. Each of the 18 input values represents the total number of skills that a particular individual may have in a particular area of technology. For instance, the raw skills database records the various programming languages in which each individual claims knowledge. This complete list of languages is compressed for the neural network into a single value, ranging from 0 to 20, denoting the total number of programming languages that the person knows. The complete set of 18 input node identifiers is as follows:

- Program Management
- Mathematical Techniques
- Technologies
- Networks/Data Comm
- Software/System Maintenance
- Software QA/CM
- College Degrees
- Professional Staff Level
- Years of Company Experience

- Systems Engineering
- Software Engineering
- Programming Languages
- Databases
- Commercial/Off-the-Shelf
- Hardware/Operating Systems
- Approximate salary
- Total Years of Professional Experience
- Scale Factor

With the exception of the Scale Factor, all of these input categories are quantifiable characteristics that describe the professional skills of the particular individual. The Scale Factor, which is assigned the value 1, 2, or 3, is introduced to account for the fact that the original skill categories in the raw data file are Boolean and do not quantify the amount of experience the individual has in the particular area. As might be expected, some individuals are more conservative than others in their self-evaluation. A Scale Factor of 3 is associated with the conservatives, while a value of 1 goes to those at the other extreme. The training results suggest that this extra input node served a useful purpose; however, should this tool be formally implemented, the Scale Factor should be eliminated and tougher restrictions on the assignment of skill values should be enforced.

The eight output classes (Secretary, Programmer, Junior Programmer, Senior Programmer, Senior Programmer/Analyst, Programmer/Analyst, Systems Engineer, and Senior Systems Engineer) represent the possible job titles an individual may have. The output nodes are binary in that the values are all either 0 or 1. Specifically, all output nodes are set to 0, with the exception of the node that matches the individual. All Programmers, then, have that particular output node set to 1, while all other output nodes are set to 0. The analog nature of the calculations, however, leads to some interesting training results. For example, if a person has skills that are strong in both programming and systems engineering, during training it is most likely that the output nodes representing Programmer and Systems Engineer will both fire rather strongly.

A loosely coupled hybrid architecture for the Skills Analyzer tool is depicted in Figure A.3. Although the neural network and the expert system are the primary components of the tool, additional pre- and postprocessing software are necessary at various junctures of the process. Data manipulation software is used, for example, to prepare the raw skills data for the neural network. Software is also required to take the neural network's data files and prepare them according to the

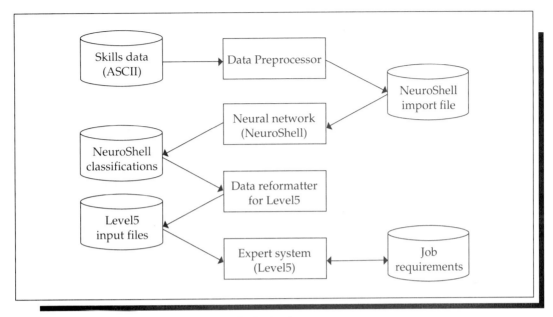

FIGURE A.3 Architecture of the Hybrid Skills Analyzer.

input files' constraints of the expert system software. Several different files are utilized to transfer the data between the various processes.

The neural network architecture is a feed-forward design that is trained using back propagation of errors, which allows development of the hybrid system to proceed with a less costly neural network shell and simplifies the development of the user interface. For example, in the NeuroShell environment, the developer has to define the input and output nodes of the neural network; however, the number of hidden nodes, the learning rate, the momentum, the biases, and essentially all other parameters are provided as defaults.

The Level5 expert system utilizes goal-driven backward chaining to assess the qualifications of job candidates against the set of job requirements provided by the user. The set of 10 jobs or roles against which the rules are designed to evaluate include the complete set of 8 job categories listed previously, as well as the jobs of Program Manager and Configuration Manager. The latter two job positions require the Management and QA/CM experience provided to the neural network, as well as some System and Software Engineering and Analysis skills. For example, an individual labeled by the neural network as being a Senior Systems Engineer will also qualify for the Program Manager job if he or she has an acceptable level of postgraduate education and various Software Engineering skills, in addition to System Engineering.

Two paths must be taken to navigate the rule base. These paths correspond to the two fundamental goals of the system: "Rqts Written" and "Select Employee." The first goal is achieved after the user provides three inputs about the staffing requirements to the knowledge base. In addition to identifying the job category to be filled (1 of the 10 identified earlier), the user must specify the minimum number of years of experience required for the job and the maximum salary. After these specifications are provided, this information is written to a requirements file and the first goal is satisfied.

The second goal must be achieved during subsequent executions of the expert system. The file input/output for Level5 implementation of the expert system allows access to one individual's skills for each pass through the system. This methodology is a bit cumbersome, but it is driven by a Level5 file access constraint and by the design goal of keeping the rules structure simple.

The process for satisfying the second goal, "Select Employee," consists of comparing the current individual's skills with the requirements specified by the user. The job requirements and one employee's skills are first read into the fact base from external files. Various conditions are then checked, and comparisons are made to see if the individual's skills adequately match the job needs. The individual's job category, produced by the neural network, is first compared to the required job/role. If it is not an exact match (e.g., Programmer looking for a Programmer job), then additional rules are checked.

If the needed role is for CM Manager or Program Manager, then other skills must also be demonstrated to qualify. Certain prerequisites are also built into the knowledge base in addition to the user-specified requirements. Each staff role, for instance, has a set of degree requirements, as well as a required amount of background in the particular area (e.g., programmers must know four programming languages). Upon completion of the evaluation of an individual against the user's requirements, a message is displayed indicating success or failure in finding a match, and the process ends. To make the required multiple executions of Level5 as painless as possible, a batch file exists to copy the next employee's skills set into the Level5 input file and then rerun the knowledge base automatically. This permits the user to deal only with Level5 input/output each time, avoiding the need to run DOS commands.

Various pre- and postprocessing software programs are also required to reformat the data as it passes through the multiple stages. Initial processing of the raw skills data is required to strip the useful portions of the data from the office database and to arrange the individual skills information in the summarized format required by the neural network. Upon completion of neural network processing, the training and test files must be segmented to place skills for individuals into separate files for Level5. These additional steps are depicted in Figure A.3. As can be seen, the processing results in the need for several intermediate files, all of which are ASCII flat files.

A.3   Training the Neural Network

Training the neural network is quite simple. This is true despite the fact that the number of training and test cases is small relative to the size of the network. The 51 individual data sets are divided into a 45-vector training set and a 6-vector test set. While the test set is clearly smaller than is normally desirable, the training set cannot be smaller without the risk of the network's memorizing the data and thereby losing its ability to generalize.

The key to fast, accurate training using NeuroShell is the use of NET-PERFECT, which helps the user decide when to stop the training process. NET-PERFECT is used to train the Skills Analyzer, effectively eliminating the risk of overtraining. At user-specified intervals during the training process, NET-PERFECT checks the current set of weights against the test set and maintains a separate file containing the set of network weights that corresponds to the least amount of error during these checks. Training can then be left essentially unattended, since we know that the set of weights optimized for the test set is being set aside by NeuroShell.

In addition to the optimized weights themselves, NET-PERFECT writes the error values computed when checking against the test set at each interval. This provides an insightful plot after training is concluded. After 360,000 training cycles have been performed, the optimal set of weights relative to the test set is computed at cycle 117,000. Upon completion of this training run, the neural network is considered adequately trained. The percentages of correct responses for the training and test sets, respectively, is approximately 95 and 80 percent.

A.4 Results

The hybrid system can be exercised by simulating the process management would use to select employees for a new project. Although the staff for a new project might normally be selected from the entire set of current employees and interviewees, we have selected only a subset of six to demonstrate the proof of concept. As will be discussed in the next section, a great deal of data preparation is required by Level5 for each person being considered. Selecting only six minimizes this overhead processing while still validating the performance of the expert system component of the Skills Analyzer.

The expert system is set up to mandate a minimum number of a particular set of skills to qualify for each job position. This required set of skills can, of course, be changed for different projects. As an example, one rule mandates that an individual must have the following skills to be considered qualified for the role of Programmer:

$$SW \text{ Languages} \geq 5;$$
$$SW \text{ Engineering} \geq 10;$$
$$System \text{ Engineering} \geq 3;$$
$$Degrees \geq 1.$$

If a Programmer is needed for the project, the user could, for instance, respond to the expert system questions as follows (user inputs are in **boldface**):

Select the type of job to be filled.
Jr Programmer
Programmer
Sr Programmer

Programmer_Analyst
Sr Programmer_Analyst
System Engineer
Sr System Engineer
Program Manager
CM Manager
Secretary
Programmer
Enter the minimum number of years experience required for the job.
3
Enter the maximum salary available for the job being filled [$1,000's].
70

When assessing the set of six candidates against these constraints, the expert system determines that no one is qualified. Inspection of the data suggests, however, that individual 6 might have been selected. A closer look reveals that while this programmer has a BS degree, knows 14 different SW languages, and has a $40K salary with 4 years of experience, the person has only 3 different SW Engineering skills and has no experience at all in Systems Engineering. (Recall that the required levels for the skills areas were 10 and 3, respectively.)

Another execution of the system can be performed in search of a System Engineer. The Skills Analyzer is asked for an individual with the required qualifications, at least 8 years of experience, and no more than a $60K salary. The system responds with a match: employee 1 with 10 years of experience, a $50K salary, and 30 different System Engineering skills. In all cases, the results from the expert system can easily be validated by comparing the skills for the set of six candidates to the requirements specified by the user.

A.5 Comments on NeuroShell and Level5

All in all, the two shells used in this hybrid system architecture—NeuroShell and Level5—are quite easy to use. Various features of each package are important. In the case of NeuroShell, it is the ability to import unformatted training data (and let NeuroShell format it), the assignment of appropriate default values for most of the training parameters, and, of course, the NET-PERFECT training optimization capability. With Level5, the simplicity of the Production Rule Language (PRL) makes the expert system rules easy to implement.

Unfortunately, the only real constraint encountered in the use of these tools introduces a severe design limitation: the absence in Level5 of an adequate set of ASCII flat file interface commands. The tool was engineered to provide maximum input/output flexibility to dBase database files. With ASCII files, however, one cannot rewind a file, open a file with anything but an explicit (hard-coded) filename, or "remember" the last record read and return to the next record of a file later during the execution of a Level5 session.

Thus, in our applications, each time employee skills data is needed from an ASCII file, the file needs to be opened and data records read from the front of the file. This constraint effectively eliminates the design option of assessing multiple employees, and ideally a variable number of employees, during a single execution of Level5. Instead, the set of six candidates must be provided individually to the expert system by a DOS batch file during separate, sequential executions of the system. Each time through, the next employee skills file needs to be copied into the file whose name was expected by Level5.

This example of developing a hybrid system follows the loosely coupled model using a neural network and an expert system shell. The training and test data can be obtained on diskette from the authors. As discussed in Chapter 15, one of the few tools now available for developing tightly coupled systems is NueX, and the implementation of the Skills Base Analyzer with NueX would be useful for a comparative study.

Index

LEVEL5 OBJECT
SMART SOLUTIONS
IN ONE POWERFUL SYSTEM

KNOWLEDGE-BASED SYSTEMS
■

LEVEL5 OBJECT® lets you incorporate expert systems technology into your applications. It emulates the human decision-making process, capturing employee knowledge so the application can make intelligent decisions for you. You get problem solving based on input from databases, end-user supplied information and queries, and values from other external sources — or any combination of these.

■ Rules ■ Triggers/demons ■ Agendas
■ Backward chaining ■ Forward chaining
■ Hypothetical reasoning ■ Uncertainty reasoning
■ Missing-data reasoning ■ Procedural logic
■ Monotonic ■ Nonmonotonic ■ OOP Methods
■ Variable search strategies ■ Logic Editor
■ Interactive Debugger ■ Historical Traces
■ Breakpoints ■ Single-stepping ■ Arrays
■ Collections ■ Sets

OBJECT-ORIENTED PROGRAMMING
■

Object oriented programming (OOP) gives you new levels of control over application design. Organize large amounts of data and procedures in an application that hides its underlying complexity — so the end result is a user-friendly application that works. And gets used!

Because objects are modular, you can reuse data structures, logic, and information — drastically cutting your application development and maintenance time.

■ Objects ■ Classes ■ Instances ■ Methods
■ Inheritance ■ Multiple inheritance
■ OODBMS ■ Databases as objects
■ Attributes ■ Properties
■ 14 Attribute types ■ Add-On objects
■ Built-in system classes ■ Object Browser
■ Pointer types

CLIENT SERVER
■

You need all the pieces to solve your puzzle. That's why LEVEL5 OBJECT gives you access to over 70 databases on remote and local platforms — enabling you to open almost all sources of data and information for analysis, integration, and decision support.

■ DDE Communications
■ Callable/embeddable ■ OLE
■ Universal SQL access ■ MS ODBC access
■ IBI EDA/SQL ■ Q+E QELIB ■ Flat text files
■ dBASE ■ Paradox ■ Oracle ■ SQLNET
■ DB2 ■ IMS/DB ■ Sybase ■ Rdb ■ SQL/DS
■ INGRES ■ SQL Server ■ Btrieve ■ Excel
■ INFORMIX ■ Tandem ■ Teradata ■ LAN
■ FOCUS ■ NetWare SQL

GRAPHICAL USER INTERFACE
■

LEVEL5 OBJECT delivers power — with a graphical user interface (GUI) that takes full advantage of the Microsoft Windows® environment. You get a complete, easy-to-use set of advanced editors, tools, and debuggers. So you can develop your own successful GUI applications quickly and efficiently.

■ Audio object ■ Video object ■ Forms painter
■ Windows ■ Menus ■ Buttons
■ Graphs and charts ■ Pictures ■ Lists
■ Tables ■ Comboboxes ■ Dynamic forms
■ Message boxes ■ Dialogs
■ Common dialogs ■ Animation ■ Drill-down
■ Gauges ■ Sliders
■ Custom help ■ Windows printing

LEVEL5 OBJECT — THE SMART SOLUTION THAT'S INTUITIVE —
MODELING THE HUMAN APPROACH TO PROBLEM DEFINITION AND RESOLUTION. THAT MEANS NO LENGTHY LEARNING CURVE — SO YOU CAN PUT INFORMATION TO WORK FAST. LEVEL5 OBJECT GIVES YOU FOUR MAJOR ENABLING TECHNOLOGIES — INTEGRATED IN ONE POWERFUL SYSTEM.

1-800-444-4303

Information Builders, Inc.
503 Fifth Avenue, Indialantic, FL 32903